Political Culture and Media Genre

Also by Kay Richardson

INTERNET DISCOURSE AND HEALTH DEBATES

NUCLEAR REACTIONS: Form and Response in Public Issue Television
(*with John Corner and Natalie Fenton*)

PUBLIC ISSUE TELEVISION: World in Action (*with Peter Goddard and John Corner*)

TELEVISION DRAMATIC DIALOGUE: A Sociolinguistic Study

WORLDS IN COMMON? (*with Ulrike Meinhof*)

Also by Katy Parry

POCKETS OF RESISTANCE: British News Media, War and Theory in the 2003 Invasion of Iraq (*with Piers Robinson, Peter Goddard, Craig Murray, Philip M. Taylor*)

Also by John Corner

CRITICAL IDEAS IN TELEVISION STUDIES

TELEVISION FORM AND PUBLIC ADDRESS

THE ART OF RECORD

THEORISING MEDIA

Political Culture and Media Genre

Beyond the News

Kay Richardson
University of Liverpool, Liverpool, UK

Katy Parry
University of Leeds, Leeds, UK

and

John Corner
University of Leeds, Leeds, UK

First published 2013 by
PALGRAVE MACMILLAN

Palgrave Macmillan in the UK is an imprint of Macmillan Publishers Limited, registered in England, company number 785998, of Houndmills, Basingstoke, Hampshire RG21 6XS.

Palgrave Macmillan in the US is a division of St Martin's Press LLC, 175 Fifth Avenue, New York, NY 10010.

Palgrave Macmillan is the global academic imprint of the above companies and has companies and representatives throughout the world.

Palgrave® and Macmillan® are registered trademarks in the United States, the United Kingdom, Europe and other countries.

ISBN 978-1-349-36061-7   ISBN 978-1-137-31462-8 (eBook)
DOI 10.1057/9781137314628

This book is printed on paper suitable for recycling and made from fully managed and sustained forest sources. Logging, pulping and manufacturing processes are expected to conform to the environmental regulations of the country of origin.

A catalogue record for this book is available from the British Library.

A catalog record for this book is available from the Library of Congress.

Typeset by MPS Limited, Chennai, India.

Contents

Illustrations

Tables

Figures

Acknowledgements

First of all, we are grateful to the Arts and Humanities Research Council in the UK, for the grant award AH/H000933/1, 'Media genre and political culture: beyond the news', which allowed us to undertake the research that underpins this book. We are very grateful to all the people who gave their time to participate in our audience response groups. We have agreed to protect their anonymity and so cannot thank them individually by name, but extend our thanks to Awesome Walls Climbing Centre, Age UK Knowsley, Shrewsbury Senior Citizens' Forum, Liverpool College School, IQ Therapies, and The Reader Organisation, for their cooperation and help in organising the groups. Thanks are due to our colleagues at Liverpool and Leeds for their support during the course of the research and writing. We would also like to thank the members of the many conference and seminar groupings to whom we have presented material from our study, often receiving valuable comment and criticism.

Finally, we are happy to acknowledge permission to reproduce copyright materials in Chapter 2 as follows. 'Spending more time with the family', cartoon reproduced by kind permission of Andy Davey; originally published in the *Sun* (London). ' "I believe in Clegg", confesses Dawkins'; 'Cameron launches "Big Idea". By our Political Staff Simon Hogwash'; 'Tea Party Candidates Romp Home in Wonderland Mid-Terms; By our Election Staff Lewis Carol Thatcher', all reproduced by kind permission of *Private Eye* magazine. 'Punches flew as the job interview turned nasty'; 'Falling prices will just worsen the shortage of new homes'; 'Cameron must beware a cunning opponent'; 'Honeymoon Suite' cartoon, 'Where do we come from?' cartoon, all copyright Telegraph Media Group Ltd 2010. 'They all jabbered at 100mph. Even old donkey Gordon', copyright *Daily Mail*. 'Hung Parliament/Strong Government' cartoon, copyright Mac/*Daily Mail*. 'Ed Miliband Gives Nothing Away in first interrogation: Labour's new leader keeps his cards close to his chest when being questioned by Andrew Marr', 'When you wish upon a star' cartoon, copyright Guardian News & Media Ltd 2010. 'People tried to put me down' cartoon, copyright Steve Bell, originally published in the *Guardian*. 'Loves me, loves me not: Clegg and the dating game', copyright *The Times*/News International, along with 'What's your big idea, Ed.?', copyright the *Sun*/News International. 'A leader to reclaim our trust' and 'Sir, I'm afraid we've discovered you've got a younger brother called Ed' cartoon, copyright Mirror Syndication International. See Chapter 2 for full details of authorial attributions and the dates of publication.

About the Authors

John Corner is Visiting Professor in Communications at the University of Leeds and an emeritus professor of the University of Liverpool. He has written widely on media history, theory and forms in books and journals, including *Television Form and Public Address* (1995), *The Art of Record* (1996) and *Critical Ideas in Television Studies* (1989). With Dick Pels, he co-edited the collection *Media and the Restyling of Politics* (2003). His most recent book is *Theorising Media: Power, Form and Subjectivity* (2011).

Katy Parry is a lecturer in communications studies at the University of Leeds, where she teaches visual communication, political communication, and media and war. She is co-author of *Pockets of Resistance: British News Media, War and Theory in the 2003 Invasion of Iraq* (2010), with Piers Robinson, Peter Goddard, Craig Murray and Philip Taylor. She has authored and co-authored journal articles in *Journal of Communication*, *Media Culture & Society*, *Sociology Compass*, *British Journal of Politics and International Relations*, *Media, War and Conflict*, and *Television and New Media*. She was research associate for the 'Media Genre and Political Culture' project, on which this book is based, and continues to publish on media visualization of war.

Kay Richardson's research is located at the intersection of media studies, sociolinguistics and politics. She has authored or co-authored papers in these areas for *Media Culture and Society*, *Multilingua*, *Journal of Sociolinguistics*, *Journal of Language and Politics*, *Language and Literature*, *British Journal of Press and International Relations*, *Interactions* and the *European Journal of Cultural Studies*. Her book *Television Dramatic Dialogue: A Sociolinguistic Study* (2010) brought approaches from sociolinguistics to the study of performed, crafted speech in TV drama. Kay Richardson is based at the University of Liverpool, where she teaches courses on language and communication.

Introduction

This book is a contribution to the growing international and interdisciplinary research on media, communication and politics. Its particular interest is in the ways that politics is dramatized, joked about and expressed within the world of entertainment, understanding that these make an important contribution to the way that political ideas, feelings and values are circulated in society. Forms of storytelling, fantasy, farce and satire provide powerful and rich indicators of the relationship between a national political system and a national political culture, acting both as expressions of, and as resources for, the wider play of imagination. Our own focus is primarily on Britain, though the scholarly context for research of this kind is an international one. The recent increase in the range and scale of media output, extending to the culture of the internet, has added to the significance of media use as an everyday practice of people acting as consumers and also as national citizens, and has deepened and broadened transnational aspects of mediated politics as well.

Taking its cue from the growing interest in both humanities and social-science research in 'political culture' (a notion defined and discussed below), our book seeks to develop improved conceptualization of how the media operate in this arena, based on empirical findings from our own recent research in the British context. Such an inquiry is made particularly pertinent at a time when British politics is undergoing a number of shifts in its party-political identity and its stylings as well as in the kinds of domestic and international challenges it faces. Questions about 'spin', party 'branding', the misuse of expense allowances by elected politicians and the broader mistrust of the political class have all variously become salient themes in the national culture, as have the various attempts of politicians to announce a 'new politics', which offers

1

fresh terms of public transparency and honesty, including those which were articulated during the 2010 election and the subsequent period of government formation and initial policy declarations. The rest of this introduction explains some of our theoretical concepts with reference to the main literatures of research (on political culture, political communications 'beyond the news', and media genre); positions national research within an international context; briefly outlines the chapter sequence; and gives a short account of the empirical materials we drew on in our primary analyses.

Political communication and political culture

There are three broad literatures of research into which our work can be placed and from which it takes its primary references. First of all, and most obviously, there is the literature of media research on the range of practices and forms we have examined. This is brought into our scheme of analysis regularly as it relates to television, radio, newspaper writing, cartoons and a range of web-based formats, and it is too diverse to benefit from an attempt at general summary here. However, our broad relationship to the other two literatures, that of media–political relations and the more focused one centred on issues of 'political culture' (even if this designation is not always the one preferred), can usefully be sketched out in general outline, to be elaborated on and developed in relation to specific chapter content.

There is vast and growing international literature on media–political relations, and what is still frequently called 'political communication', although use of this established term often implies a dual focus on political media management and political journalism that is misleading in relation to the primary concerns of this book. Nevertheless, the wider set of questions about how 'politics' and 'media' interconnect, particularly insofar as public knowledge and civic understanding are at issue, are ones to which we want to connect the analytic findings of our study. These questions are becoming more frequently asked within political science, despite a longstanding tendency to overlook media systems when discussing political structures and processes, or to regard them as fitting only for marginal, sub-specialist attention. However, for some time they have been asked within the developing interdisciplinary area of media and cultural studies, where they have been addressed at different levels of generality but with a growing body of empirical, including historical, investigation, as our references later in this introduction indicate. Within the broad 'political communications' literature, there has been a marked tendency to see the relationship of media to politics in terms of a cause for anxiety, as 'media logic' (see, for instance, the account in Dahlgren, 1995) or the effects of 'mediatization' (Mazzoleni and Schulz, 1999; Strömbäck, 2008; Livingstone, 2009) become more central to policy formulation and to the whole business of political claims-making and political performance. Those societies in which the media are most intensively commercialized or are undergoing further commercialization have often produced a strong 'critical' literature of this kind, but in recent years even European nations with previously strong public service commitments in broadcasting have seen these commitments reduced, so it is not surprising that the critical perspective is internationally familiar and dominant in many publications and conference proceedings. Not everyone has seen a comprehensively negative tendency however. Some have commentated on the increased inclusiveness of political mediation through simplified, dramatized and personalized formats and the very large number of people who now have access to political information and debate (although the very terms, systemic and discursive, upon which popular 'accessibility' has been achieved is the departure point of criticism by others).[1] Continuing and emerging kinds of 'critical' journalism have also been noted, placing those who hold power under questioning and scrutiny. More recently, the potential of 'new media' to resist the techniques of media management, which dominated in previous decades, to allow the increased flow of 'leaks' and 'unofficial' sources of information (including those from people who would not previously have had any means of public exchange) and to permit new forms of political engagement, has been one of the most intensively researched themes in the whole area of international media research.[2]

Quite where the borderlines of 'the political' lay, how far it is viewed as a quite specific, professionalized realm of action or as a dimension of broader public and private life, has been the subject of debate not only within research upon political communication but within the main body of political science itself. In particular, the relationship of a political system to the economic, corporate and legal systems, nationally and internationally, have been regular points of attention, not surprisingly so given the dynamics of globalization, the effect of which has been to reduce national autonomy, the space for independent national action, in a number of ways not always formally acknowledged.[3] Some writers have used the term 'politicality' (see, for instance, the usage in Haines, 1979; and Buckley, 2010) to indicate the various aspects, and different 'strengths', of the political that can be identified in particular activities and discourses, some of which might not be self-identified as being to do with politics at all but are part of the way in which politics is constructed and related to from the broader locations of social space and everyday life. The term has the advantage of displacing any unified and stable sense of 'the political' in favour of a more contingent and constitutive set of elements. Although our primary concern in this book is with the portrayal of professional political activity at a national level (the 'political' in its major institutionalized forms), these more extensive connections with the 'elements' are very important to parts of our analysis, as our central use of the term 'culture' indicates.

If 'politics' is by no means a term indicating self-evident boundaries, then to place 'culture' after it risks blurring matters further and this brings us to our second range of conceptual and analytic reference points. 'Culture' often suggests, sometimes with great imprecision, the wider, diffuse area of meanings and values surrounding a given activity or sphere (e.g. football culture, youth culture, drugs culture). It often does so in awkward relationship to the idea of 'culture' as essentially about the arts and expressive activity. The two meanings frequently leak into each other, not surprisingly given that, as in our study, questions essentially about aesthetic form are often connected back to questions about underlying social values. Sometimes the leakage has a strategic convenience (as, for example in the meaning of the title 'European City of Culture', which is an arts-led usage but one with a strongly affirmative 'local ways of life and values' resonance). Sometimes there is uncertainty or ambivalence as to quite which emphasis is being placed (the idea of 'working-class culture' is notorious for generating debates around this uncertainty). 'Political culture' can be used to indicate the area that surrounds the activities of politicians within the formal political system, to be a designator of 'their' world, variously perceived by the rest of society, and inhabited mostly by politicians, professional administrators and, perhaps only as part-time residents, by political journalists. In Britain, the term 'Westminster Village' conveys something of the self-enclosed and institutionally focused nature of the idea, as does the notion of the 'political class' as indicating an elite separate in important ways from the rest of society. However, 'political culture' also has an established usage in political science and political sociology (see, for instance, Almond, 1956; Somers, 1995; Berg-Schlosser, 2009) as a term indicating the wider range of orientations, norms and perceptions within which a political system is embedded. The usage is sometimes to be found in comparative work on different political systems and is routinely subject to debate about how best to research it sociologically (again, see

Berg-Schlosser, 2009). It is then of interest how this usage, one close in its general descriptive profile to the sense in which this book will use the term, relates to the idea of 'civic culture', the sphere of meanings and values that embraces all who are citizens.[4] Lacking the explicit core reference to political structures and processes, 'civic culture' is a more diffuse, dispersed idea, ranging from the perspectives surrounding types of committed civic action to the less self-conscious, intermittent and partial sense of the 'civic self' that informs everyday life for many people. This is a 'civic self' routinely invoked by, for instance, paying taxes, responding to various changes in national and local government regulations and attending to media accounts of political persons and events.

We shall keep the ideas of 'political culture' (in its broad and narrow meanings) and of 'civic culture' in focus throughout this book, their relationship through media practices, and often their overlap, being a part of our investigative agenda since our material connects both with the sphere of professional politics and the broader setting of values and patterns of awareness, consent and concern within whose framing terms the business of this sphere, as 'public business', is organized and conducted. However, there is a third notional space we want to consider too, that of 'popular culture'. Again, this lacks a focused centre and is immediately diffuse in implications, although it is now routinely seen to be framed in terms of the entertainment and leisure industries and those cultural productions, including media productions, which have met with sufficient levels of market success to justify their description as 'popular'. This gives it a pronounced 'arts and expression' emphasis rather than that sociological–anthropological emphasis ('practices and values') activated in uses of 'political' and 'civic' culture. Always a contested area in terms of its definition and values through its very etymology (see Williams, 1976; Hall, 1981), 'popular' culture carries a resonance, of the choices of 'ordinary people', which cannot easily be ignored within the conventional terms of democratic society.

One of the growth areas in recent research on media–political relations has been the examination of how politics relates to 'popular culture', constituting a special focus within the framework of those broader questions concerning the media and politics relationship, and the more general connections with the 'cultural', which we noted above. We indicate some of these studies below and then at points in the following chapters, since they are a primary reference point for much of our argument. They give emphasis to the political significance of the entertaining, the comic and to the apparently trivial, whereas the framings of 'political culture' and 'civic culture' have tended to exclude or marginalize these in favour of the 'serious'. However, throughout the book we shall regularly return to the ways in which all three designated areas, with their recognisable centres of gravity, interconnect, and the ways that the changing forms of this interconnection carry implications both for what 'politics' is now and how 'the media' portray it.

Mediated politics: in the news and 'beyond the news'

In media–political relations, it is the journalistic treatment of politics that has conventionally received the lion's share of attention among political communication scholars. And although, in Britain as elsewhere, media coverage of political life spreads well beyond traditional print and broadcast news discourse, it is important to note that a great deal of this range takes the national news agenda as its point of departure. In this section we comment on 'political news' as a contemporary cultural phenomenon, to provide us with a baseline of our own for the purposes of later discussion. Our primary point of reference is to Britain, but as our indicative references show, the British experience has considerable international resonance.

Political journalists can 'enjoy' close relationships with politicians in what has been referred to as a symbiotic and mutually beneficial relationship (Louw, 2005); however, issues of perceived spin and obfuscation from politicians, along with hostility and combative questioning from journalists, can lead to each blaming the other for public disaffection and cynicism about politics. Politicians might agree that journalists should hold them to account and interrogate their policies, but they can become antagonized by what they see as the media's insatiable appetite for gaffes and scandals, dubbing it a 'feral beast tearing people and reputations to bits' (Blair, 2007: see also Lloyd, 2004). Journalists in turn counter that their critical, inquisitorial approach is necessary to combat the pre-tested, packaged and highly spun versions of policies that politicians present to the public via the news domain.

Political news does not just cover, then, the serious 'hard news' of governance, or reasoned debate between political elites, but gaffes, trivia and revelations about politicians' behaviour and character 'behind closed doors'. The ever-shifting professional values and presumptions of 'what counts' as political news, with the serious 'hard' subjects apparently making room for more personalized 'soft' subjects and tabloid treatments, make any definition prone to certain strains and fuzziness around the borders. Furthermore, battles for control over where the lines are drawn and conflicting messages from politicians and journalists on what counts as politically relevant information appear to be increasingly contested in the public arena. The manoeuvrings of mediated politics, characterized variously through the years as pseudo-events (Boorstin, 1961), spin, packaging (Franklin, 1994) and 'PR-ization of politics' (Louw, 2005), can become the subject rather than the covert processes of political news.

The dominance of the 'agenda setting' elite politicians in the news has traditionally relegated ordinary citizens or the public to a minor role in mediated political life; a tendency that, certainly in TV news, has been found to reinforce the perceived distance and disconnection between official political news and the public's own experiences and activities (Lewis et al., 2005; Couldry et al., 2007). As Dahlgren writes, citizens as spectators 'cannot easily translate journalistic information into civic knowledge and practices', a fault not only of the way political life is organized but also of 'how the news portrays citizens, giving very few clues to support civic identities and agency' (Dahlgren, 2009, p. 130). As noted earlier, where political news discourse fails in encouraging civic engagement, a number of authors believe that features of popular culture could enhance democratic life, both where its influence has seeped into political life, even redefining 'what constitutes politics' (ibid., p. 137), and in popular entertainment formats (van Zoonen, 2003, 2005; Coleman, 2006). For example, politicians may choose to appear on non-news TV formats, such as chat shows, to avoid the penetrating questioning of political interviewers, but such appearances can feed back into the news cycle if they 'slip up' or choose to announce a new policy. However, politicians should beware of circumventing the traditional routes for announcing policy, since snubbed political journalists are keen to point out politicians' transgressions to the public. The politician meanwhile gambles that the popular talk show will receive a larger audience than the political commentary of the journalist. But the 'non-political political interview' also contributes to a style of politics in which both the politician and presenter perform their roles as media celebrities in a more relaxed and wide-ranging setting than afforded by the restricted, sound-bite culture of the news. On the internet, publicized webchats with politicians, within discussion forums such as Mumsnet, can target effectively a certain section of the electorate, addressing their particular concerns while also promoting their own efforts at digital interactivity. The terms 'personalization of politics', 'lifestyle politics' and 'celebrity politician', linked intrinsically to the dominance of TV as the defining medium for political life, have now received a good deal of attention

(Delli Carpini and Keeter, 1996; Marshall, 1997; Bennett, 1998; Blumler and Gurevitch, 2001; van Zoonen, 2005, 2006; Campus, 2010; Mancini, 2011), with the performances and personae of politicians deemed fundamental to understanding and appreciating mediated political culture (Corner and Pels, 2003; Higgins, 2010). As our interest resides in those notional mediated spaces between news and popular culture, we have not set out to measure further expansions of 'soft' into 'hard' news coverage. However, our remit does allow for a cross-generic investigation into those spaces where symbolic expressions and interpretations travel and morph into politics as entertainment. As politicians, journalists and citizens adapt to the always-on news cycle, or 'political information cycle' (Chadwick, 2011a, 2011b), of the new media environment, it can be argued that the very nature of politics changes along with wider cultural and technological shifts.

To introduce a cultural framing in this context is to recognize that public interest in political affairs has a variable character, and that citizens access the 'political' in different forms and at different levels. Undoubtedly, they access politics as information and opinion, mediated 'officially' via news journalism and associated editorial comment, and less officially via online sources. They also access it through comedy programmes, drama, newspaper cartoons, reality TV, blogs, online forums, Twitter streams and satiric newspaper columns, many of which are designed to offer pleasure as much as, or even more than, to enhance their understanding of 'the political' and perhaps mobilize them to political action.

As our earlier comments suggest, our study thus belongs within what can be described as the 'cultural turn' in the political-communication field, a more comprehensive placing of mediation within the broader settings of social values and expressivity exemplified by such studies as Street (1997), Corner and Pels (2003), van Zoonen (2005), Jones (2005, 2010) and Mazzoleni and Sfardini (2009). The next two sections of our introduction deal respectively with the concept of 'genre' and with genre research in its international context.

Media genre

In the mediated space that is positioned somewhere between official political news and popular entertainment there exists, as we noted above, a variety of media formats in which political issues, events and people are approached through commentary, comedy, satire and debate. The genres that offer expressive and imaginative treatments operate differently at varied positions on the 'elite'/'popular' spectrum of taste, and are of interest to us when they rely on substantive thematic content with a specifically political focus, in whole or in part.

The notion of 'genre' is a relatively unfamiliar one within the literature on political communications, although as the above-mentioned 'cultural turn' in international work continues, this is likely to change. One reason for its absence is that established work in the area, particularly on media and elections, has been centrally if not exclusively concerned with the modes of political journalism. Here, although there are important variations in formal organization and market demographics to be registered, ideas of generic-level variation might seem beside the point given the relative singularity of focus. However, since our own project centrally involves drawing comparisons and contrasts across very different ways of representing politics in speech, image and writing across diverse media, ideas of the generic are at the core of our approach. Recognising, if only approximately, what 'kind' of thing a given item of mediation belongs to informs a sense of what kind of formal 'rules' it might follow in its construction, what kinds of satisfaction it might give and what kind of criteria might be most appropriate to judgements of its qualities. In relation to politics and the political, it provides an indication of the expressive range, scope and level of detail likely to be found, and the modes of address and tones that will be employed. Notions of genre provide basic templates both for media practice and for media use. Although in their more intensively commercialized varieties they have been regarded as formulaic constraints on creativity, they are better approached analytically as frameworks enabling certain types of discursive work to be done effectively, building on recognized precedents but allowing originality. An example that demonstrates an occasion when the political world and a commercialized variety of TV genre collided rather uncomfortably was Gordon Brown's appearance on the celebrity chat show *Life Stories with Piers Morgan* in February 2010, in which he talked with great emotion about the death of his daughter in front of a studio audience that included his tearful wife. Appearing within a TV genre associated with celebrity revelations opened up novel space for the incumbent prime minister to show his 'human' side, but it also highlighted just how far Brown had moved, from conventional political TV, into a popular form of programming with its own distinctive 'rules' and highly stylized qualities. The idea of generic 'affordance' may be used to register this capacity.[5] The medium of TV has already attracted significant work on the 'working through' of public issues in genres beyond the news – how generic recipes and remediated interpretations of events work to invite responses from audiences, and how audiences also 'work through' those public and private concerns in their conscious and unconscious engagements with the generic material (Ellis, 2000; see also Corner, 2004). Annette Hill has usefully developed the notion of 'genre work' (2007) to further understand how audiences respond to generic techniques in factual programming and especially the 'feral genre' of reality TV (2007, p. 215). Our study takes these ideas up within a much broader frame of reference and with reference to a wider range of examples.

International contexts and national comparisons

The global communication and entertainment industries undoubtedly influence what particular national audiences get to see, hear and read across the mediascape, and public policy internationally is generally supportive of increased marketization in these industries (Thussu, 2007). With due acknowledgement of homogenising trends originating at this level, and allowing also for the transnational affordances of the internet as a medium and channel of communication, intensive focus on national levels of media production and consumption remains the most appropriate starting point in the cultivation of this particular research field, a necessary basis for convincing cross-cultural explorations, of a kind which is now seriously under way.

The 2011 special double issue of *Popular Communication*, 'Not Necessarily the News: Global Approaches to News Parody and Political Satire', provides a timely collection for international contextualization of similar kinds of non-news forms. It has articles on TV news-parody formats in France, the USA, the UK, Australia, Italy, Germany, India, Israel, Palestine (now YouTube online archive only), Iran (Voice of America, via satellite to Iran), Hungary, Romania and Denmark. There is certainly evidence from this material of extensive transnational programme flows, with countries buying, borrowing and adapting formats like that of Britain's *Spitting Image* (ITV, 1984–1996) or America's *The Daily Show* (Comedy Central, 1996–present) (Baym and Jones, 2012). *Spitting Image* was the original inspiration for France's *Les Guignols de L'info* (News Puppets, Canal+, 1988–present – see Doyle, 2012), which has in its turn been acquired as a format in India, broadcasting there as *Gustakhi Maaf* (Excuse the Transgression, NDTV India, 2003–present – see Kumar, 2012). In other research, Hamo et al. (2010) demonstrate considerable similarities between the tactics of politician–interviewees in 'mock interviews' of the 'Ali G' kind, in both Israel and the UK.[6] Yet the authors in *Popular Communication* are also keen to show how news-parody programmes, whether imported or home-grown, fit into national cultural traditions and contexts. In India, for example, the considerable differences between the Hindi and the English language news-parody offerings on TV (*Gustakhi Maaf* versus *That Was the Week That Wasn't*, CNN-IBN, 2006–present) speak to a linguo-cultural divide between the rural population and an anglophone urban elite, as a legacy of British colonial rule, while also building on much older Indian dramatic and satiric traditions (Kumar, 2012).

National starting points, including our own, are desirable in the first place, because, viewed as a contribution to cultural study, the research requires a focus close to citizens' experiences of reading, watching and listening to media discourse. With the exception of (parts of) the internet, these experiences are nationally conditioned. In the second place, as a study of *political* culture, it relates to understandings of domestic national *politics* – this being the most significant kind of politics for most people. The genres and formats themselves may or may not be 'home-grown' ones, depending on the country, but in focusing on Britain, our own research has begun with a country which, like the USA, has a strong tradition of originating a lot of its own broadcasting programmes and formats, both for domestic consumption and for export. Its exported formats have included *That Was The Week That Was* (BBC, 1962–1963) and *Spitting Image*, both programmes highly relevant to the subject of this book. Other genres covered here (press parliamentary sketchwriting is a significant example – see Chapter 2) seem to have few equivalents in other countries (Crabb, 2010; Richardson and Corner, 2011).

The international success of the American TV drama *The West Wing* in the noughties shows that it is not only political TV *formats* that can be imported but also actual *programmes*, raising questions as to whether the non-American audiences for these programmes interpret them exclusively with reference to America as a foreign country, or also derive meanings that impinge on their understandings of politicality in more general ways. Van Zoonen's (2007) research on audience responses to audiovisual political fiction, using the international resource of Internet Movie Database discussion forums, explores how viewers from a variety of backgrounds construct their 'political selves' in their modes of comment on both feature films and TV drama series, including *The West Wing*. More recently, the success of Danish imports *The Killing* and *Borgen* suggests that sectors of the British public have an appetite for international drama with substantial political content, despite the vast majority of viewers being unfamiliar with the represented political culture and its language.

Countries vary therefore in the extent of their political media outputs overall, as well as in the range of genres that they offer, and the balance struck between serious and light-hearted modes of address across and within mediums, genres and formats. The balance of commercial as against public service values at the institutional levels of media ownership and media regulation play an important part in determining the specific configurations available in any given polity, as do variations in language and literacy conditions. Yet there are also similarities, because the same basic forces are at work: the state's need to manage public opinion; politicians' needs for publicity in a context of party and individual competition; media commercial interests; media public-service commitments. It is the relative weighting of these forces that varies from country to country. Israel and the UK are both parliamentary democracies with a 'mixed economy' of public service and commercial broadcasting: both have introduced mock interviews to the generic repertoire, and involved politicians as interviewees (Hamo et al., 2010). The political dispensation in contemporary China is of a very different character: here, commercial considerations rather than democratic principles have seemingly fostered more open alternatives to traditional, monologic, state propaganda such as *Duihua* (*Dialogues*, CCTV, 2000–2004). But for Zhong (2004), the hierarchy between the main voices and the supporting ones in *Dialogues* is too strong, the main voices are too like-minded, the topics are too safe to merit the programme's branding as a real alternative to the standard fare on Chinese TV.

The generic system is constantly being modified by new options as a result of broader market and technological as well as aesthetic shifts, and any assessment of it, including the one we present in the following chapters, is necessarily provisional. We now briefly summarize the material to be found in those chapters.

The sequence of chapters

Our study is presented through five core chapters. The first three chapters present and discuss specific textual materials; the fourth deals primarily with audience responses to particular items from our corpus (we give more information about the corpus at the end of this Introduction), while the fifth chapter is a thematic synopsis, identifying the most significant matters of political substance to have emerged from the research across the range of distinct generic forms.

The three textual chapters address, respectively, broadcast, print and internet genres. Although the internet can be used as a distribution channel for any genre via websites, programme downloads and podcasts, we recognize that particular genres have their origins in one or the other, and this has been the basis of our divisions.

Chapter 1, on broadcasting, covers both radio and TV, allowing us to focus on genres such as the 'panel show' (*Any Questions*, *Question Time*), which are common to both media in appropriately customized forms. Broadcasting shows politics at its most performative, with embodied and envoiced imitations of politicians (for dramatic or comic purposes) appearing alongside performances by politicians themselves. Chapter 2, on the press, takes most of its material from the national daily (including Sunday) newspapers – editorials, cartoons, sketch columns and other authored column writings. It also includes some items from the fortnightly satirical magazine *Private Eye*, which has long provided its own distinctive contribution to national political discourse. Comic textual design is of particular interest to us in this chapter, both written and illustrated, and forms a point of connection with our treatment of comic discourse in other media.

Chapter 3, on web formats, concentrates mainly on the political 'blog post', as a genre which owes its existence to the internet. So-called 'social media' (Facebook, Twitter) are now regarded as central to the likely development of online public communication, but blogging has shown itself capable of adapting to these new conditions while remaining distinctive, and this certainly includes political blogging.

It is in relation to online media that references to media 'audiences' have come to seem so problematic (though feeding back into older theoretical concerns about media 'consumption' and media use). We pick up on some of the key issues in Chapter 4, our audience chapter, notably around the increased opportunities for public participation in political communication by citizens, beyond those associated with traditional media such as the published 'letter to the editor' in a newspaper. However, the core of the chapter focuses on taped discussions we held with respondent groups convened for the specific purpose of discussing textual extracts.

Chapter 5 is a thematic chapter that allows us to complement the form-driven analyses of the textual chapters with discussion of the topics that these forms take as their subject matter, paying particular interest to those political subjects, feelings and values that cut across generic space. This also places in a more developed context the comments of our respondents as cited and discussed in Chapter 4.

We end the book with a chapter that attempts to draw together some of the key findings from the research and assess its significance not only in relation to contemporary British political culture but also its contribution to the international agenda of research in this area, with some suggestions for how this agenda might be further developed and extended.

Before proceeding to our substantive chapters, however, we present a short overview of our corpus of materials from across the media landscape, and our collection methods.

Notes on data collection

We collated a selective yet varied corpus of material, initially from TV, radio, national press and the blogosphere, across a spectrum of formal and informal engagement with political life in Britain. Here, we provide further description and rationalization of the corpus selection.

Primary data collection took place throughout 2010, although our survey of political culture and media genre ultimately covers a broader scope in its interests, beyond the more systematic auditing undertaken at points throughout the year. We conducted three audits of selected media materials: the first period covered the four weeks of February 2010; our second covered five weeks, running from 15 April to 19 May, to cover the general election and its aftermath; our third autumn sample captured the main political-party conference season and Comprehensive Spending Review, running from 18 September to 8 October, and restarting on 17–24 October 2010, providing another four weeks' worth of materials.

Selection was discerning in its scope because of the sheer scale of the amount of material on offer in the national mediascape. From the national press we collected all the front-page headlines (where politically themed), parliamentary sketch-writing, the main political column or comment piece, editorials and editorial cartoons in five national newspapers (*Sun, Daily Mirror, Daily Mail, Guardian* and *Daily Telegraph* – along with their Sunday equivalents).

From radio, we recorded about three hours each week: two weekly studio-based shows on media and politics (*Media Show*, BBC Radio 4; *Week in Westminster* or *Beyond Westminster*, BBC Radio 4); a Friday night news-oriented comedy show (*The News Quiz* or *The Now Show*, BBC Radio 4); a political panel show with participating audience (*Any*

Questions, BBC Radio 4), along with its corresponding phone-in show (*Any Answers*, BBC Radio 4).

Because of its importance as a source of political representations in British cultural life, we collected between 17 and 19 hours of recordings each week from free-to-air TV channels. We selected two daily (weekday) shows: one directly concerned with the machinations of Westminster (*Daily Politics*, BBC 2); and one popular daytime talk-show incorporating newspaper reviews and audience participation through phone calls, e-mail, Twitter and SMS (*The Wright Stuff*, Five TV). The core audit sample additionally included: four weekly political shows (*Question Time*, BBC 1 (with its participating audience); *This Week*, BBC 1; *Andrew Marr Show*, BBC 1; *The Politics Show*, BBC 1); a comedy panel show (*Mock the Week*, BBC2 or *Have I Got News for You*, BBC 1) and a current-affairs documentary series (*Panorama*, BBC 1). We added to these regular programmes a number of more occasional broadcasts, some of which are brought into our analysis later. For the February audit, this included the four-part reality TV series, *Tower Block of Commons* (Channel 4), Gordon Brown's appearance on *Piers Morgan's Life Stories*, and the one-off drama *On Expenses* (BBC4). During the election period this included the three Leader Debates and the three-part Channel 4 satirical show, *Bremner, Bird and Fortune*. In the autumn audit, *Daily Politics* (BBC2) was frequently extended beyond its usual 30 minutes to cover the party-conference speeches and reactions in September and the Comprehensive Spending Review in October.

From the UK blogosphere, we selected four regularly updated and popular blogs from across the political spectrum (*Dizzy Thinks, Paul Waugh, Liberal Burblings, Luke Akehurst*). Our core selection of blogs represents a small 'dip' into the variety and expanse of the UK-based political blogosphere; however, they provide a range of insider and outsider status and a spread of political partisanship while being among the most popular in their particular category of blog (Dale, 2009).

In surveying the broad mediascape throughout a year-long period, we argue that our study offers a more nuanced picture of the meanings and values in public circulation than a study focused on one specific genre would be able to do. Along with recording the date, title and media format for each of the materials, we devised a two-level coding schema to identify key elements of interest. The Primary Coding level provided a macro-level summary of the prominent Political Themes or Subjects and the dominant Communicative Modes of expression for each media output. The Secondary Coding level captured the detailed substance of the media content under the main headings of Political People, Issues,

Institutions and Values, along with space for notes on key visuals. This allowed us to plot a broad profile of political references, themes and modes of articulation. We refer the reader to Appendix 2 for more details on the coding scheme and further notes on how we utilized the database as a resource, providing a general profile of political themes and modes of articulation across the media forms and formats we sampled.

1

Broadcasting Beyond the News: Performing Politics

In democratic political systems, broadcasting has from its origins been attributed with key roles in mediating between government and citizens. Its nature as a way of recording and transmitting speech and then (with TV) images, including through 'live' programming, have given it a special and powerful place in the history of media–political relations (for a recent historical account see Hilmes (2011)). Although the extent and character of broadcasting's public service responsibilities vary from country to country, and are subject to change over time, all governments impose some level of duty towards the polity, a duty which broadcasters interpret through considerations of their own, convergent or divergent, agendas of public communication (Freedman (2008) reviews the different policy frameworks in their economic settings). These agendas are more or less commercial according to national context, and more or less influenced, if not by bottom-up demands direct from viewers and listeners, then at least by a professionalized orientation to viewing figures and other proxy indicators of what makes political content in various generic formats relevant and interesting to them.

Political *news* on the airwaves has always attracted the most academic attention in political-communication research, as the core component in the fulfilment of broadcasting's democratic obligations. As with print media, in political news on radio and TV the conduct and performance of government is mediated to national audiences, along with the variously supportive or critical voices of participants inside and outside of the political apparatus. Within these conditions of political 'visibility', the extent to which, and the ways in which, elected rulers can pursue *unpublicized* governance is a pressing question, as is evident in the level of outcry when leaders are discovered trying to 'conceal' important actions from public scrutiny or when past concealment is revealed.

From the perspective of our own interest in genres of political communication, broadcast news typically is articulated across distinctive formats that are separately and collectively worthy of analysis – anchor speech to microphone and/or camera; voice-over film package; the live two-way; the news interview. Our inattention to these formats here is not because they lack importance, but because our focus is on the broadcasting of politics and political themes past the point where 'news' stops and other genres begin, while recognising a degree of generic permeability and format transfer. Thus, although interviewing of politicians may take place as *segments* within *items* within news *programmes*, the specific properties of the 'accountability interview' format (Montgomery, 2007; see also Clayman and Heritage, 2002), where something more penetrating than the provision of information/opinion is sought by the interviewer on the public's behalf, may also be found in other contexts, including as current-affairs programmes in their own right (*Jeremy Paxman Interviews*, BBC 1, April and May 2010).

Arguably, broadcast news is the genre most likely to preserve a rhetorical stance in which politics and its reportage are independent of one another, consonant with the formulation 'media coverage of politics'. But if news is reframed as just one of the possibilities in a spectrum of genres, and the framework is shifted to 'mediated politics' as a more satisfactory way of understanding the relationships involved, then we can begin more carefully to unpack the ways that broadcasting's generic repertoire configures relations between citizens and embodied/en-voiced performances of politicality. The role of the inquisitorial interviewer is just as much a political role in this perspective as is that of the interviewee, not because of any ideological stance on the part of the former, but because of the democratic functions performed by such interviewers within mediated politics.

It is also important, within this framework, to allow for mediated politics as a resource not only for civic engagement (e.g. allowing for participation in debates over political issues and values) but also, and perhaps at the same time, for general entertainment (e.g. through drama and comedy). Politicians are one group of people among many others, whose appearance and actions can be mocked for the sake of humour, where the humour is regarded as a self-sufficient outcome quite separate from any civic value. Not all politically based humour on TV and radio is satirical in intention or effect. Yet even in genres where an entertainment objective takes precedence over a civic one, civic sensibility may nevertheless be nurtured: the material may, as a side effect, help to increase political knowledge, provide resources for deliberation of political issues, or help to foster greater attention to political matters more generally (see, e.g., Cao, 2010). Of interest here is how news and non-news broadcasting works with the *emotional* attachments of citizens, along with their cooler rationalities, in the fostering of civic dispositions, whether those dispositions are cynical/rejecting/disengaged or engaged/affirmatory/partisan, in whole or in part.

The generic repertoire

What is the best structure to adopt in presenting the range of broadcast genres where audiences encounter politics and politicality? What sequence of programmes and/or formats is most useful for indicating key aspects of mediated politics across both radio and TV? These questions presented a significant challenge in the writing of this chapter. The most obvious approach would have been by medium, separating radio from TV. But this was too mechanistic for our purposes, and would have involved an unsatisfactory separation of very similar formats, such as the TV show *Question Time* (BBC 1, 1979–present) and the radio show *Any Questions?* (BBC Radio 4, 1948–present). We therefore adopted an aspectual approach, focusing on aspects of (political) *performance* in broadcasting. This focus takes its justification not only from our interest in political performativity more generally, but also from the fact that it is with the broadcast media, much more than either print or online media, that we derive our sense of politicians and other persons in the political world as embodied human beings, with faces, voices and mannerisms.[1] Their social identities become more complete for us through our para–social interactions (Horton and Wohl, 1956) with their live and recorded public performances, and those performances in turn become resources for subsequent characterizations in further broadcast contexts.

The dimensions of performance in which we are interested, specifically in relation to *broadcast* genres, are fourfold. Our first principle of differentiation is between primary and secondary performance. Primary performance is that which takes place when a politician is engaged in some on-stage business, and is required to present a public version of him- or herself. The most-discussed British examples of this in recent times were the three televised *Leaders' Debates* of April 2010, which took place as part of the 2010 General Election campaign (ITV 1, Sky News, BBC 1, 2010).[2] Secondary performance involves the imitation of a public figure by an actor, an impressionist or a member of the public (*Bremner, Bird and Fortune*, Channel 4, 1999–present), or else the creation of fictional politicians, designed to fit requirements of story and theme in a dramatic context (*The West Wing*, NBC, 1999–2007; *The Amazing Mrs Pritchard*, BBC 1, 2006). A second significant difference is that between performances of a 'public' and that of a 'private' self. Performances of the former take place when viewers and listeners are given access to the in-role self, appropriate to the public context. Performances of the latter are also possible, as when, in 2010, Prime Minister Gordon Brown gave an interview to Piers Morgan in the latter's *Life Stories* series (ITV 1, 2009–present), which we discuss below. In the opening-up of private life to public attention, politicians can be seen as accommodating themselves to the conditions of contemporary celebrity culture, ever more interested in the private affairs of the famous. Thirdly, we differentiate between comic and serious performances. Although, beyond mild attempts at humour, a politician is very unlikely to indulge in deliberately comic self-presentation (with someone like London Mayor Boris Johnson as a possible exception here), video or audio clips of their gaffes and misfortunes can often be rekeyed and made to serve humorous functions, as on the comedy panel show, *Have I Got News For You* (BBC 2/BBC 1, 1990–present), while impressionists like Rory Bremner make a living from their ability to produce versions of politicians that can be put to comic/satiric purposes (*Bremner, Bird and Fortune*, Channel 4, 1999–present). The serious self-performance of actual politicians is complemented by actorly versions of these in 'serious' drama–documentary (*The Deal*, Channel 4, 2003; *The Kennedys*, ReelzChannel, 2011), or by fictional politicians such as *The West Wing's* Josiah Bartlet (NBC, 1999–2007). Finally, we are attentive to the differences between, and the distribution of, dialogic and monologic modes of address by politicians to one another, to intermediaries and to the electorate. The traditional political speech (in origin a pre-broadcasting genre of political communication) has a vestigial presence in the contemporary mediascape, wherever national audiences are given access to fragments of speeches in the form of 'soundbites'. But the more prevalent dialogic contexts, with or without audience participation, can be adapted to include monologic components, publicly performed statements of opinion and belief where any 'response' from an interlocutor has the status of an optional extra.

As this discussion shows, the four dimensions of broadcast political performance here identified (serious and comic, public and private, self and other, monologic and dialogic) are ones which interact with one another to produce specific generic forms and particular programmes, where some programmes are more or less singular in respect of format throughout (*Jeremy Paxman Interviews*), while others are composed of discrete segments, each of which might be distinctively formatted (*Bremner, Bird and Fortune*). Segmental broadcasting also lends itself very usefully to cyberspace remediation (Bolter and Grusin, 2000) via 'clips' – on YouTube, on the broadcaster's own website, or on other blogs and websites (bearing in mind issues arising from considerations of copyright in this regard). In any period, there is merit in identifying traditional as well as innovative ways of trying to engage with the audience–electorate, if only as part of an effort to anticipate future developments. Thus, the discussion below also tries to work with a sense of the familiar in relation to the novel forms of political broadcasting, with perhaps slightly greater emphasis on the latter.

Performing the political self

Serious, public personae

It is not only the elected politicians, or the candidates for elected office, who offer in-role performances of their civic selves in broadcast programmes, but also the intermediaries (journalists, interviewers, programme hosts) and the participating citizens. And although we are drawing a line for expositional purposes between 'private' and 'public' selves, certain aspects of identity have public relevance and can be invoked without loss of privacy in the course of serious political discussion. It is as parents, welfare recipients, job seekers, pensioners, workers, business people, shareholders, home owners, customers, savers and so on that citizens have a stake in politics and government.

Within a civic perspective, politicians seek opportunities to put across their own arguments while concealing anything they regard as better not exposed to too much scrutiny – better for them, for their party or for their country. Broadcasters seek to get as much information as possible into the public domain, to interrogate the sense and ethics behind particular proposals, to hold politicians to account. Broadcasters are also likely to care more than politicians about the *popularity* of political programming, as well as, if not instead of, its value for democracy. If the intrinsic fascination of political talk for the sake of better civic involvement is not enough on its own to draw the crowds, then extrinsic considerations become relevant. More extensive revelations; greater theatrics; insights on the personal man or woman behind the public persona; on TV, greater use of visual resources to support the verbal discourse, are all potentially useful here.

Whatever the content of the talk – foreign affairs, the economy, law and order, housing, education, social welfare and so on, there is a self-presentational task to accomplish in broadcasting to the nation. Where the context is a politically serious one, that task calls for the display of commitment to civic values, conditioned by the speaker's place in the polity. The expectations in respect of a prime minister are very different from those in respect of a fringe party by-election candidate, though both might legitimately describe themselves as 'politicians'. The individuality of the politician–persona is variable too: some politicians are able, over time, to establish a distinctive 'voice', while others, with limited opportunity to occupy national airtime, may restrict themselves to a dutiful on-message repertoire, with scant hope of indexing their deeper identities and characteristics in so doing.

The serious, public political self is the default identity for the purposes of political broadcasting. To perform in this mode requires a rather one-dimensional persona, a speaker who holds him or herself to the designated speaking position of politician, citizen or intermediary. These speaking positions have representational obligations. The politician speaks for his or her party, and sometimes for the government. The citizen may be an official spokesperson for an interest group, or positioned as an exemplary 'teacher', or 'senior citizen', or 'jobseeker', etc. The intermediary carries responsibilities in respect of the broadcasting institution.

Mainstream political broadcasting deploys performers in all of these positions, in varying configurations of interaction according to genre and format. Rather than plot the entire territory, we will take a route through it, which identifies dominant features for this mode of performance so as to better understand significant variations which offered themselves in our datum corpus, drawn from the British national mediascape of 2010. The play of tradition and innovation is of interest here, and to a lesser extent the relative prominence of particular genres.

'Question Time': a case study

The weekly *Question Time* is a flagship programme in Britain's public service repertoire. We start with this because of its status, because it involves exemplars of all three speaking positions, and because it represented the most traditional end of the generic spectrum in 2010. It has been broadcasting since 1979; its radio equivalent is *Any Questions?*, on air since 1948, with only four permanent chairs in that period.

Question Time currently is normally configured as follows. The neutral chairman is the eminent celebrity broadcaster David Dimbleby who sits in the middle seat with panellists to either side around a semicircular table facing a studio audience. The five panellists always include a representative of the Conservative and Labour parties, and very often a Liberal Democrat as well (the Liberal Democrat 'slot' can also be filled by a representative of a minority party or a national party from Scotland or Wales). The other two panellists are citizens, but distinguished from those in the studio audience by their personal standing in public life – an eminent journalist, for instance, and more recently a celebrity from the worlds of entertainment or sport. The citizens in the studio audience pose questions to the panellists when invited by Dimbleby to do so and these form the basis for the discussion of a current affairs topic. In its one-hour slot, between four and six topics can be covered in this fashion. The questions have been preselected but the panellists do not know what they will be until they are delivered. Follow-up questions and comments are more spontaneous and responsive to what panellists have said. The proceedings are not broadcast live but neither are they edited before airing and there are no retakes during recording. Some interaction between panellists is facilitated.

The voice of the politician in 'Question Time'

Politicians on the *Question Time* panel, as engaged participants in public life, come to the programme with knowledge of what the main news topics of the preceding week have been, and when the questions are put to them their experience and preparation around these topics allow them to deliver initial short monologues to the studio and home audiences. They speak primarily as individuals, in command of their own beliefs, feelings and opinions, though their individuality is of course constrained by their obligations to the party they represent. The following example (and other examples in this section) are drawn from the edition broadcast on 25 February 2010.

The question is: *'Should RBS pay 1.3 billion pounds in bonuses when they lost 3.6 billion pounds last year?'*. Peter Hain, a senior member of the governing Labour Party (Secretary of State for Wales) is the second person to offer a response:

> Well, I agree with a lot of what Elfyn said.[3] Frankly, bankers are the only people who've made politicians look popular in the last year or so, and that's saying something after what's gone on. Look, what's happening here is that the government – and this takes up a point that was made from the back earlier on. The government has had to rescue the banks from what has been a worldwide banking implosion.

We all know that, it started in America and it came rushing round the world like a blizzard. And

[Heckling from the studio audience disrupts Hain's fluency temporarily; Dimbleby suppresses heckler]

And in the course of that the Royal Bank of Scotland has at least reduced its losses significantly from around twenty-four billion to three billion, has started to repair the damage done and has started to get itself into a proper situation. I wish they weren't paying any bonuses at all. As it happens, nobody earning over thirty-nine thousand pounds is getting an entire cash bonus. And the Chief Executive of the RSBS, Stephen Hester, has foregone his own bonuses. But I wish bankers would start realising, especially when taxpayers' money, your money, has bailed out the banks, that they would behave much more responsibly as individuals.

The background to this issue is that as a result of the financial crisis in 2008–2009, the British government became the majority shareholder in the Royal Bank of Scotland Group, saving it from collapse. In 2010 the company's management sought to pay bonuses to staff, as was their normal practice, though not quite to normal levels. This seemed to much of the public not only to offer reward for failure but also, self-servingly, to protect one set of privileged individuals – bankers – when other citizens had lost jobs, homes and savings as a result of the crisis. Hain speaks personally when he says 'I agree with a lot of what Elfyn said', and 'I wish bankers would... behave much more responsibly as individuals', and when he adds, as a self-deprecating grace note, a joke at the expense of both bankers and politicians. But as a part of the British government, he is expected to speak protectively in relation to his party's executive actions. He can defend the original bailing out of the banks, including RBS, which appears to have improved while within state ownership. He has a bigger problem when it comes to the bonuses. His on-message approach is not to defend them (though he does try to dial down their scale), but to 'outsource' responsibility from the government to the industry, and to individuals in the industry, making it a moral issue for them. But it is then precisely this outsourcing of responsibility for which he/his party/his government will come under attack as discussion proceeds.

The programme permits considerable amounts of 'play' across individual and collective framings by politicians and other panellists, depending upon the topic and the participant's relationship to that topic. In the same episode, the behaviour of one of the panellists, Nigel Farage of the UK Independence Party (UKIP), *is* the topic:

> Are Nigel Farage's rude and attention-seeking remarks about the new President of the European Council not conclusive proof that UKIP, and he, have become nothing more than a boorish national embarrassment?

UKIP is an ultra-nationalist, anti-European party, attracting just enough electoral support to return some members to the European Parliament (for which turnout is notoriously low).[4] Farage had been the leader of the party between 2006 and 2009, was the party's elected representative for South East England in the European Parliament, and led the UKIP group in that Parliament. During the preceding week he had reportedly said publicly to the President of the European Union, 'you have the charisma of a damp rag and the appearance of a low-grade bank clerk'; 'you have a loathing for the very concept of the existence of nation states, perhaps because you come from Belgium, which is pretty much a non-country'. He is subsequently taken to task on the programme for failing to 'get' the conventions that prevent proper politicians from engaging in personal abuse, however strong their disagreements, though he disputes the existence of these conventions in Westminster.

The voice of the citizen in 'Question Time'

The voice of the citizen in *Question Time* is distributed through different elements of the participation framework. Questioners in the studio audience launch the topics, more privileged citizen–panellists participate in the response to the questions. Other members of the studio audience offer comments and follow up questions on invitation from Dimbleby. General principles of public civility, along with the specific interactional conventions of the show, exercise some control over the passions that may underpin audience contributions. For example, the questions are preformulated in writing, and read aloud by the speaker so that any 'attitudinalising' they convey is inscribed into the wording of the question but very much less into the embodied delivery. Linguistically speaking, there are degrees of attitudinalising at this stage, from neutral, through subtly implicit, to explicit:

- How damaging is the bullying allegation to Gordon Brown and the Labour Party in the run-up to a general election?

- Should the Royal Bank of Scotland pay 1.3 billion pounds in bonuses when they lost 3.6 billion pounds last year?
- Are Nigel Farage's rude and attention-seeking remarks about the new President of the European Council not conclusive proof that UKIP, and he, have become nothing more than a boorish national embarrassment?

The first of these can be heard as a more or less dispassionate interest in the fortunes of the ruling party, following some potentially damaging revelations about the conduct of its leader in his professional life. The second, while not expressing in so many words the speaker's own personal outrage at the payouts, points towards shock as an appropriate reaction to the facts (a reaction that most of the panellists duly produce, to varying degrees). The third is explicitly condemnatory of one particular individual in public life, the panellist Farage.

The posing of questions gives limited scope for the expression of personal belief, feeling and attitude, but there are resources for doing so in other parts of the discourse. Audience members can choose to disrupt the programme's conventions, they can make the verbal expression of personal involvement more explicit, or they can theatricalize their contribution through the manner of its vocal and kinesic expression.

The audience has no permitted voice when panellists are delivering their initial statements in response to questions: if they heckle, as during Hain's contribution quoted above, they are not offered the microphone and their interruptions attract reproof by Dimbleby, who thereby reasserts the norms. Nevertheless, something like 'strength of feeling' has been performatively accomplished.

Greater verbal, vocal and kinetic displays of feeling are not treated as disruptive or improper during the open discussion phase of any topic, though the collective self-restraint of the audience, and Dimbleby's chairmanship, ensure that this does not mutate into polyphonic confrontation that is indifferent to the discussion's status as a managed display, as a coherent product for public consumption.

The voice of the broadcaster on 'Question Time'

The hosting/intermediary function in political talk shows, including interviews, requires a professional broadcaster, though the credentials of actual hosts vary in the kind of professional expertise they offer. Those closer to the journalistic end of the spectrum (Jeremy Paxman, John Humphreys, David Dimbleby, Jonathan Dimbleby, etc.) bring a kind of authority that is weaker when individuals further away from the world of news and current affairs take on these responsibilities. The names above are those of individuals who have accumulated their authority over many years of performing in their intermediary roles.

The professional broadcaster who currently hosts *Question Time* is David Dimbleby (his brother Jonathan hosts *Any Questions?*). His familiarity to British audiences makes him a celebrity too, though well away from popular-culture stardom. As a host, he consistently plays it safe, sticking to familiar conventions of neutralism while maintaining formal control over discursive proceedings. This leaves little scope for displays of individuality for a casual viewer or listener to notice, despite his being more well known than many of the panellists; in later sections of this chapter we will have something to say about hosts who foreground their individuality to a greater extent.

In this discussion of a flagship programme with undisputed public service credentials we have explored the performative-role configuration and noted how this configuration enables the display of earnest civic identities. Our analysis shows that role–performance tends to repress the individuation of particular speakers. Yet complete elimination of individuation is neither desirable nor possible. Farage's individuality is assured through the episode's substantive attention to his flamboyant behaviour in public life, while Dimbleby's contribution to the series over a long period of time has engendered some conflation of the role and the person, almost in spite of Dimbleby's chairmanly restraint.

Beyond 'Question Time'

A familiar metaphor of *weight* is often used to discriminate between different programmes featuring performances of the serious, public, political self. If *Question Time* is 'heavy', then so too are one-to-one interviews between politicians and journalist–presenters like Jeremy Paxman and Andrew Marr. The *Leaders' Debates* of April 2010 (during the election campaign) were even heavier – because of their novelty in British politics, the rules were even more rigidly codified preparatory to the live broadcasts.[5]

In contrast, various formats can be viewed as lighter than *Question Time*, in tone if not in substance. To achieve greater lightness while remaining essentially serious rather than comic in purpose might involve one or more of the following: inclusion of more celebrities, including celebrities with professional lives well away from the civic sphere; inclusion of fewer politicians or even their exclusion; greater acceptance of opinionated contributions from intermediaries; provision of greater opportunities for audience contributions; contextualising discussion within programmes where politics is not an exclusive or central focus; a more colloquial phrasing of introductions, questions and links.

A programme that meets many of these criteria is *The Wright Stuff* (Five, 2000–present), a two-hour daytime chat show on a commercial TV channel, free to air in all British homes. A host, Matthew Wright, sits at a desk with three guests to his left (screen right), facing a studio audience: two of the guests are drawn from a regular panel, including, for example, Anne Diamond, Christopher Biggins, while the third is a special guest, generally with something to promote. Politician panellists are rare and this is far from being an A-list celebrity talk show, but the subjects discussed by host, panellist, and home audience include some which are political or have political aspects: 'Has the Coalition damaged the Lib Dems?' (20 September 2010); 'Are big families a no-no if you're on benefits, as one cabinet minister claims' (8 October 2010); 'Benefit cheats – will the Coalition really cut their money off? Should they?' (9 October 2010). *The Wright Stuff* uses a phone-in format to involve the public: twenty-first-century programmes of this type now obviously include email, text message and Twitter inputs, as well as telephone calls by landline and mobile phone. Written contributions however, while displayed on screen, do not generate interaction as the phone contributions do.

How do the voices of politicians, citizens and intermediaries in *The Wright Stuff* vary from those in *Question Time*? Those of the politicians disappear, except when they are quoted or referenced by panellists and callers. Those of citizens, including the celebrities on the panel, become more prominent. The voice of the broadcaster becomes more engaged and opinionated. All of this was apparent in the episode of 21 October 2010, when *The Wright Stuff* tackled the serious subject of national budget cuts, for 15 minutes of airtime between 10.00 and 10.15 a.m., in its fourth segment. The newly elected government's much-anticipated Comprehensive Spending Review (CSR) was publicly announced on 20 October and the plans to reduce the public sector and drastically economize on a number of social benefits, to shrink the national deficit, were extensively discussed throughout the national mediascape. *The Wright Show*'s participants on the following day were Wright himself, along with a British radio and TV presenter (Terry Christian), an American pop star (Kimberly Wyatt) and a British actor (Gemma Bissix).

With no politicians participating in the episode, their voices are present only indirectly. George Osborne's voice is heard in this way (Osborne, as the Coalition's chief finance minister, presented the CSR to Parliament). Hosts, guests and callers take up not only the substance of the CSR in their discussion but also one particular aspect of its rhetorical framing: Osborne's suggestion that 'we're all in it together', where 'we' are the citizens of Britain and all of 'us' will feel the effects of the cuts. Matthew Wright, as host, is the first to recycle this trope, and to do so with ironic scepticism, deploying the idea that Osborne's personal wealth will protect him at least from pain:

> Now, the spending cuts. How are they going down with you, the Great British Public? Are you resigned to the pain? After all, we are 'all in it together', as George Osborne kept telling us, though I should imagine, with a four million pound personal fortune already in the bank and twenty million pound in the family's coffers, we're not all quite in the same camp as the chancellor.

In the phone-in part of the segment some callers themselves also reference Osborne's representation as one which spuriously assumes the equality of citizens, though Michael, below, has heard it as coming more generally from the government rather than specifically from Osborne:

> MICHAEL: [...] this 'all in it together' is really getting on my nerves.
> [...]
> The Tories and the big business people, we've know that they've been avoiding tax for years, for donkey's years, but they've just, they keep saying, 'all in it together', so why don't they just shut up.

Terry Christian, whose sympathies are with working-class people from a left-wing position, takes a different approach, when he quotes from the previous day's parliamentary proceedings, not Osborne, but the Coalition politicians collectively. In his characteristically strong Manchester accent, he objects on moral grounds to the enthusiasm with which they greeted the cut proposals – and Wright gives him some support:

> CHRISTIAN: Well, I think whatever your political stripe, if you'd've actually watched what was going on in the House of Commons, and they were all *cheering*!
> WRIGHT: It was pretty sickening.
> CHRISTIAN: Oh, it was ugly.

From what has been said so far, it might be expected that the voice of the citizen in *The Wright Stuff* would be more unbuttoned than on

Question Time, because contributions come less from the studio audience, which is itself part of the show's staging, and more from callers watching the programme in the privacy of their own homes. Although the time devoted to political topics is less overall than on an episode of *Question Time* (a maximum of one political topic per episode), 15 minutes on a topic is roughly equivalent, even slightly longer. And of this 15 minutes, the entire amount is distributed between host and citizen voices, to the exclusion of politicians. Panellists differ from callers inasmuch as the former are celebrities and are physically present in the studio. Of these two different types of citizen, the callers are more likely to bring their personal circumstances as well as their civic values and rationalities to bear in their contributions. Some panellists (e.g. Kimberley Wyatt in this episode) are not British citizens, but citizens of some other polity, and this influences the terms on which they can respond to the topic.

Although the performing voice of the politician is conspicuously absent in *The Wright Stuff,* there are many politically oriented TV and radio shows where that is the dominant voice. We have already examined one of these, *Question Time,* to illustrate in some depth what we mean by the performance of a serious, public, political self. We will conclude this section with a briefer discussion of one other programme, *The Week in Westminster* (Home Service/Radio 4, 1929–present).[6] This is a topical magazine-style politics programme on BBC Radio 4, which runs all year except during parliamentary recesses. What makes it interesting for our purposes is how the political voice in this show differs from the one on display in *Question Time.* The political voice on *Question Time* has a front-of-stage character; the one made available on *The Week in Westminster* is more concerned with the *backstage* of politics. Public revelation about the political backstage can seem to be democratically worthy, for example, in claiming to address the leadership's 'real' plans and their motives, as against what they themselves prefer to tell the electorate. But this can also come across as contributing to a democratic deficit, an exclusion of the ordinary voter, by putting on display what only insiders and political 'anoraks' might conceivably be interested in. *The Week in Westminster* also serves the purpose of deeper *analysis* than is possible on other programmes, with a role for intermediaries not so much as hosts, but instead as experts on the world of politics, with much greater expositional responsibilities, for instance, on 18 September 2010, on political issues surrounding the replacement of Britain's nuclear deterrent. The host is a different journalist each week, usually from a newspaper or other periodical such as the *New Statesman.*

Jackie Ashley in the quote below was working for the *Guardian* when she took responsibility for this episode:

JACKIE ASHLEY, PRESENTER:
As MPs pack their bags for the party conferences, it's no surprise that the issues coalition parties disagree on are the focus of attention. There's a clear division on Trident, the Coalition government has pledged to replace the nuclear weapons system while the Liberal Democrats within the Coalition retain the right to explore alternatives (*Ashley's voice strikes a note of surprise on this statement, with a rising intonation on 'alternatives'*). So there was a major explosion at Westminster when the BBC reported a leak suggesting the replacement for Trident could be delayed until 2015, after the next General Election. The former defence spokesman John Lewis believed that Liam Fox the Defence Secretary would never stomach such a move:
[Lewis recording]
To dampen down Tory fury we saw the strange spectacle of Nick Harvey the armed forces minister insisting the decision to replace Trident had been taken, in other words the leak was wrong. But he then added that as a Liberal Democrat he's personally opposed to the renewal of Trident:
[Harvey recording]
And to compound the confusion, the Liberal Democrat leader Nick Clegg left open the question of whether what's called the Continuous At-Sea Nuclear Deterrent would remain:
[Clegg recording]
So what's going on? Was the apparent leak just a lot of kite-flying, designed to appease the Liberal Democrat conference, or is the future of the replacement for Trident really in doubt, or at least in the long grass?

Note that this is not framed by Ashley as a discussion of the policy issue of whether Trident should be replaced, but as a meta-discussion of whether the decision has been taken or not. 'The decision has been taken' favours the Conservative manifesto position. 'The decision has not been taken' favours the Liberal Democrat position. Ashley's approach picks up from the news agenda by focusing on strains within the Coalition, while attempting to achieve greater insight into these tensions by going 'behind the scenes' – and behind the headlines.

The politicians who are recruited to appear on *The Week in Westminster* are not normally those from the front benches, but backbenchers with greater time at their disposal and more freedom to go off-message in relation to their party's official agenda. In the studio, Ashley discusses the Trident issue with one Conservative MP (Sir Malcolm Rifkind) and one Labour MP (Gisela Stuart). As party loyalists, they behave predictably inasmuch as Rifkind plays down the extent of internal divisions in the Coalition while Stuart plays them up. But both are given more latitude thereafter to approach the subject in their own terms. Rifkind, for example, is allowed to explore in some depth the idea that the more important issue is which departmental budget (the Ministry of Defence or the Treasury) will be expected to pay for Trident's replacement.

In summarising this section we can say that *Question Time* is the most high-profile part of a spectrum of programming in which 'heavier' programmes (such as *The Week in Westminster*) and 'lighter' ones coexist. It is the performative implications of this range that we have focused on. At the lighter end of the spectrum, civic roles take on greater personal colouration for hosts, guests and audience members, as we have shown. More serious programming also complicates role performance, but in a different way. The obligations of party representation that politicians on *Question Time* so evidently carry are weakened here, and such speakers are afforded greater scope to turn a constructively critical eye on their own parties – safer here, apparently, from the risk of being found either hypocritical or disloyal.

Politicians performing as private selves

When politicians agree to appear on *Question Time* and *The Week in Westminster*, they do so to further their own and their parties' needs for public recognition. For the most part their personal lives are not deemed relevant to these discussions. But the more prominent national politicians are also celebrities and as such their private lives may attract interest in their own right. Less prominent politicians may also attract gossip-column style interest if their private lives are in some way out of the ordinary. Private lives of politicians can be relevantly illustrative of 'character', in a positive or a negative way, but the dangers of parading domestic virtue which is then undercut by revelations of imperfection are very well known.[7]

In February 2010, with only months to go before a national general election, Gordon Brown the Labour Prime Minister, appeared as a guest in the third season of the celebrity interview series *Piers Morgan's Life Stories* (ITV 1, 2009–present).[8] In previous seasons, Morgan had interviewed, for example, TV talent-show judge Sharon Osborne, and former tennis star Boris Becker. With a licence to pry, Morgan asks Brown about the sporting injury that cost him the sight of one eye, his courtship of wife Sarah Macaulay Brown, and the death of his infant daughter Jennifer in 2002, as well as about his career in politics. The facts behind these events in Brown's private life were already in the public domain: what Morgan is interested in is the telling, circumstantial detail and the emotional response – venturing into areas that elsewhere would be taboo:

It was the era of free love, Gordon: how free was your love?

The voice of the broadcaster in this series is that of chat-show host, not political interviewer, and the exchanges between Morgan and Brown are mainly co-operative. If some of the questioning, as here, is more intrusive than the guest is used to or comfortable with, this can be dealt with by evasiveness coloured by laughter, which Morgan allows, shares – and moves on. The extent of Brown's sexual promiscuity as a young man is never made fully explicit despite strong indications that he did indeed 'play the field' at that age like other heterosexual males of his generation.

Discussion of the equally intrusive subject of Jennifer Brown's birth and death in 2002 does not call forth such evasiveness. The bereavement does not raise any moral issues and Brown is required to be frank about emotions not facts. The programme shows a short film, including to-camera testimony of Brown's brothers and wife, telling the story of his family life, foregrounding Jennifer's death. As the film concludes, the studio camera focuses again on Brown, so that the pathos of the narrative as it affected him can be seen in his face at this tender moment. He folds his lips inwards, then relaxes them. Morgan waits for about five seconds before pursuing the subject with him:

I remember that time very well, Gordon. I remember the press conference you gave, which we saw there, where you were so happy, and I talked to you in that period. But looking back on that […]

While Brown is talking about the initial happiness at Jennifer's birth, the camera focuses on Sarah Brown in the audience, silently wiping away her tears. The Prime Minister explains how the child failed to thrive in the days after her birth. His chin begins to quiver, he may even be shedding a tear (many commentators thought so), as he tells the later part of the story, their realization that she would not survive; he then pulls himself through without 'flooding out', ending on a more confident note in referring again to his relationship with his wife.

Among the politicians, it was not only Gordon Brown who sought to offer the public a more personal side in 2010, and it was not only the chat show format which proved useful for the greater display of private selves in broadcasting. A commonly voiced criticism of politicians is that they are not like 'us' – their social backgrounds as well as the world of politics itself, insulate them from the values and concerns of ordinary people. The show *Tower Block of Commons* (*TBOC*) (Channel 4, February 2010), addressed this criticism by recruiting five volunteer politicians to experience life in the tower blocks of housing estates, as temporary guests of some of the country's poorest citizens. This was a political version of something like *Wife Swap* (Channel 4, 2003–present), offering an entertaining as well as informative look at what its experiment produced, containing generous measures of confrontation and embarrassment figured as more real than anything these same people might display in the more conventional contexts and genres of political broadcasting (see Corner et al. (2011) for more extensive discussion of this series).

The terms of the series' opening commentary are, in many ways, indicative of the broader vocabulary and evaluative assumptions for discussing politics in contemporary British popular culture:

COMMENTARY A group of MPs are finally about to come face to face with the kind of voters they claim to represent.

TIM LOUGHTON (Conservative MP for East Worthing and Shoreham): 'Whether we convince people that politicians are all normal people, I very much doubt'

(inserted scene shows Loughton outside a general store in heated exchange with a man, who says to him 'you want the bottom line – assholes!')

IAN DUNCAN SMITH (Conservative MP for Chingford and Woodford Green): 'There'll be lots of surprises I'm sure'.

MARK OATEN (Liberal Democrat MP for Winchester): 'I think they're going to hate me'.

COMMENTARY For eight days and nights they will be living a real life...on Britain's overcrowded and rundown housing estates...Filmed over the past twelve months at different times and on different estates, these MPs have to survive without parliamentary expenses...without the help of taxpayer funded staff...with no pre-prepared soundbites...no spin...no room for any political manoeuvres and none of the safety and security of the Houses of Parliament...

This is the MPs' new second home...

What will happen when those who have the power to make a difference finally confront the harsh reality of the Britain that they have helped to create?

(Shot from flat window of Mark Oaten lying prone on the grass around the base of the tower block in apparent despair.

FEMALE RESIDENT (OATEN'S HOST):

Look, one day he's been here. And look at him, he can't take it. What's he going to be like at the end of the week? He's going to want a noose.

COMMENTARY And when they finally return to their privileged lives...will they provide political solutions for the people they have left behind?

This commentary suggests that, shorn of their reliance on sound bites, spin, expenses and staff (self-evidently, the core 'props' of the career politician), these representatives of the elite will live a 'real life' for a few days. Their face-to-face contact with those who live in deprived housing will be an unprecedented moment of truth in their previously cocooned political careers. In a repetition of the term which, of course, the entire approach takes as the key marker of its generic identity, they will confront 'harsh reality'.

The series is made particularly interesting for our project by the way in which it explores elite–citizen relations through focusing on politicians as specific persons, bodies who now have to eat and sleep in entirely different circumstances from those they are familiar with. Just one example of this can be taken from episode two, after a scene in which Mark Oaten has been supermarket shopping with his host resident (Sloane) to see how far they can make the household budget go, and then been appalled to see her spending £40 on cigarettes. Later, over the evening meal, this exchange occurs:

SLOANE: I felt bad for taking £40 of cigarettes and that's my luxury.

OATEN: I felt uncomfortable when I saw 40 quid go across.

SLOANE: But then...you've got to think of other...we've all had the expenses scandals...I thought, I'm a nosy sod, you know, press Google and off you go....and I was gobsmacked, you had an enormous list of expenses. You claimed for two irons.

OATEN: I can't have an iron in Winchester and in London at the same time.

SLOANE: But why should you claim an iron off the taxpayer? By the time you filled in all the forms wouldn't it be easier, you know what, just to go to Argos, £14.99 for an iron?

The sequence above has already been prepared for by an earlier scene in which Sloane is seen on the internet (following what seems almost certain to be 'cueing' by the production team), noting down the figures for Oaten's parliamentary expenses and remarking that the sums and items involved are such as to make her think the whole thing is a 'piss-take'. At one level, the issue in this sequence is about how politicians, through their lack of awareness, have produced the economic situation in which the residents of poor housing live their restricted lives; at another it is about having two irons at the taxpayers' expense. Oaten and the other politicians in the series are attempting to 'redeem' the negative personification of the political class as too simplistic or even false both as it applies to them and to the system.

TBOC's performative aspect goes well beyond that of other programming discussed in this chapter. The participants are required to do the work of 'being politicians' in unfamiliar and uncongenial settings, often projected as forms of private interaction. It displays different dimensions of discourse, as terms and perspectives are applied to engage with and debate the conditions on the estate and also at least partly to defend the integrity of official politics against the charge of deception and corruption.

The two examples discussed in this section demonstrate very different ways of bringing the 'private' into the 'public' domain. While Gordon Brown has agreed to talk about his private life, moving out from behind the conventional concealment of such personal matters, Mark Oaten and the others have volunteered to 'be' themselves rather than just talking 'about' themselves in public. Brown is invited into a dedicated media performance space – a studio – while Oaten et al. are 'in the field'. It is the contrivance in making the 'field' in question an unusual and challenging one for them which gives their performances such resonance – and our contrast also draws attention to the fact that the ostensibly 'artificial' media studio is, in normal circumstances, very much the natural habitat of the politician as public self.

The comedic political self

In the kinds of programming mentioned so far there is scope for some humour around the edges of the serious discussion. Politicians need to cultivate common ground with citizens, and it helps them if they can show they have a sense of humour. They can deliver comic lines themselves, or 'take a joke' at their own expense, within limits, wary as anyone might be of chronic loss of face. What passes for humour in otherwise serious formats can as a result be rather laboured, as in this example from the first of the televised *Leaders' Debates* (ITV 1, April 15 2010) during the election campaign:

I'm grateful to you, David, [Cameron] by the way, for putting up all these posters of me and about crime and about everything, everything else, er, em, you know, there's no newspaper editor done as much for me in the last two years, because my face is smiling on these posters [titters from audience, a weak smile from Cameron], and I'm very grateful to you and Lord Ashcroft for funding that (Alistair Stewart, the host, then breaks across rising laughter to reassert his authority over the proceedings).

Brown wants to remind the audience of the Tory campaign posters designed to criticize him and his party; his 'joke' is that they helped his cause more than their own, because they used a photo of him smiling (he is recurrently ridiculed for ineffective use of the 'smile' in public). But the delivery of this line is much less fluent than his more serious flow of talk in the debates, and is unlikely to have done much to enhance his reputation for humour.

Mockery of politicians behind their backs, so to speak, is another matter. The serious selves that they so assiduously cultivate for programmes like *Question Time* are readily undercut, and can in other contexts (including, increasingly, online contexts) be made to seem *ridiculously* pompous, pretentious, misguided, naive, deceitful or otherwise wrongheaded.

In broadcasting, such mockery is designed into the format of several programmes, the most high profile of which is *Have I Got News For You (HIGNFY)*. This panel show, in the first episode during the election campaign, screens for comic purpose a short clip from a Labour press conference:

ROBERT WEBB, celebrity host of *HIGNFY*:
    Here's a press conference where Gordon is asked about his wife Sarah:
    (Film clip. Close-up on Brown.)
BROWN: She's the love of my life and we work well together and we like going round the country together, and I'm looking forward to the campaign.

(Cut to medium shot of Brown, Peter Mandelson and Alistair Darling at the press conference desk.)

MANDELSON: There you are, isn't that nice. Thank you very much indeed (collecting up his papers as a further gesture of closure).

(Brown, Mandelson, Darling all smile, audience offers restrained laughter at the incongruous tone of the final comment.)

[*HIGNFY* panellists and audience laugh loudly.]

HISLOP: He's just *so* patronising. It's like he's a ventriloquist, isn't it? Webb (caricaturing Mandelson, with a sweep of his arm): 'That's enough about people who aren't *me*'.

With comedians waiting to pounce on any detail, the politicians' very seriousness then becomes a liability in an awkward double bind.[9]

Imitating political performance

Our starting point here is an appreciation of the fact that politicians collectively, and many of them also individually, are familiar figures in the mediated cultural landscape. Their appearance and behaviour provide accessible resources for a range of appropriations in the service of art and entertainment (some of which may have a public service character), articulating themselves to the 'real world' on different levels, as appropriate to the nature of the project.

Dramatic appropriations

Fictional politicians in dramatic productions for stage or screen can be given whatever attributes the themes and storylines of the work require, to be performed appropriately. Such characters are not restricted to texts with a main focus on politics. The science-fiction series *Dr Who* among others has featured elected political leaders, as well as autocrats. The relatively recent series *The Amazing Mrs Pritchard* (BBC 1, 2006: for further discussion see Corner and Richardson, 2008; Cardo, 2011; Nikolaidis, 2011) was more overtly political, with an eponymous heroine who progresses from apolitical supermarket manageress to elected Prime Minister within the first episode, spending the remaining five episodes attempting to conduct the business of government and handling the responses of her nearest and dearest to this change in their fortunes.

Imaginative drama of the sort represented by Pritchard coexists with productions designed to retell actual political history, which thus require performers to produce their own versions of, for instance, Margaret Thatcher and Tony Blair (e.g. *The Deal*, Granada, 2003). Cinema too has both kinds of production, with *Dave* (Warner Bros., 1993) on one side of the divide and *The Iron Lady* (Film 4, 2012) on the other side (*Primary Colours*, Universal, 1998, is an interesting intermediary case, indicative of a sliding scale of creative transformation, rather than a dichotomy). In both media, dramas offer opportunities for the incorporation of broadcasters as characters, when they can be performed by actors (Michael Sheen plays David Frost in *Frost/Nixon*, Universal, 2008). Alternatively, broadcasters who are not main characters help to provide appropriate mise-en-scène detail; a 'true story' production might then rely on actual recordings at the time (*On Expenses*, discussed below, uses a clip featuring the BBC's political editor Nick Robinson in this way). Both fictional political dramas and true stories might also recruit real broadcasters to play themselves in cameo appearances (as Kirsty Wark, a presenter for BBC2's *Newsnight* programme, did in *Pritchard*).

Both imaginative political drama and the true-story kind were on air during 2010 in the UK, though new productions on mainstream channels were rare. Imaginative drama was represented by series five of *Number Ten* (BBC Radio 4, 2008–present) with Damian Lewis as Tory Prime Minister Simon Laity. True-story political drama was represented by *On Expenses* (BBC 4, 23 February).[10]

The plot of *On Expenses* begins when an American journalist living in the UK, Heather Brooke (a real person, not a fictional creation), is frustrated in her attempts to elicit any information on British MPs' expenses. It climaxes when the Speaker of the House of Commons, Michael Martin, is forced to resign. In real life, Brooke's initiatives were eclipsed by the *Daily Telegraph*'s scoop, and this is acknowledged in the play.[11] Thematically, the play reproduces what by then was a very familiar censorious frame, though the construction of Martin as a 'bad guy' who sought to protect parliamentarians from public scrutiny is tempered by humour and even sympathy. He is shown playing bagpipes in the solitude of his office and drinking IRN-BRU, a non-alcoholic pop branded as Scottish. These traits, and others, foreground Martin's Scottish ethnicity to an extent that encouraged a comedic interpretation. At his downfall, he is shown alone in the hallways of Westminster, delivering a denunciatory monologue, which is directed at the elite club he is now leaving. This gives us, in a credible Scottish accent and dialect, Martin's view of himself as a social class outsider, set up by the political (also social) elite as the scapegoat for its collective sins.

Here is our transcription of that monologue (with apologies for the eye dialect):

> Everything I did. All the flak I've taken: 'Gorbals Mick'. You know what's really insulting about that? The place where I grew up made the Gorbals look like Center Parcs. And I fought my way out of there. I fought my way into this job. And by God, every minute I've been in it I've fought for yous. And this is the thanks I get! To be stabbed in the back, in the place where I should command absolute respect! [Shouting] Ya greedy, ungrateful bastards! Ya wasna worth it! Any o' yous. None o' yous. [Quieter] You really think getting rid o' me's gonna let yous off the hook? Ah, hah, hah, hah.

The monologue device functions like a Shakespearean soliloquy in allowing 'Martin' to speak out loud thoughts that were certainly attributed to him at the time. It also permits the dramatist to make explicit the dramatic irony that Martin, as the defender of MPs, eventually comes to a similar conclusion as the general public about their greed, as a result of his own fall from grace and what he reads as their disloyalty to him. The viewing public also knows that Martin's final prediction holds good.

Comedic appropriations

Comedic versions of politicians were very much in evidence throughout 2010 in British broadcasting, the heightened levels of visibility and the increase in claims-making performances surrounding both the election and the first months of the new government providing an expanded range of targets.[12] The one-off 'comedy docudrama' *Miliband of Brothers* (More 4, 24 September 2010) offered the most innovative approach to political programme-making, seeking to put performed caricatures of two real-life politicians to serious purpose. The programme concerned the rivalry between the two brothers, David and Ed Miliband, for leadership of the Labour Party, a rivalry culminating in the unexpected election of Ed at the Labour Party Annual Conference on 25 September (the day after the broadcast).

The show's pre-title sequence encapsulates its key characteristics:

> (Actor playing David Miliband enters foyer of TV company with an assistant, talking into a mobile phone):
> DAVID: The figures speak for themselves. I thought it was good news. Yeah yeah...
> Well, if they want to go with the one-horse race, we'll run with it.

(Within the larger scene, another suited figure is seen sitting in the background.)

DAVID: What the hell are you doing here?

ED: I'm doing the lunchtime news interview. What about you?

DAVID: Great! (Sits down in exasperation and turns to assistant to say:) Nice one, seriously, I mean that.

(Studio manager with clipboard enters foyer.) Mr Miliband?

(Both suited figures stand up.)

Interview sequence 1: (Neil Kinnock, ex-leader of the Labour Party, in a well-appointed committee room): *David's response to Ed running has, to my astonishment, been deeply resentful.*

(The two brothers with their assistants and broadcasting staff walk down corridor towards studio.)

DAVID TO ADVISOR: Why didn't I know he was doing it as well? Pretty important information. Kind of crucial, actually. And yet...no...

ED (to studio manager, walking alongside him): I'm the warm Miliband

Interview sequence 2: (Andrew Rawnsley, political commentator, in book-lined study): *Among Tony Blair's people Ed Miliband was known as the emissary from Planet Fuck because he was the only member of the Brown acolytes who didn't tell them to fuck off.*

(The make-up desk in the studio dressing room, the two brothers seated alongside each other.) David to Ed: Don't want any of your nonsense about Iraq – that spiel about how you were always against the war.

Interview Sequence 3: (Oona King, ex-Labour MP and former schoolfriend, in sparsely furnished room/studio): *They cannot be the same after this. Politics will tear you apart and I've seen it happen and I can feel it happening between them.*

(The TV studio, with cameras and the two seated Milibands, greeted by a female interviewer.)

INTERVIEWER: Right if we can just have a few words for level pitch.

ED: I'll start, testing, testing, one...

DAVID: This is a time of real change and we face some challenges but I think under my leadership the party really can begin to...

(Ed swivels on chair and kicks David on shin.)

DAVID: Ow! Did you just kick...? (To interviewer.) Did you just see that?

(Cut to colour-faded shot of two young boys kicking each other on swivel chairs.)

OFF-SHOT VOICE: Boys, Please!
Main title and then subtitle, Like father, like sons
(Post-titles opening scene: a dinner party at the home of the father,
Ralph Miliband, with political argument in full swing.)

Many single-programme dramatizations have a comic dimension, as we
have already suggested in relation to *On Expenses*, but few display the
level of overt comic distortion of politicians and political activity shown
here. This distortion portrays events within the generic terms of the
comedy 'sketch' familiar in its political versions from *Bremner, Bird and
Fortune*, rather than those of the 'reconstructive' dramatic realism used
widely by other dramas in which real politicians are portrayed. It does
not so much ask its audience to believe that events might have happened 'like this' (the 'reconstructive' offer) but to play around with the
comic fantasy presented in the light of what *is* known about the brothers
and their running against each other for office. In this fantasy, the sibling rivalry is constructed within caricatured terms of political publicity
(e.g. the tactical search for media advantage; Ed trying to set up a frame
for his own evaluation by declaring himself as the 'warm' one), political cant (David's interrupted test speech), and reductive biography (the
brother's political identity shown to have childhood, family roots).[13]

The programme is also unusual in its mixing of dramatic with documentary elements. The three short interview segments indicated above
all put 'strong' testimony into the mix, though their interweaving with
the comic narrative briefly raise questions of their own seriousness. This
is especially true of the contribution from Rawnsley, the nature and
language of his anecdote carrying the possibility of 'spoof' (especially,
perhaps, given its strong links with the typical situations and speech of
the popular political sitcom *The Thick of It* (BBC4, 2005–ongoing).

As suggested above, the caricaturing deployed in *Miliband of Brothers*,
while innovative in the use to which it is put, connects with a more
familiar tradition of performative mockery in British media involving
vocal imitation of specific politicians. In 2010, such mockery could be
found in radio on shows like *The News Quiz* (BBC Radio 4, 1977–present)
and *The Now Show* (BBC Radio 4, 1998–present), with more sustained
impressions provided at intervals throughout the year by Rory Bremner
in the regular programme *Bremner, Bird and Fortune* as well as the election
specials, branded as *The Daily Wind Up* (Channel 4, 2010).

The News Quiz is a long-running comedy panel show on BBC Radio
Four, the 'older sister' of the TV series *HIGNFY*, already mentioned
above, though reaching a much smaller and more elite audience. During
a series, each episode goes out weekly (Fridays at 6.30 p.m. repeated

Saturdays at 12.30 p.m.). Comedian Sandi Toksvig is the current host; the rest of the cast is not fixed from week to week, though there are some regulars. Series 72, from which the following extract is taken, was on air during the autumn of 2010. The basic generic format involves getting the four panellists to answer a series of cryptically worded questions on topical events, starting with the most newsworthy ones, which are frequently political. The contestants are expected to produce witty performances as they elaborate their replies; this is managed interactively, giving the talk a conversational joke-making tenor and drawing the studio audience into its sociability: the broadcast audience is invited to appreciate, and imaginatively inhabit, the good-humoured ambience. Toksvig's opening 'puzzle' question to Jeremy Hardy concerns the CSR already mentioned above in relation to *The Wright Stuff*, while Hardy's answer refers to the cheers with which the Chancellor's announcements of cuts was greeted by the government benches. (Our quotes here are slightly edited for fluency and focus and the audible audience laughter has been omitted):

TOKSVIG: Jeremy, where can we say 'The Axe Man Cometh'?
[...]
HARDY: ... I don't like to think badly of people just because I disagree with them, and I think there probably was a time when some Conservatives were motivated by some sort of decency... in war time, for example, there was a coalition, we were all under Churchill [...] we literally were all in it together. But in those days at least the Conservatives knew not to cheer when it was announced that Coventry had been bombed. We don't live like that. I mean I am, literally, in debt to a building society for two hundred thousand pounds. Eventually they'll get it back, I don't know when. They don't really care because I'm paying the interest anyway. But eventually they'll get it back. But I don't suddenly, arbitrarily decide: 'Well, that's it. That's it, I'm in debt. It's two hundred thousand pounds, that's it. No more lavatory paper for me! I shall just rub my arse on the wall from now on.'
TOKSVIG: That's an image which is going to stay with me for some time!

Hardy, who is well known for his left-wing sympathies (compare Terry Christian's response in *The Wright Stuff*, quoted earlier) uses the show's format and his own performative talent to derive humour from political policy and political ideologies, satirising the substantive basis of political action. Underlying his humour here is the makings of a genuine debate about the extent to which both national and personal debt can be 'lived with' without resort to drastic measures. The third panellist to join in this round of comment is Rory Bremner:

> BREMNER: The person I feel sorry for is Vince Cable. Do you remember Porridge? Do you remember the prison officer, Barraclough? That's Vince Cable: [Northern accent] 'Well, I, I, I, I'd really rather you didn't cut child benefit, actually, but if you absolutely have..., I suppose it'll be all right'. [The disfluency here is part of the vocal effect.]

Bremner is a satirist and impressionist and his response here makes use of the latter ability in channelling another political celebrity, Vince Cable, a senior Liberal Democrat holding the Cabinet post of Business Secretary in the Coalition. Bremer achieves his depiction of Cable by mediating him as 'Barraclough', an inept and diffident but likeable prison officer in a 1970s TV sitcom trying, unsatisfactorily, to maintain authority and discipline over confident, manipulative and clever inmates – a rather dated cultural reference, but not too much so for the programme's main audience. Bremner as satirist hears Cable as someone equally ineffectual in influencing his coalition partners to mitigate the extremity of their plans.

Our analysis of selected material from across the genres brings out strongly how the communicative profile of broadcasting, as a system grounded in the transmission of recorded speech and images, works with and upon the political. It installs a variety of professional political performances right at the centre of diverse non-news output, whether through the direct participation of politicians, the use of material taken from news programming or various approaches to dramatic and comic imitation. The politician as personality, as behaviour, demeanour and voice becomes effectively the core of 'the political' as heard and seen. These modes of mediation underwrite the audience's sense of familiarity with politicians as a collectivity, but there is in addition a powerfully *individuating* effect in the quantity, range and congruence of performative representations clustering around a small group of key individuals at the heart of the political scene. This would normally include the major party leaders, but it might not (Nick Clegg initially struggled for public recognition); it might include people slightly to one side of national government (Boris Johnson is a pertinent example), and it might also include broadcasters (for our period, Jeremy Paxman, John Humphreys, and David/Jonathan Dimbleby are the main contenders here). Individuated citizens, as representative proxies for the 'general public' are not unknown, though their fame may be transient. Gillian Duffy, when represented by Gordon Brown as a 'bigoted' woman in the spring of 2010, was the most famous member of the public or more precisely, considering the date, the electorate, though her on-screen performances were confined to news material. The 'bigotgate' incident which drew Duffy to public attention is discussed in Chapter 5.

Around this core, other 'civic' voices, including those of professional broadcasters and types of participant are organized and forms of comment and dispute undertaken. Generic work in print and web forms can only accomplish these levels of immediacy and embodiment in partial ways, in the case of the web largely by adopting modes developed in broadcasting. The representations we have examined also involve a powerful sense of 'audience' (live and through transmission), an assumption of a 'shared event', through collective listening and/or viewing, which maps on to 'civic space' and civic identities more directly than those forms working with more individualized modes of reception. Thus it is in such genres that the convergence of 'audience' with 'public' is at its strongest (Livingstone, 2005). We discuss this at greater length as a point of theoretical interest in Chapter 4 below.

2
The Political World in
Print – Images and Imagination

This chapter looks at a selection of printed, non-news mediations of British politics collected during our research period.[1] We give particular emphasis to a category that we have called 'colour writing', of which parliamentary sketches are a core example, and to that long-standing vehicle of critical political expression – the editorial cartoon. We also give briefer attention to other forms, including newspaper 'leaders', a genre of writing in which it is opinion rather than information as such which is given priority and where the newspaper's own identity, as well as its views, are given strong visibility. We conclude with some examples of parody from the satirical magazine *Private Eye*, examples which take a more elaborate and sustained approach to comic design than most of the other work we examine.

Following the design of inquiry pursued throughout the book, we want to ask a range of questions of the material selected. What can be said about its discursive and aesthetic organization? What is the stance taken by it towards politicians and political issues and which aspects get selected for emphasis? In what ways are elements of comedy introduced? How is the relationship with readers managed? What kinds of sentiment and ideas are assumed and what kinds appear to be projected by the items themselves?

Of course, newspapers are the oldest 'modern' medium of political communication and in Britain, as elsewhere, the range of papers available has a distinctive political and demographic profile evidenced not only in the views they put forward but in the vocabulary and the styles they employ. Here, questions of what the audience might already know and their general level of education (including their levels of literacy and comprehension) as well as their socio-political disposition produce what, at its ends, is a sharply differentiated spectrum of generic practice.

The relationship that newspaper readers have with their newspaper is clearly physically different from that of being the viewer or listener of broadcasting and from the various modes of online engagement. It allows for different modes of perusal, varying in context and in level of intensive or relaxed attention. While being cautious of generalization here, we can also note that in many cases it involves quite close relationships of identity between paper and reader, daily renewed relationships, which many papers are keen to reinforce through various interpellations of the reading community ('our readers') and opportunities for feedback and comment. Online manifestations of the same or similar content, appearing under the recognisable newspaper 'brand', allows for a more 'chanced upon' reading and space for immediate and public comment, while broadening accessibility of the material for international audiences.

'Colour writing'

What we are terming here the 'colourists' are the writers who produce for many British newspapers regular accounts, often in the form of a 'sketch', of parliamentary and political life.[2] The way they do this is at some remove from the predominant forms of news journalism, having a primary commitment to entertaining through the kinds of caricature and the (often elaborate) conceits through which they render the people and events that constitute 'the scene'. In this sense, they can be likened to the cartoonists this chapter will discuss later (see Hoggart, 2010, on this resemblance), although the detail with which they can assemble their portrayals (often 'lampoons') within a narrative frame and the range of evaluative commentary that they can bring to bear are of a different order.

Political sketches, the core of 'colour' writing, have a long history, traceable back to the days when attendance at parliamentary sessions was not possible for writers and therefore when speculation and imaginative invention were necessary (see Richardson and Corner, 2011, for a more detailed historical account with examples). Over the last 50 years, sketch-writing has undergone a number of major shifts as a cultural practice, reflecting in part radical changes both in the nature of official political culture and in the broader popular culture within which newspaper writing makes its address to readers. Although it can focus attention on the more private, informal and 'backstage' aspects of political life, sketch-writing gives primary attention to the public arena of parliamentary business, conferences and media appearances.

The inherent 'theatricality' of performance here provides writers with their principal points of reference. In this regard, it is interesting that Colin Welch of the *Daily Telegraph*, perhaps the first of the modern sketch-writers when writing regularly in this vein in the 1950s,[3] was described as 'treating the view of the Commons from the Press Gallery as though he were looking on to the stage from the stalls and reviewing a performance which was part high drama and part cabaret' (*Daily Telegraph*, 2004).

In looking at how examples of written sketches contribute to the mediation of national political life, we are concerned with two, related, dimensions of their generic character. These might be labelled tone and positioning. Tone indicates the kinds of mood established in the writing through its use of tactics of description and address. A dominant characteristic of tone in a lot of the work we examined, across different authorial styles, was the sense of amused, curious and often condescending detachment with which it observed the different 'spectacles' of political life as well as its more intimate, 'glimpsed' moments, a detachment which it invited the reader to share. By positioning we mean both the kinds of normative alignment or disjunction with the political structure, processes and issues established by the writers and that anticipated with their readers. These accounts, permeated as they are with a sense of the theatrical, and often farcical, character of political business, rarely shift to defined terms of criticism (in the manner, say, of political columnists, bloggers, or of some satirical approaches). Their positioning is also generically framed as a confident one at the level both of the personal grounding and the social articulation, taken up without argument in a manner often suggesting assumed peer relations with those elites whose practices they 'sketch'. Contemporary sketch-writing has also to be seen in the broader context of 'comedy culture' and the changing borderlines of what is acceptable by way of personalized comment, its language and themes, within that culture. Here, the introduction of more deliberately 'vulgar' moments and the more extensive referencing of popular entertainment (films, TV, music) would show some differences with the writing of previous decades.

Our first example is from the *Daily Telegraph*, on 16 April 2010, the day after the first of the televised *Leaders' Debates* had taken place. It is the opening of a piece by sketch-writer Andrew Gimson.

Punches flew as the job interview turned nasty

THREE middle-aged men last night submitted themselves to a job interview, with the selection panel consisting of many millions of voters, minus anyone who popped out to make a cup of tea or turned over to watch 'Welcome to Lagos' on BBC Two.

Almost at once the three candidates started to fight among themselves. Like pumped-up boxers, they hurled punches regardless of how this might appear to the viewers.

Personally we enjoyed the fight, even if it went on for longer than was strictly necessary. Adversarial politics is a vital part of our tradition, and brought out the differing characters of the three men far better than an uninterrupted exchange of high-minded platitudes would have done.

Gordon Brown tried without much success to hide how furious he is at being forced to reapply for the job.

Gimson starts his piece by immediately employing a principal device of the sketch-writer, the diminishing of 'the political' as a sphere of action by a description that transforms it into emphatically lowly terms. As readers, we are asked to consider a job interview, which turns into a punch-up and the first, short sentence of the title plunges us into a contemplation of this (highly public) affray. In another characteristic move for this genre, however, Gimson notes his own personal enjoyment in watching the contest, noting the less productive alternative in which the three men might have exchanged 'high-minded platitudes'. Within the strategically reductive terms of the account, these are presented as the *only* options for contemporary political behaviour. Gordon Brown, within this view, is an angry middle-aged man suffering the indignity of having to reapply for his job. Both the politicians and the event are re-framed to their great disadvantage.

Quentin Letts, writing of the same event in the *Daily Mail*, again on 16 April 2010, provides our second example.

They all jabbered at 100mph. Even old donkey Gordon...

Here in the vast media hall (size of a Sealink ferry's car deck), it was like the Henley Royal Regatta for spin doctors. They were everywhere! Striking poses at the coffee bar, lurking behind the sandwiches, peering over shoulders at our computer screens.

Indeed, as I bash this out, some Labour apparatchik is in my other ear, insisting that 'Cameron was rattled'. Go away, you annoying man!

The leaders' debate was a grand prix of ear bending, a gymkhana of schmoozing, the Artifice Olympics. But the debate itself, surely, was pretty good.

At the risk of sounding like Young Mr Grace, I'd say they all did very well. Maybe Gordon Brown was a bit of a copy-cat, repeatedly grunting 'absolutely'. Maybe David Cameron's face was a bit too John West salmon a colour. Maybe that Clegg man gassed on too much, wiggling his head as though he was a breakdancer.

But the whole thing was zestier than U.S. presidential debates. Better TV.

The gig got off to a breathless, game-show start. Alastair Stewart, presiding, almost exploded with excitement.

These are the opening few paragraphs of a much longer article. Letts' positioning in the piece is complex, as a consequence of his decision to render it as an account of an occasion involving a *series* of events. The last event in the series is ongoing, and Letts is a participant in it as well as a reporter of it. In a reconstructed chronology the sequence is simple enough. The participants arrived, the debate took place, the accredited press produced their post-event assessments. For this, they spent time in a room shared with political functionaries deployed by their parties to talk to the journalists about the proceedings on partisan lines. However, these events are recounted in reverse chronology, allowing Letts to start the piece 'Here...' and even move into the present tense: 'as I bash this out...'. He becomes a character in his own story, reproducing as direct speech his words to one of those functionaries: 'Go away, you annoying man!'

In relation to his directly political references, Letts sets himself up in judgment over the spin doctors in post-debate mode ('annoying') while being more positive about the three onstage performers: 'But the debate itself, surely, was pretty good'. This is despite the measured disrespect of the opening, which is comfortable in placing the prime minister as an 'old donkey', confident that most *Daily Mail* readers will find this judgement easy to accept. Indication of positive alignments into which the reader is also encouraged is offered by framing the evaluation of the debate in imaginary dialogue ('surely'...) with a doubtful but per-suadable interlocutor. A little reluctantly, a serious, affirming point is made 'against the grain' of the genre's usual thrust. Of course, it is the value of the debate as *performance* that Letts is judging, more than its political substance, an orientation further reinforced by the choice of the term 'gig', in the fourth paragraph framing the event primarily as entertainment. In contrast, the negative judgment of the spin doc-tors is emphasized, through repetition emphasising their sheer numbers and their hyperactivity, the connotations of particular verbs ('lurking') and nouns ('apparatchik'). Sports metaphors (Henley Regatta, grand prix, gymkhana, Olympics) add entertainment value to the description, while also suggesting suspect practices (ear bending, schmoozing, deceit). Another aspect of evaluation can be seen in the variation in the naming of the three leaders. Clegg is treated as less well known than Cameron and Brown. The straightforward given name plus surname formula used for the two main party leaders significantly contrasts with 'that Clegg man' for the Liberal Democrat leader.

Letts' alignment with *Daily Mail* readers is deserving of further attention – for instance through the colloquial phrasings periodically deployed ('bash'; 'a bit of a copycat'; 'gassed on'; 'gig'), underpinning a greater feeling of closeness between writers and readers. The range of cultural references also speaks to the basis of that relationship in shared knowledge. The Sealink ferry and Henley Royal Regatta are likely to be accessible to most of the national audience, with the former providing the more 'vulgar' point of entry, and taken together are indicative of mainstream affiliations. But the allusion to 'Young Mr Grace' connects out to popular culture via the catchphrase of a character from the iconic BBC TV sitcom, *Are You Being Served*. Since the series finished 25 years ago, the use of the reference gives emphasis to a bonding with a middle-aged audience.

Our third example is taken from the writer, Ann Treneman, at the time the only woman among the political sketch-writers on the major dailies. This is from her piece in *The Times* on 8 May 2010, two days after Election Day,[4] when in the light of the inconclusive election results, speculation began about the series of alliances that might develop between the Conservatives, or just possibly Labour, and the Liberal Democrats.

Loves me, loves me not: Clegg and the dating game

Spare a thought for Little Nicky Clegg. He had believed he was a contender. But now, the morning after the nightmare before, he was merely a pretty face lusted after by the other two for their own selfish reasons. Thus he did the only thing he could: he played hard to get. For yesterday we saw three men playing a very public game of power dating.

Later in this chapter we return to the way in the Clegg–Cameron alliance was referred to in erotic terms, as either a 'civil partnership' for instance, or in a more hostile phrasing as the 'Brokeback' coalition (e.g. Littlejohn, 2010). This was widely taken up in those genres which have scope for

imaginative development, particularly after the Number 10 press conference of 12 May (projected within the erotic/marital frame as a 'wedding
day'). Here, Treneman describes a 'dating game' (a distinctive version,
'power dating') in which Clegg is placed as the woman in relation to
two suitors. Later in the piece, this idea is developed further:

> Our love-hate triangle now moves to Downing Street where Gordon
> is fuming. He disliked Nick, but he hated Dave. How dare they talk of
> love! Such was his fury that he knew he had to do the hardest thing
> of all – act. Thus at 12.40pm, Gordon strode out of No 10. He looked
> straight into the camera (and thus into the eyes of Nick) and did all
> but throw himself at Nick's feet. He even told Nick that he respected
> him (yes he did, even though everyone who has ever dated knows
> that this is a bad line). Then he gushed about their wonderful new
> life together.

This language and narrative are taken straight from the pages of popular romantic fiction, although, as often in sketch-writing, the figurative
analogy is not simply a comic embellishment worked upon the political
behaviour it describes, it is used to *illuminate* aspects of this behaviour.
In doing so, it identifies weaknesses of character and of action in what
has been happening.

Moving into a later period of the year, the fourth example is provided by Simon Hoggart, writing in the *Guardian* on the Monday (27
September 2010) after Ed Miliband had achieved a surprising success in
the Labour Party leadership, held at the start of their September conference. Once again the judgemental tone is reserved for the character of a
political leader, assessing his performance in a televised moment, rather
than in Parliament. We quote here from the first few paragraphs.

**Ed Miliband Gives Nothing Away in first interrogation: Labour's
new leader keeps his cards close to his chest when being questioned by Andrew Marr**

Ed Miliband faced his first rite of passage as Labour leader this
morning, being questioned by Andrew Marr. He seemed nervous to
begin with, like a young man (and he does look very young indeed)
at his first job interview. You could imagine his mum brushing the
dandruff from his shoulders and straightening his tie. His legs were
apart and his hands clasped between them.

In short, he looked like a geek. He had some good news for the
middle classes, but they will probably beware of geeks bearing gifts.

Ed had a tough task ahead, to spend half an hour saying absolutely nothing and giving nothing away.

Except how much he loved his brother, David. 'He has shown extraordinary generosity to me,' he said, several times. 'He is a fantastic person.'

Almost everything he said was in accordance with my law of the nonsensical reverse. For instance, just after he won, he said he was 'passionate about Britain'. Since declaring that he was passionate about the Maldive Islands would have been absurd, it was perhaps unnecessary to make the point in the first place.

He felt we should have great respect for nurses. ('I despise nurses with every fibre of my being.') He thought strikes should always be a last resort. ('Get the lads out, then talk to management, that's my plan.').

He was, he told us, his own man ('I am a puppet, ready to be manipulated by anyone who can grab my strings'). He was the change that Labour needs ('No real problems in our party. Leave well alone I say'). Unity was his watchword ('Let's fight each other – it's always fun!').

As we have seen in some of the earlier examples, the establishing of a diminishing image early on is part of the strategy. Here, the 'young man at job interview' analogy is not just put forward but elaborated with references to posture and an attentive mum. This turns to the more directly abusive description of him as a 'geek', part of whose role here is to allow the joke about 'geeks bearing gifts'. The account then moves into what is its defining humorous move – setting off what Miliband says against the absurdity of saying something very different. This punctures the seriousness of Milband's claims-making and its broader target is the tendency of many politicians towards banality and the statement of the obvious when offering general accounts. Hoggart sees that the project is almost entirely about 'saying nothing' and within these terms Milband's performance might be deemed a tactical success. The parenthetical remarks, which illustrate, by the contrasts they provide, the 'obviousness' of what is actually said, have a further, subversive edge to them too, as if some of them might be truer to perspectives really to be found in sections of the Labour Party – on strikes, change, and unity – than those articulated by Miliband. In sum, these opening comments place a quiet but deeply critical frame around this first media appearance of the new leader.

Although, as we have noted, sketch-writing is a central and regular form of 'colour' writing, it is not the only place where rhetorical moves self-consciously involving distortion and a relationship with the reader constructed around humour can occur. Clearly, many columnists have a signature style of this kind and when they are writing of public events their accounts get close to those of the sketch-writers, if only for specific passages.

Here is the opening paragraph from a column ('The coalition must tackle the shortage of new homes') by Boris Johnson for the *Daily Telegraph* on 18 October 2010, written in relation to the Coalition government's policy on housing.[5]

> Watch out, folks, we are about to be hit by a snowstorm of economic data. So put on your goggles and look out for the one big hurtling fact that really matters. The key point you need to remember during this week's spending announcements is that the population of the UK is set to rise by an incredible 10 million over the next 20 years. That is more than the population of Greater London crash-landing on a land mass half the size of France.
>
> Not since industrialization, not since medieval England recovered from the Black Death, has there been anything like it. Thanks very largely to Labour's deliberate failure to control immigration, and to higher birth rates, the Big Society is about to get very big indeed.
>
> What jobs will we all do? Where will we all live? And what effect will that extra demand have on the cost of housing?

This is written in a colloquial register of exhortation and exaggeration within which Johnson has created a distinctive identity. Telling the reader to 'put on your goggles and look out for the one big hurtling fact' creates a comic book (or *Wind in the Willows*) image at the same time as it confirms the writer as warmly 'chummy', someone a reader can bond with. Again, as in some of the work discussed above, an engaging 'shock' analogy is offered ('crash-landing'), together with self-conscious historical overstatement ('Black Death') to establish a position about the existing situation. This then, via a sequence of the most generally resonant questions, leads into the sustained and seriously argued section of the column.

We have noted significant variations in the tones and the stances taken by sketch-writers, together with the nature and elaborative intensity of the various 'conceits' through which they carry out their portrayals. Even where partisan alignments can be detected, however, the generic 'rules' of the sketch really require that no explicit argument, or indeed any but the briefest intrusion of a 'serious political point', breaks the comic frame, a frame that marks out the political world as one having a dimension of intrinsic absurdity within which specific examples of behaviour and action nevertheless display their distinctive farcical aspects, worthy of close identification and comment. As we see in the last example, it is possible for other kinds of columnist to work within this generic recipe for passages and then to shift, often quite abruptly, into a more propositional, and more sober, register of writing.

Editorial voices

We want to turn now to take a brief look at another, established, genre of non-news writing – the editorial column, or 'leader'. This is of interest for a number of reasons, not least because it is where a newspaper is often most explicit about its own views and political positions and where it seeks a relationship with its readers not at the level of individual contributors but at the level of the identity of the title and the institution generally. We have chosen to look at the way in which three newspapers in our corpus covered Ed Miliband's election to leadership of the Labour Party, a situation already commented upon in the extract from Simon Hoggart's sketch given above. For our purposes, the value of looking at editorials here lies not only in their specific generic properties but also in the fact that they allow us to engage with tabloid newspapers, an engagement which is not possible in respect of parliamentary sketch-writing and only intermittently possible in respect of political cartoons, as we discuss later. All three newspapers cited are the editions of Monday 27 September 2010.

The Sun

What's your big idea, Ed?

THERE is only one way Labour's new leader Ed Miliband can prove why he shouldn't be called Red Ed.

He must stand up to the union bully boys who put him in power.

Mr Miliband starts with a clean slate and *The Sun* wishes him well.

The country needs a proper Opposition to hold the Government to account.

But responsible opposition means being constructive and not just mouthing slogans.

Mr Miliband must reach out to millions of *Sun* readers alienated by Gordon Brown.

To do that he must confront those to whom he owes his job – the militant unions and his party's Left.

Second, Mr Miliband must prove that he is not the puppet of the trade union barons. He must speak up against politically-motivated strikes such as those on the London Underground and British Airways that cause misery for millions and damage the economy.

He must condemn irresponsible TUC rabble-rousers warning of riots.

...It was Gordon Brown's reversion to Old Labour that lost the party the last election.

Ed Miliband must not make the same mistake.

This clearly works as an open and aggressive warning to Miliband to stop the activities that have (in the newspaper's view, rightly) led to him being called 'Red Ed' within the right-wing stretch of the political spectrum. The editorial works with a number of established prejudices, articulated within evaluative phrases that are not thought to need further argument for support ('union bully boys', 'mouthing slogans', 'puppet', 'rabble-rousing'). The idea that the paper 'wishes him well' would seem rather strained in such a context, and it is more that the country needs a 'proper opposition' than any positive evaluation of what Miliband stands for that leads to this qualified, gestural affirmation. The marginal nature of the victory, and the sense that it was the union vote that decided it, are central to the overall feeling that he is a politician whose independence, let alone whose political wisdom, is greatly in doubt. The *Sun*'s prescriptive tirade (with its repetitions of 'must') appears to be more concerned with identifying the unions as the cause for 'misery' and as Miliband's primary problem. Interestingly, among the moves urged on Miliband, as part of avoiding the pitfalls of 'Old Labour', is a 'reaching out' to *Sun* readers, thus bringing the identity of the newspaper and its readers centrally into the debate about the national political future.

The Mirror

A Leader to Reclaim Our Trust.

ED Miliband's victory to become the 10th post-war leader of the Labour party is a remarkable achievement.

Such was the manner of his triumph – taking on the party's Prince Regent, who also happened to be his elder brother – that no one will ever doubt his grit and determination (even if it could mean a rather frosty atmosphere round at Mum's this Christmas). His first task is to neutralise the clichés spouting from the Tories that his win means a lurch to the left, that he is a union stooge.

Mr Miliband must be his own man, beholden to no special interests, only to those of the British people.

He must re-establish Labour as the home of fairness. His campaign clarion call for a 'living wage' should be the first of many bold, imaginative and fiscally sound initiatives Labour would deliver when back in charge.

Mr Miliband is a consensus politician. He can be a strong, decisive leader but still utilise the strength in depth at his disposal.

... We wish him well.

The *Mirror*'s position is initially in sharp contrast to that of the *Sun*, while giving an impression of being in dialogue with its rival tabloid newspaper. The win is seen as a 'remarkable achievement' and a positive tone is established from the start. Personal qualities of 'grit and determination' are seen to be evident from the manner of it, including the competition against the elder brother. The *Mirror* precisely warns against the negative views that the *Sun* endorses, although its remedy is essentially for him to avoid the policies which would reinforce these views. As with the *Sun*, a clear independence is urged on him against constraints from within his own party. The values of 'fairness' and a commitment to greater attention to levels of poverty are supported along with the idea of consensus (again, pulling against the perceived dangers of a factional orientation). Instead of the *Sun*'s clear anxieties, the *Mirror* projects the potential for progressive change based on the qualities perceived in the campaign, although this is qualified by a sense of the need to recognize 'the reality of the markets' and to have an economic policy that combines social justice with growth. In contrast to the *Sun*, the measured well-wishing appears sincere.

The Daily Telegraph

Cameron must beware a cunning opponent

The natural response to Ed Miliband's victory over his brother in the Labour leadership contest is to congratulate him. We do so, while also recognising that the new Leader of the Opposition won his position as the result of the most breathtaking ruthlessness. David Miliband was more hurt than alarmed when his younger brother entered the contest in May. He did not foresee the skill with which Ed would flatter, cultivate and cajole the different Labour constituencies – above all, the trade union leaders – in order to thwart David's lifelong ambition.

This was a virtuoso display of political cunning, and one that David Cameron should study carefully, instead of listening to Conservatives who assure him that 'Christmas has come early' thanks to the choice of the 'unelectable' Ed Miliband. The new Labour leader was relaxed and assured on TV yesterday. Labour would not 'lurch to the Left' under him, he insisted. He occupied the 'centre ground' of British politics and recognized the need for restraint in the public sector; he would not oppose the Coalition just for the sake of it.

.... As for the myth of Ed Miliband's deep-rooted niceness, the Government must make sure that the British public does not buy into it. Certainly, many Labour MPs no longer do so. Saturday's wafer-thin victory was a political triumph of sorts; but the calculated humiliation of David Miliband by his younger brother was not the act of a nice man.

Here, by contrast with the two leaders in the popular newspapers, the emphasis is strategic and tactical, focusing not so much on the future possibilities for Miliband but on the appropriate response to the victory that should be taken by David Cameron. In some ways more directly than the *Sun*, the *Telegraph* condemns the 'utter ruthlessness' that was behind Miliband's election. 'Flattery, cultivation and cajolery' are seen as the principal forms of behaviour upon which his success is based. The editorial develops its strongly Machiavellian line on events, noting the ease and dexterity with which dubious claims have already been made by Miliband on TV. The *Telegraph*'s demographic position (with a broad middle-class and middle-aged to elderly readership) also seems to suggest that issues of 'niceness' be addressed, in a way that would be entirely out of context in the other two editorials. By emphasising the way in which he behaved towards his brother ('calculated humiliation'), the *Telegraph* seeks to advise its readers not to slip into thinking that there are any redeeming virtues in this area.

As with the examples of 'colour' writing, there is a considerable stylistic range employed in the various newspapers' approach to civic stance-taking. This is clearly very much to do with their sense both of their own political and social identity and that of the readers they address. Matters of value predominate in what is a strongly judicial, indeed often a magisterial, exercise driven by questions, rhetorical and real. What can act as a positive marker? Where do risks lie? Of what should we be most suspicious and who deserves our trust? What can be 'taken as read' and what needs a more careful appraisal and recognition of complexity? In cuing their readers towards imperatives for 'ways forward', the editorials display, in the performance of the role of their paper as a civic actor, properties of 'voice' and of social positioning quite distinctive in relation to the wide variety of other forms of writing that newspapers carry.

'Visual damage': the art of the political cartoon

Martin Rowson, regular cartoonist for the *Guardian* and the *Mirror*, has referred to the art of caricature as 'a type of voodoo – doing damage to someone at a distance with a sharp object' (2009, p. 153). The caricaturing of political leaders in political cartoons is merely one element of the imaginative capacities of this graphic form: by drawing on dimensions of fantasy, reality, allegory and metaphor, the cartoon can offer a distinctive appraisal of political people, behaviours, events and structures via a diverse range of visual styles, attitudes and moods, usually with comic effect. As a visual form of political commentary, the political cartoon originates as a regular newspaper item in the late nineteenth century, and is now stabilized as a daily multiple-column feature within the leader and comment sections of the 'quality' newspapers, and less consistently within the pages of the mid-market and tabloid titles.[6] Regularly printed in colour across all newspapers, this primarily pictorial mode often integrates text; in titles, captions, speech bubbles and labelling of content (both to aid identification and to draw out allegorical connections). As a more recent development, political cartoons are also available in digital form via the newspapers' sister websites, with the *Guardian*'s cartoons regularly garnering around 100 written viewer reactions in the few days that the pages are open to comments. The internet has increased visibility for cartoonists' work at a time when scarce employment opportunities had led some authors to fear the decline of the political cartoon alongside the shrinking readership of traditional quality newspapers (e.g. see Seymour-Ure, 2001; Danjoux, 2007).

Political cartoons have an ephemeral quality, often making elliptical references to topical subjects and news events that might prove difficult to appreciate fully in the subsequent years or even months. Conversely, the sharp observations of a cartoonist can endure beyond the life cycle of a news story, or even a political career, with certain caricatures recurring and becoming familiar to regular readers (e.g. Steve Bell's depiction of John Major wearing Y-front underpants over his trousers). Despite the often instantaneous and brutal 'bite' recognized in a momentary glance, only those acquainted with the particular cartoonist's stylistics, favoured cultural allusions and recurring tropes are likely to pick up on the full array of meanings and insinuations. Rather than explicate further on the broad generic and thematic features found during our audit periods, we present a selection of cartoons as indicative examples, with analysis focused on aspects of visual design and the varied modes of engagement with political realities.

An election-campaign period offers a particularly fruitful time for visual satirists; as political candidates strive to promote their identities and characters to gain public recognition and approval, cartoonists concurrently subvert, distort and exaggerate character traits to humorous effect (Edwards, 2001; Seymour-Ure, 2001; Conners, 2005). In the cartoons we have audited, there is, not surprisingly, often an emphasis on *political persons*, in particular the three party leaders during the general-election campaign and the autumn election of Ed Miliband to the leadership of the Labour Party.[7] This makes personal characterization and caricature the principal depictive mode. Yet portrayals of distinct moments in a campaign and political caricature can also extend to implications concerning the nature of institutions or structures, in spite of the limitations of the static visual frame.

Our first cartoon, by Martin Rowson in the *Guardian*, directly comments on the power of TV to raise the public profile of political leaders, and we include it here because of its distinctive visual style and cultural allusions (see Figure 2.1). The setting, as so often in work in this genre, is imaginary, but here the fairy-tale story of Pinocchio and his creator Geppetto provides the inspiration, along with Clegg's newfound standing as a 'real politician' – alluded to as a consequence of his equal billing in the televised *Leaders' Debates*. The fairy-tale genre of literature is a densely allegorical form of storytelling, and some of its principal markers are utilized here, with the top-left title imitating the beginning of the story, 'When you wish upon a star...', the scenery a simple wooden house with stars in the sky. But unlike the more realistic portrayals of party leaders, which were found in other cartoons at the time, Rowson uses the devices of extreme exaggeration and distortion (in the dark eyes and large lips of Vince Cable as Geppetto),[8] politicians depicted as animals (Cameron as the fox), or as inanimate objects (Clegg as a wooden Pinocchio). The 'fat cat' beside Cameron, peering in at the window, is also a condensed representation for high-earning, big-business interests who have close relationships with political leaders; his proximity to Cameron and possible interest in Clegg providing a neat visual device

Figure 2.1 Guardian, 19 April 2010. Copyright: Martin Rowson/Guardian News & Media Ltd 2010

that implies potential developments in the tale, as Clegg progresses on his journey of self and political discovery.

The political figures are not so easily recognisable to those readers with only a passing interest in politics, and Rowson also rewards a familiarity with the Pinocchio story and its own sinister undercurrents. Rather than appearing overjoyed with Clegg's transformation, Cable is depicted as shaking the boy-Clegg, an elder father-figure who has lost control of his creation or 'puppet': 'The Tellyfairy's promise has come true! You have turned into a real politician!' A promise coming true is a usually a celebratory proclamation in the fairy-tale genre, here subverted by Rowson into a more ambivalent statement, imbued with a cynicism directed at the nature of mediatized politics. Rowson's use of Pinocchio to depict Nick Clegg is perhaps the most vivid example of innovation during this period, a symbolic construct that was devised for portraying the electoral campaign but one which worked even better when portraying the activities of the government that followed.[9]

Editorial cartoons in the broadsheets have received criticism for their 'elitist' tendencies, often requiring high levels of topical knowledge, recognition of political character traits and a wider literary or cultural understanding to decipher their meanings. Although digital access to editorial cartoons may now be starting to challenge Seymour-Ure's earlier claim that cartoonists such as Mac in the *Daily Mail* reach 'a readership of about the same size as all the broadsheet cartoonists added together' (Seymour-Ure, 2001, p. 353), it is still the case that those cartoons aimed at the mid-market newspaper readership reach a considerable audience and offer interesting points for comparison with the 'qualities'. The example by Mac below (Figure 2.2) presents a quieter form of cartoon, with simplicity of composition, strong use of symbolism, and sparing use of colour or text. This cartoon accompanied a front-page editorial on the eve of the election (5 May 2010), filling the top half of the page while the headline read, 'Vote DECISIVELY to stop Britain walking blindly into disaster', with the capitalized 'decisively' also in red type. Such prominent positioning for the cartoon is unusual, although the promotion of editorials to front-page status is common during the final days of an election campaign. The political message is unambiguous in this case; a blind Britannia walks to the edge of the cliff, with the thunderstorms of a 'hung parliament' towering above. In the opposite direction, to the right of the frame, the sun shines on 'strong government'. In employing the traditionalist female personification of Britannia, Mac signals a visual appeal to national pride, here depicted in immediate peril rather than resplendent and proud. Eschewing caricature and captioning, Mac's tone is a serious one, contingent on the editorial's direct message, which is to 'vote Conservative' and avoid the prospect of the 'shabby compromises' of a coalition government. The two options are presented as clearly opposed, a condensation of a political argument that fears a Labour–Lib Dem

Figure 2.2   Daily Mail, 5 May 2010. Copyright: Mac/Daily Mail

coalition and hopes for an outright win for the Conservatives; albeit an argument expressed in non-party terms as a choice between 'hung parliament' and 'strong government', thereby raising the sense of crisis to an institutional rather than party-political level. There might be thought to be some symbolic 'excess', and even reduced impact, in the signalling of the precise nature of imminent peril, with the impending stormy weather a rather insignificant threat when compared with that of walking over a cliff by proceeding a few paces further down the path!

Our third example shows a nicely enigmatic style of comment, alluding to the formation of coalition government as a marriage between party leaders Cameron and Clegg (Figure 2.3). The cartoon contains no direct reference to either political person, yet the metaphor of romance was heavily, and often heavy-handedly, utilized across the mediascape during this post-election period; Ann Treneman's column in *The Times* discussed above is one illustration (see also Parry and Richardson, 2011). Christian Adams' cartoon for the *Telegraph* provides a subtle portrayal, one in some contrast with many other depictions of the coalition as a civil partnership, marriage or showbiz coupling. It employs a wry take on the 'political honeymoon' period. The signifiers in the cartoon all allude to two lovers (honeymoon suite, champagne, a red rose, 'do

Figure 2.3 (Christian) Adams cartoon, 15 May 2010, *Daily Telegraph*. Copyright: Telegraph Media Group Limited 2010

not disturb' sign), yet the political content (an already-lit bomb) sneaks into the cartoon's serene setting through its placement under the trolley tablecloth. Very much a 'cartoonish' bomb in its appearance, here it is labelled with the potential problems for the new coalition (tax, Europe, cuts, National Insurance). The mood in this example is whimsical rather than cynical, with elements of farce introduced as an inherent dimension of the coalition agreement and, more generally, of coalition politics.

As even the selection we offer here shows, the aesthetic design of cartoons varies enormously across the different artists and newspapers, quite apart from the different positions taken up towards politics and the political class. Below (Figure 2.4) we reproduce a cartoon from a later period in the year, following the election to the Labour Party leadership of Ed Miliband, an event that we discussed above in respect to both sketch-writing and newspaper leaders. This image by Patrick Garland is more gentle and subtle in approach than the ones we have discussed earlier, taking its cue from Paul Gauguin's 1897 post-impressionist painting, 'Where do we come from? What are we? Where are we going?'; cross-referencing the news story of a major exhibition of the artist's work at Tate Modern in autumn 2010. The painting is an allegorical piece about

Figure 2.4   (Nicholas) Garland cartoon, 29 September 2010, *Daily Telegraph.*
Copyright: Telegraph Media Group Limited 2010

the 'human condition', offering a portrayal much influenced by the artist's experience of life in *fin-de-siècle* Tahiti. With its figures replaced by those of leading Labour Party politicians, including many from the last Labour government, the dreamy softness of the depiction loses its spiritual force to confer a sense of ridiculous disorientation and uncertainty, with Miliband appearing pathetically low in leaderly qualities, amid a group of colleagues lost in introspection. In Gauguin's original, each of the figures represents past and future incarnations, their troubled expressions betraying the flaws and anxieties of their particular situation – in choosing to adapt this painting in fine detail, Garland offers a nuanced treatment of the key themes of Labour's past and future, as covered in Miliband's speech. As often with Garland's work, the pursuit of a 'high art' analogy and a delicacy both with colour and line produce an engaging and effective image.

In strong contrast to this is another image looking at the same event, this time by the *Guardian*'s cartoonist, Steve Bell (Figure 2.5). Bell has developed a strong reputation as an original artist (Plumb, 2004; Dodds, 2007), not least because of the series of comic strips he has produced alongside his single cartoons. His anger, often leading to a deliberately

Figure 2.5 Steve Bell, 29 September 2010, *Guardian*. Copyright: Steve Bell – all rights reserved

'vulgar', viscerally explicit and highly distortive depiction of political leaders, has also been commented on across a run of British politics which stretches from early Thatcher to Cameron. Here, he offers a multi-frame take on Miliband's post-election address to the conference, working a connection to the lyrics of *The Who's* classic song 'My Generation', which was a huge success when released in 1965. The departure point for this approach is the fact that Miliband's speech drew strongly on the idea of a 'new generation' of Labour politicians now becoming influential in the development of party policy. The song is based on a call and response structure, with some stuttering introduced at the start of the lines, which run:

People try to put us d-down
Just because we g-g-get around
Things they do look awful c-c-cold
I hope I die before I get old

At the end of each line the response – 'talking 'bout my generation' – is sung.

The penultimate frame breaks the song pattern to introduce a cliché of political speeches, repeatedly used by Miliband in his speech ('and I tell you this'), and then to follow it with a negative pronouncement about Gordon Brown's own negative pronouncement at the Labour Party conference of 2000 (Brown's precise words were 'There will be no return to Tory boom and bust'). Brown's claim was clearly belied by the economic events of the last years of his leadership and introducing it here signals not only the past failures of the Labour Party but the possibility that the making of promises that cannot be kept will continue. The double negative of the formulation calls attention to this 'history repeating itself' factor at the same time as its very syntax gives a sense of underlying absurdities. It is interesting the first seven frames place Miliband in full body profile or three-quarter profile, with the last one showing a more decisive turn to front on. Without risking over-reading here, this has the effect of showing Milband's performance as 'observed' as it is projected across the podium, before the last frame aligns it with the live audience in the hall addressed 'directly' and across one part of its lateral range.

We finish our selective analysis of cartoons in this chapter with two taken from the popular press, the *Mirror* and the *Sun*, both within a day or so of each other. Just as the genres of non-news political writing in newspapers varies considerably with the assumptions made about the readership's political disposition, education and range of cultural references, so political cartoons, too, vary. In particular, the multi-layered allegorical styles much favoured by the 'quality' press are not to be found extensively in the mid-market and popular press. Here, and especially in the latter, a more one-dimensional and direct (rather than allusive) approach is employed. We can see this in the different 'takes' offered below on the running against each other for party leadership of Ed and David Miliband. We have looked both earlier in this chapter and in other chapters at the way in which this high-profile version of sibling rivalry was given varied generic expression. In the *Mirror*, the treatment is reduced to a basic joke form, the idea of the shock that might be caused to another David, David Cameron, were he to find out that he had a brother Ed too (Figure 2.6). The visual work illustrates the idea without elaboration, in the simplest of line illustrations with a caption and with both the place (10 Downing Street) and the addressee given written identification to avoid any puzzle or misunderstanding (we have our own evidence of readers struggling to make sense of more 'difficult' cartoons, and this is discussed in Chapter 4).

In the *Sun* it is not so much a joke event as a basic irony that is worked with, in this case the political cliché of 'spending more time

Figure 2.6 Kerber and Black, 28 September 2010, *Daily Mirror*. Copyright: Mirror Syndication International

Figure 2.7 Andy Davey, *Sun*, 1 October 2010. Cartoon reproduced by kind permission of Andy Davey

with the family', used about those who find themselves removed from front-bench politics. The irony is of the caption against the act depicted, an enraged David sticking needles into a voodoo doll of his brother (Figure 2.7). Both cartoons stay at the level of a humour created around political personalities rather than venturing into an engagement with political values and political ideas.

The play of the cartoonist's art on political life allows a directness, often a 'cruelty', in the treatment of political persons and events that has connections with the kinds of caricature produced by 'colour' writers but has an immediacy and vividness of its own. The critical force, and perhaps the anger, behind some cartoons is not found so often in the writing we have examined, where a modulated sense of fascinated, amused distance (of writer to topic and by implication of reader to topic too) is the norm. Cartoonists do not activate a mediating authorial position in the often marked way that 'colour' writers do, their strategy is to engage us with the immediacy of their visualizations, with the judgements and perceptions that went into constructing them elided from the representation (e.g. the difference between our seeing an 'absurdly confused Miliband' and being told, through description and appraisal, how Miliband was absurdly confused). This final example neatly recalls Rowson's comment cited at the start of this section, of cartoonists' practice as a 'type of voodoo', delighting in its capacity to disturb and cause damage to inflated egos or deficient politicians. In this sense, despite the visual form being arguably more 'open' to interpretation, they share with the sketch-writers an assumed positioning of superiority and judgement, in which those holding powerful positions of public office are caricatured as nervous interviewees, old donkeys and near-naked nymphs. As our examples show, as well as carrying out significant cultural work on political persons and local situations, some cartoonists are able to make powerful connections with a sense of the institutional and systemic order and with broader political ideas and clashes of value.

Parodic modes

Some of the written examples we have discussed above involve a temporary move into parody, a form in which the discursive design of a familiar (political or more broadly cultural) style is imitated for critical purposes. A particular way of speaking, or form of official writing or genre of popular culture, for example, can be subjected to attention of this kind. More extensive kinds of written parody are only infrequently found in newspapers but the fortnightly satirical magazine *Private Eye* regularly includes them in its survey of the political scene. Their mode of humour, and their contribution to a certain section of political culture in Britain, is significant and worth briefly examining through a few instances. One dominant strategy in *Private Eye* writing of this kind is to portray one event or circumstance within a discursive framework 'borrowed' (parodically) from the way in which another event or circumstance has been portrayed in public media.[10] Here, for example, is Nick Clegg being written about in terms borrowed from coverage of the biologist Richard Dawkins' controversial scepticism regarding the existence of God, given worldwide attention following the publication of *The God Delusion* in 2006 (Dawkins, 2006). The issue is 14–27 May 2010, which went to press after the election but before the coalition agreement had been confirmed. This is a period, of surprise and speculation, which we have already referred to extensively elsewhere in the book.

'I believe in Clegg', confesses Dawkins
By Our Religious Staff The Rev. A.N. Wislon
The world's best-known atheist Prof. Richard Dawkins has shocked his thousands of followers across the world by announcing that he

now believes that Nick Clegg is the Messiah, capable of saving the world.

'I admit', he said, 'that there is no scientific evidence for the existence of such an omnipotent and benign being as Clegg. But these are matters of belief, not of rational proof.'

'I personally feel that Clegg is all around us, holding out the promise of a better life and a better world, if we will only have the courage to follow him'.

'It's silly to think of this wonderful Supreme Being as an old man with a long, white beard. That was his predecessor, Ming Campbell'....

These sentences, the first four paragraphs of a six-paragraph item, take the phenomenon of 'Cleggmania', a consequence in large part, as we have noted, of the public response to the first of the *Leaders' Debates*, and 'graft' it on to the terms of an already established public issue around Dawkins, one which is given a reverse rendering ('belief' instead of 'doubt'). The effect is the familiar one in political comedy of taking what seems to be an 'inflated' claim or reputation and pushing it to the point where it becomes self-evidently ridiculous (in the process, undercutting the seriousness and status both of Clegg and of Dawkins, and also of Menzies Campbell, the MP and, for a brief period, Liberal Democrat leader).

Our second example shifts the focus to political *ideas*, rather than the personal characteristics of political leaders. It concerns the dominant Coalition policy of 'The Big Society', launched with enthusiasm by David Cameron. This edition of *Private Eye* is from 23 July–5 August 2010. It imitates a news story as if from an excited political editor of a Conservative newspaper:

Cameron launches 'Big Idea'
By our Political Staff Simon Hogwash[11]

In what was described as the largest ever shake-up in how Britain is run, groups of individuals will now be encouraged to set up their own governments on a local basis.

With the help of grants and advice from the central authorities, local groups, including faith-based charities and small businesses, will be allowed to set up broadband networks, raise taxes, arm local militias and, even, if they wish, reintroduce the death penalty for selected offences.

In a speech today, the Prime Minister, Mr David Cameron, told stunned reporters, 'For too long central government had dictated to British people how they should run their lives, often in a quite arbitrary way.

I want to put an end to this top-down approach and give power back to the people'.

The strategy here, the first four paragraphs of nine-paragraph item, is to work at times quite closely to the phrasing through which 'the big society' was introduced and reported by supportive newspapers but then, in a standard discursive move, to push the examples of local autonomy to the point of the ridiculous and beyond. The move to the ridiculous is indicated early on by the idea that the new localism will involve the establishing of 'governments' and it is clinched in the quickly escalating list of activities over which the 'groups' will be able to exert authority. The location of such devastating information within the context of an otherwise conventionally toned piece of policy reporting in which elements of the real policy (e.g. reference to 'faith-based charities') are embedded, provides the contrast which is at the centre of the whole piece. The primary purpose is clearly to take Cameron's idea of 'giving power back to the people' and, by *reductio ad absurdum*, show something of the banality if not the civic risk that underlies it.

A final example is taken from the issue of 29 October–11 November 2010, focusing the apparent absurdities of politics abroad, in the 'Wonderland' of the United States.

Tea Party Candidates Romp Home in Wonderland Mid Terms
By our Election Staff Lewis Carol Thatcher

A group of eccentric Tea Party attendees, including the Mad Hatter, a White Rabbit, a Dormouse and a girl called Alice, are set to pull off an incredible victory in Wonderland.

Despite clear evidence that all the candidates are clinically insane, voters across Wonderland are flocking to them in their thousands. These are just some of the Tea Party's radical credos:

- The Mad Hatter believes that President Obama is a Muslim sent by Satan to encourage masturbation.
- The White Rabbit refuses to allow any coloured rabbits into his burrow.
- The Dormouse is permanently asleep.

- Alice is a hot-diggety born-again Hockey mum whose children have yet to be born but who believes in having the occasional drink from the bottle so that she can either 'walk tall' or 'support a smaller state'. (That's enough Tea Party, Ed.)

Again, the strategy is one of mapping one discourse on to another. Here, Lewis Carroll's *Alice's Adventures in Wonderland*, with its own account of the Mad Hatter's tea party, provides the basis for an account of the recent success of the Tea Party in US politics, with some of the views expressed by Party members taken and pushed even further into the extreme. The account is written as by a British columnist supportive of the new initiative (a lightly disguised Carol Thatcher). The sense of hectic farce that informs much of *Private Eye's* parodic exercises is also evident.

Summary observations

Newspapers and magazines comprise a wide range of non-news genres in which elements of the political receive regular articulation. This range shows strong differentiation in relation both to the political affiliation and the demographic profile of readers, a set of alignments reinforced by the nature of newspapers and magazines as selectively purchased sources (a pattern which is likely to become more prevalent in broadcasting as the shift to multiple subscription channels continues). The shaping play of generic work upon politicians, political events and that broader, dispersed spectrum of political factors which, in our Introduction, we called 'politicality', shows a considerable diversity, with a common vein across columnists, sketch-writers and, most obviously, cartoonists, of the comical. Frequently, politics is 'placed' in its more absurd, even farcical, aspects, often with a politically partisan inflection but sometimes within a framing that finds comedy in the behaviour of politicians from all parties. A key strategy is that of exaggeration and distortion, taking existing deficiencies, inconsistencies or moments of excess or lapse and working them into self-evidently absurd versions. The tone of work runs from the gentle (even the affectionate) right through to the aggressive and the angry. Across the majority of the writing, however, there is little by way of implied general alternatives to politics-as-it-is, indications of change (nearly always implicit) are at the level of specific policies or specific parliamentary practices. The flaws and weaknesses of specific politicians is the most regular point of reference, combining both ideological and more personal criteria. Here again, however, what kind of person might better perform the role of politician (wiser, less vain, less in thrall to either big business or the unions, more consistent and honest) is left almost entirely gestural, a matter of presumed contrasts with the dominant characteristics on display. There is thus a sense in which a lot of the critical edge carried by the writing works finally more as a complement to the political world as represented in the mainstream news – a concurrent strand of release for a routine dimension of disrespect and distrust transformed, or semi-transformed, into *amusement* – rather than as a serious subversion of that world. This is even true of the stronger and more sustained kind of derisory attention provided by *Private Eye* (called the 'licensed jester' working within a 'Politics of the Fool' by Colin Seymour-Ure in his own invaluable review of how this magazine works) (Seymour-Ure, 1972).

The depth and richness, including the capacity to engage with concepts and complexity, on display in newspaper and magazine non-news writing and drawing makes a significant contribution to British political culture, reflecting (and often amplifying) its uncertainties, contradictions and shifts. Of course, questions have been raised about the survivability of this type of work in the context of a mediasphere increasingly dominated by new media applications, including those supportive of broadcasting. In this context, the profile that has been selectively examined in this chapter may be exposed to more radical changes in its conditions of production and supply than much else that has been taken for analysis in the book.

3
Politicality and the Web – Tracking the Cross-Currents

Summarising the opportunities for 'political mediations' in the rapidly evolving, multifaceted space of the web presents a number of complications, due in part to its immense capacity to embrace and adapt material from across a broad range of traditional media platforms. Indeed, on one level, the web is difficult to treat as a medium separate from older forms of media, as ever-expanding broadband capabilities allow it to develop as a conduit for TV, radio and even cinematic productions (through iPlayer, podcasts, YouTube and LoveFilm), while content displayed under 'brands' of mainstream print media often shadows its offline 'older sister' in terms of genre, format and style (e.g. editorial cartoons, *Private Eye*). Moreover, the web enables audience connectivity and shared responses to 'real-time' broadcasting and other content through social-media sites, such as Twitter, live blogging, official and unofficial forums, and comment threads. Leading political blogs, or 'influentials' (Perlmutter, 2008), with their more personalized approach to reporting on political events, present a relatively definable – though evolving – communicative space through which to venture into the wider political mediascape online. Political blogging is therefore at the centre of the following account.

The selection of blogs in our original 2010 sample was never intended to represent the UK political blogosphere in a comprehensive manner, but rather to offer a set of markers and exemplars for the forms of mediation found (*'offer' appears twice*) in this internet-based format. Following the general pattern of our inquiry into treatments of politics and the political across the mediascape, this material is here used to explore the kinds of images, language, themes and personas that are posted, linked and re-posted in UK blogs. With this point of departure, we examine not only the character of blogs as generic form, but also the character of mediated British politics in its online manifestations.

Blogging as a political genre

Compared to other media formats and genres discussed in this book, the 'weblog' is a relatively new concept, non-existent before the late 1990s, and evolving into in its recognisable configuration as a 'blog' largely with the help of the initial tool that facilitated the creation of blogs, *Blogger* (boyd, 2006, para 9). Although in the early 2000s newspaper and broadcast media regularly felt the need to explain for audiences what a 'blog' might be, the practices and products of blogging have now gained a taken-for-granted status, acquiring an entry as both verb and noun in the *Oxford English Dictionary* (OED) from March 2003. The online OED currently defines a weblog, or blog, in this context, as: 'A frequently updated web site consisting of personal observations, excerpts from other sources, etc., typically run by a single person, and usually with hyperlinks to other sites; an online journal or diary' (OED, 2011). As a verb, to blog, the OED has: 'To write or maintain a weblog. Also: to read or browse through weblogs, esp. habitually' (ibid.). Despite the vagueness of these definitions, there are significant pointers here towards the *sociability* of blogging: blogs are 'frequently updated', personal observations, with hyperlinks; in some cases treated as an online journal. Likewise, blogging as an activity is here deemed to include the habitual *reading* as well as the writing of blog entries.

The interconnectivity of blogs – their conversational tone, authorial presence (albeit pseudonymous in some cases), and regularity of updates – is crucial for understanding their role as forms of mediation found. But the notion of a 'community' of bloggers can also elide hierarchies, as well as political and cultural differences. The word that generally reflects this, 'blogosphere', gained an OED entry in 2009: 'The cultural or intellectual environment in which blogs are written and read; blogs, their writers, and readers collectively, esp. considered as a distinct online network'. Jodi Dean prefers the term 'blogipelago' to highlight that not all blogs are created equal, or operate collectively: the term 'reminds us of separateness, disconnection, and the immense effort it can take to move from one island or network to another' (2010, p. 38). Dean's plea to remain alert to both the solidarities and absences in the various networks of blogs reminds us that certain groupings can emerge along distinctly political grounds. Past research has suggested that blogs promote other blogs with similar ideological views and political partisanship (Perlmutter, 2008, pp. 35–37), providing support for a related concern with 'cyberpolarization', whereby online groups communicate largely with like-minded people and may become more extreme in their views (Sunstein, 2001; Kolbert, 2009).

In terms of appearance, despite certain features now associated with blogs, they are also diverse in nature and ever-adapting, partly in an attempt to maintain their relevance in a contemporary media environment defined by social, cultural or technological flux. David Perlmutter describes a blog as '(a) written in the style of a personal essay, journal entry, diary or memoir, (b) interactive, (c) containing posts of varying length in reverse chronological order, (d) embedded with hyperlinks within text, (e) providing permalinks and allowing trackbacks, and (f) listing other blogs (blogrolling)' (2008, p. 61). We would add that moving and still images (including screen grabs) are also commonly embedded within the text (sometimes referred to as in-line linking when the image 'belongs' to another website), rather than necessarily accessed via a link. RSS feeds and links to social-media sites such as Twitter and Facebook are now regular features, enabled by the interoperability of web software (Naughton, 2011).

Another approach to blogging shifts the focus onto the practices of blogging, rather than comparing the form of the blog with possible antecedents, such as diaries or journalism. 'What is communicated, the content of blogs, is secondary or tertiary to the fact of communication' (Dean, 2010, p. 46). If the blog 'post' is an attempt at connection, as argued by both boyd (2006) and Dean (2010, pp. 47–48), then it falls between orality and literacy as a form of expression, and is an essentially performative action: 'Blogs emerge because bloggers are blogging' (boyd, 2006, para 31). A very small amount of technical know-how is needed to claim the identity of a 'blogger' in a way that is hard to challenge. Requiring no crew, cast, producer or editorial committee, a blog generally carries its author's name (or pseudonym) on its personalized masthead, announcing a sense of authorship, autonomy and prerogative within the defined space of the blog's URL. But the projected autonomy of bloggers has limits. Along with their own tagline, menu bar, recommendations from other influential bloggers, blogroll and Twitter links, blogs with any pulling power will also share webspace with advertisers, may be supported by a dedicated service like MessageSpace, or by a parent institution such as a newspaper or a political party (see below, *Contexts of blogging in UK politics*).

With a focus on psychoanalytical terms, such as 'drive', 'affect' and the 'gaze', Dean's theoretical perspective on bloggers' subjectivities (see also Siapera, 2008) focuses on the negative aspects of fragmentation and instability. But where Dean sees distraction, entrapment and submission to neo-liberal circuits of communication, others take a more positive view, characterising the 'magpie' tendencies of such montage practices as creative, participatory and technologically savvy (e.g. see Jenkins, 2006; Shirky, 2008; Coleman and Blumler, 2009).

It is not our intention here to take a position in this context on the optimistic and pessimistic conceptions of contemporary communication technologies, but Dean's critically imbued insights point to certain factors relevant for our analysis. If content is secondary to the 'fact of communication', is this evident in our material and how does it affect the form and content of what is displayed? How do political bloggers perform their own identities within their blogs? Where and how do political blogs place themselves within the interconnected and turbulent media environment? What variety of political mediation functions do blogs perform? Notwithstanding Dean's claim that blogs do not 'target an imaginary community of everyone (in the nation, state, or city)' like mass media, but enable 'the production of content potentially accessible to anyone who happens to find it' (2010, p. 46): are there ways in which blogs do imagine their audience?

For now, we will note that the task of defining the diverse range of blogs continues to provoke disagreements among bloggers and blogging experts, and turn our attention to UK political blogs.

Contexts of blogging in UK politics

While the potential powers of popular social-networking sites such as Twitter and Facebook are emerging as an area for study in the British context, as forces for political engagement and influence (Chadwick, 2011a, 2011b; Anstead and O'Loughlin, 2011), the blogosphere is now comparatively well established, with notable moments of penetration and visibility in the mainstream press (Beckett, 2009). A small number of political blogs appear to have stabilized as leaders in their field (*Guido Fawkes, Iain Dale*), renowned for their readership and assumed influence within the Westminster village, even to the extent that the idea of parliamentary lobby passes for bloggers has been proposed (Singleton, 2010). Lobby access carries extensive privileges of access to journalists, and the prospect of including bloggers provokes concerns for traditionalists. One House of Commons insider suggests: 'There will be far more scope for mischief and trivia if you let bloggers in' (ibid., para 6). The characterization of the blogging voice as essentially *mischievous* is one that we shall revisit later in this chapter. First, however, a more general overview is in order.

The 2009/2010 *Guide to Political Blogging in the UK* listed 1,800 active blogs in its directory, up from 1,300 in 2008, with new entries replacing inactive sites every month (Dale, 2009, p. 6). In the same 2009/2010 edition, editor Iain Dale admitted that political blogging 'is not yet a mass activity' and that they are viewed as 'geeky' by politicians and the traditional media, but the top four or five blogs receive more than 100,000 unique visitors each month (pp. 17–18). The variation among them is a matter of political orientation (left/right; conservative/progressive); of affiliation (institutionally affiliated or independent; affiliated to a media organization or to a political party/lobby group); and of multiple or unitary authorship.

Britain's 'Premier League' has been dominated by right-leaning blogs in past years, whether independently run (*Guido Fawkes, Iain Dale*), independent but supportive of the Conservative Party (*ConservativeHome*), or media-run blogs (*Spectator Coffee House – The Spectator* is a weekly right-of-centre magazine). By 2010, the *Guide to Political Blogging 2010/2011* listings indicated that the seemingly untouchable top four had finally been infiltrated by a left-of-centre blog: arriving in at No. 3, *Left Foot Forward* was edited at the time by Will Straw (son of former-Home Secretary Jack Straw), and promotes itself as a non-aligned 'evidence-based' blog for progressives, focused on scrutinising policy and statistics. Inspired by the *Think Progress* site in the US, *Left Foot Forward* presents its mission and beliefs in a wholly earnest manner (http://www.leftfootforward.org/about/).

Left-of-centre, progressive and liberal blogs have more recently started to challenge the dominance of right-leaning blogs, with *Labour List* and *Lib Dem Voice* compiled by various activists within the parties. Many MPs and party-political candidates in the recent general election also have their own blogs, along with local councillors and campaigners. The political blogosphere encompasses a range of actors with varying degrees of institutional alignment; from the lone voice expressing their own personal opinion, to party-affiliated sites with multiple contributors, as well as media-affiliated sites with established journalists offering perhaps more personalized content in comparison with their regular contributions in broadcast or print media.

The traditions of blogging position bloggers as 'outsiders' with respect to official politics and journalism but, as the above survey suggests the adoption of blogging's recognisable non-mainstream voice (geeky, specialist, opinionated, rude, maverick) will be harder to sustain for some writers more than others. Although bloggers were represented as a threat to the lobby journalism system in the comments cited earlier about the 'mischief' that bloggers would inflict if they were admitted on the same terms as accredited journalists, some lobby correspondents are themselves already bloggers – Paul Waugh of the *Evening Standard*, Ben Brogan of the *Telegraph*, Nick Robinson of the BBC – and their blogs are among the most successful (Dale, 2009, p. 71). Lines of differentiation between 'inside' and 'outside' are becoming harder to draw.

Institutionally based or independent, what blogs offer is space for the recognisably individualized voice or voices. Even the names or taglines for blogs hint at their more personalized take on political events, with an apparent self-awareness of their original 'political anorak' or obsessive status: while elected officials and established writers might simply use their own names, others signal their playful or 'outsider' standpoint with an often ironic nomenclature. Right-wing blogs favour the display of an angry or frustrated disposition (*Underdogs Bite Upwards*; *Grumpy Old Twat*; *Constantly Furious*); left-leaning blogs offer a more sincere stance in their branding (*Next Left*; *Left Foot Forward*; *Progress*) and Liberal Democrat blogs emphasize a thoughtful if rather hesitant approach (*Mark Reckons*; *Caron's Musings*; *Disgruntled Radical*). Of course, these are generalizations that could be countered with different examples, and the end of the Conservatives' long spell in opposition could see a shift to less vitriolic branding in the next few years. In all cases, it is a sense of arch knowingness that pervades; a nod to public perceptions of the online 'ranters', and to the prejudices of political foes. One of the most consistently popular blogs in the UK political blogosphere, *Guido Fawkes*, written by Paul Staines, makes clear in its tagline the favoured attitude and target: 'Tittle Tattle, gossip and rumours about Westminster's Mother of Parliaments'. The 'about' section of the website offers a clear indication of Guido's deliberately mischievous form of political engagement: 'The primary motivation for the creation of the blog was purely to make mischief at the expense of politicians and for the author's own self-gratification. [...] to create a more fun, gossipy and acerbic "anti-politics" form of commentary'.

The most popular political blogs tend to be frequently updated, with multiple postings a common feature on weekdays – weekend blogposts are read and re-posted by fewer people and so, as a general rule, there is less blogging activity over the weekend. On the other hand, the pulling power of Sunday political programming for drawing in heavyweight political interviews (BBC1's *Andrew Marr Show* and *Politics Show*, and Sky's *Sunday Live with Adam Boulton*), together with the favouring of

Sunday newspaper editions for scoops, serializations and 'exclusive' features, means that bloggers can appear behind the curve if they miss posting on a Sunday. Re-postings by other bloggers are considered a key indicator of a blog's success, with blog posts consisting of numerous links to other websites, acting as 'signposts' to other sites while also indicating their own role within the 'distributed network' of the internet (see Rettberg, 2008, p. 61). Linking and interactivity between blogs are key determinants in rating popularity and authority: for example, wikio.co.uk ranks blogs according to the number and weight of incoming links from other blogs, with the 'weight' of a link dependent on the popularity of the linking blog. Websites that index blogs in this way, such as Wikio, Reddit, Technorati or Digg, allow users to monitor blog activity and popularity in real time (with 'Twitterati' offering a comparative function to indicate the issues that bloggers are tweeting about), but such sites also produce end-of-year reports on trends in the international blogosphere (http://technorati.com/state-of-the-blogosphere). Wikio's system of ranking is included in Iain Dale's annual UK political-blogging guide, along with another poll of favourites voted for by bloggers and their readers. A reliance on this kind of indexing, and the fact that a Google search will recommend the blogs primarily with the most links, only contributes further to the 'power law' identified by Clay Shirky (2003): that popularity and perceived influence become concentrated in the power-elite of bloggers, while others form a 'long tail' of those with fewer readers. Arguably, the evolution of the 'social' and the 'personalized' web (in which 'eyes' for websites are directed via social-media sites and filtered based on browsing history), away from the 'search' web, characterized by the dominance of search engines (providing instant access to information in a vastly expanding web), could disrupt or ameliorate the aforementioned 'power law' identified in the early 2000s by Shirky. (See Pariser (2011) for further details on the evolution of the personalized web.)

UK political blogosphere in 2010

The volition of UK online political mediation had to contend, in 2010, with a general election that was a climactic moment in the nation's political history. Bloggers themselves predicted a role for online voices in breaking significant 'game-changing' stories during the general election campaign (Dale, 2009, p. 18; Linford, 2009, pp. 70–73). In the *2009/2010 Guide to Political Blogging*, there was palpable excitement that the blogosphere, along with 'new social networking technologies', would exert real political influence during the election, at the very least by the politicians themselves exploiting digital media to connect with voters (Linford, 2009, p. 70). By the time of the 2010/2011 edition, compiled after the general election, there are a few accounts detailing the blogosphere's impact on the election campaign or results, with Will Straw rebutting the claims that this was simply another 'television election' rather than an 'internet election' (2010, pp. 101–106). Despite his detailing of examples of 'viral' stories and successes, Straw concludes: 'The mainstream print and broadcast media broke most of the big stories, as their training, experience, and resources gave them a platform that the blogosphere could never match' (p. 106). One clear development between the publication of the 2009/2010 and the 2010/2011 edition of the blogging guide is the rise to prominence of social media, especially Twitter, as part of the UK blogosphere, rather than as a threat to its survival. The integration of well-known 'Tweeters' as contributors and Twitter 'moments' into many of the guide's short chapters only serves to highlight the necessity for rapid adaptability for those publishing and presenting material on digital platforms. It is difficult to find evidence that blogs as such initiated material that affected the election: mostly they *reacted to* and *pointed out* material originating elsewhere, on or offline. As digital media content is increasingly sought out via mobile phones and tablet computers, the original 'wordy' look of the blog is outshone by seductive fresh interfaces and touch-screen moving images; maintaining or attracting audiences requires adaptation to changing practices, interactions and technologies.

Data and analysis

Our own approach to the exploration of this area, as in the previous chapters, is grounded in textual analysis of particular examples, so as to develop a better understanding of common features as well as more idiosyncratic ones. The complications discussed in the preceding pages of this chapter led us to favour an intensive approach: we focus here on one subset of political blogs, audited throughout 2010, and within this sample, on their involvements in a particular media event – 'Bullygate'. We begin by spelling out features of our four selected blogs, and follow this with a brief account of the 'Bullygate' episode as this has come to be understood in (short) historical perspective.

The narrowness of the blog selection has the advantage that it facilitates attention to their use of hyperlinks and other formal intertextualities. Not only does this expand the range of material beyond a relatively modest archive of blog texts, but it also pays attention to a key feature of such texts – their self-conscious positioning in public communicative space. Furthermore, our core selection of blogs itself provides a range of insider and outsider status and a spread of political partisanship while being rated as among the most popular in their particular category of blog at the time of selection (Dale, 2009).

The core sample comprises *Dizzy Thinks, Luke's Blog, Liberal Burblings* and *Paul Waugh's* blog. *Dizzy Thinks* is a right-leaning blog, written by Phil Hendren. Although the title sounds more like a wishy-washy Liberal blog, Dizzy's tagline asserts a more knowing, Tory, stance: 'opinionated arrogance'. Dizzy is rated at No. 4 in the top Conservative blogs of 2010/2011, dropping a place from the year before. For our left-leaning blog, we chose *Luke's Blog*, written by Labour Party activist Luke Akehurst. Elected to Labour's NEC in September 2010, Luke's masthead reads: 'Just for the record: all the views expressed here are entirely personal and do not necessarily represent the positions of any organizations I am a member of' – indicating a more serious stance than that of Dizzy. *Luke's Blog* is rated at No. 7 in the top 100 Labour blogs of 2010/2011, a fall of two places. For the Liberal Democrats, we selected the characteristically Lib Dem-titled, *Liberal Burblings*, maintained by Paul Walter, an activist from Newbury who, like Phil Hendren, has a full-time job outside of politics (in computer logistics). Indicative of the volatility in such polls, *Liberal Burblings* had been ranked 10 in the 2008/2009 list of Lib Dem blogs but has since dropped out of the ratings. To represent the media, we chose Paul Waugh's blog, which at the time was hosted on a mainstream media's website, and produced while Waugh was employed as the deputy political editor of the London-based *Evening Standard*. In the 2010/2011 *Guide to Political Blogging*, Waugh is No. 1 in the list of top Non-Aligned Blogs, and rated No. 2 in Media Blogs (collated before his move to *PoliticsHome* in November 2010). This selection of four blogs thus encompasses: right, centre and left politics; one journalistic voice and three politically partisan voices. The sample includes those with insider status at the centre of British politics (Waugh is a lobby correspondent), party activists with established links in the blogosphere, and those more on the periphery. These four blogs come closer than many we could have selected to the original idea of a blogger as someone writing as a single voice, rather than compiled through collaborative but unaccredited efforts (see Beckett, 2009, on the use of interns by popular blogs), or those with direct links to, or funded by, a political party (MPs' own blogs were excluded). For this reason we also avoided collaborative projects, or community blogs, such as *ConservativeHome*, *Left Foot Forward*, or *LibDem Voice*.

A case study: bloggers and Bullygate

The 'Bullygate' episode of February 2010 was an intense and short-lived mediated 'fuss', even a scandal, according to point of view, about the behaviour and character of the then Prime Minister Gordon Brown, constructed out of 'old' and 'new' media resources. Although the event as such died away quickly, it contributed to a legacy of understanding in the mediated public sphere of reasons to be negative about the Labour Party and its leadership at a crucial point in the election cycle.

Bullygate (we will from here on drop the inverted commas) offers an illuminating case study, due to the ways in which its key thematics played out across the mediascape. Brown was alleged to have bullied and behaved with extreme rudeness towards his staff, and also to colleagues. The ensuing debates turned partly on the accuracy of the accounts, partly on the characterization of the prime minister's alleged conduct as 'bullying', under either a common sense or a legal sense of that term, and partly on matters of possible explanation and excuse for conduct, which could be illegal, immoral or both. The implications of the story bore directly on questions of *leadership*: at the centre of the allegations was a particular book, Andrew Rawnsley's *The End of the Party*,[1] launched around 21 February 2010, which sought, among other things, to reveal the private (and emotional) life of a current prime minister. There were some interesting ramifications in the mediascape as a consequence of the revelations. The accusations against the prime minister led to the involvement of Christine Pratt, the founder of a bullying helpline. She based her right to be heard not just on her credentials of professional expertise, but also on claims to 'backstage' knowledge of actual events at 10 Downing Street. Yet her relative inexperience in the world of mediated politics seriously undermined her own projected persona in the debate, as well as the impact of her intervention. Long-standing political gossip about Brown's bad temper off-camera had fed into his 14 February 2010 appearance on the chat show *Piers Morgan's Life Stories*, where he was able publicly to downplay charges in respect of his 'bad' emotions (anger) and play up potentially 'good' ones (grief) – good, at least, in their potential to incite sympathy from the public rather than its disapproval (see Chapter 1 for more discussion of this programme). International interest in the affair was such that it also provoked an unusual visual articulation from a Taiwan media organization, which then circulated extensively online. This clip, portraying British public figures as crazed CGI videogame characters, capitalized on the power of political news to offer *entertaining spectacle* to viewers and listeners within and beyond national media spaces. Our own interest in the affair lies in exploring the forms of political expression performed by political bloggers in their responses to Bullygate.

Andrew Chadwick has detailed this short-lived but intensely covered episode in his forensic study of how it played out in the 'political information cycle' across the UK political mediascape, and he provides a useful hour-by-hour narrativiation of how certain developments in the story gained public attention (2011a). While Chadwick closely tracks the Bullygate story across a wide range of print, broadcast and online material, his interest lies in power shifts between a range of elite and non-elite actors, who collectively and individually produce content in a 'hybridized media environment', and in the kind of 'work' that such a range of actors undertake in guiding the narrative flow and meanings: 'The combination of news professionals' dominance and the integration of nonelite actors in the construction and contestation of news at multiple points in a political information cycle's life span are important characteristics of contemporary political communication' (2011a, p. 3). However, Chadwick's study does not seek to explore the particular qualities or personalized styles found within the political mediations; for example, the linguistic choices made in the commentary, choice of visual images, or further restyling of the Bullygate scandal in the blogosphere or broader media environment. Nor is Chadwick primarily concerned with the more playful treatments of the story, outside of the political information cycle. In this sense, our study is complementary to Chadwick's, with a distinguishable focus on *generic form* in the present chapter, while being rather more modest in its scoping of media material.

The Bullygate mini-saga really got underway on 21 February, as Rawnsley's much-hyped book serialization in the *Observer* prompted a number of defensive media appearances from senior Labour politicians to counter the claims against their leader. Brown's own pre-emptive and deeply personal interview with Piers Morgan had aired on 14 February. While Brown had sought to convey himself as passionate yet impatient in the stagey interview, rumours of his intemperate behaviour had circulated for many years (e.g. 'MP claims "raging" Gordon breaks three phones a week by hurling them at the wall', *Daily Mail*, 14 April 2008), and allegations suspiciously similar to those made by Rawnsley had appeared just a few weeks earlier in the *Mail on Sunday* on 31 January 2010 ('Angry Gordon Brown "hit out at aide and yanked secretary from her chair"', Simon Walters). But the timing of Rawnsley's book serialization and publication, just a few months before an anticipated election, and in the context of dire polling for Brown's perceived character traits as party leader and prime minister, along with the subsequent intervention of Christine Pratt from the National Bullying Helpline, meant that the story progressed from a mere background rumbling into a full-blown political storm, most intensely experienced during 21–24 February 2010.

This in itself makes the Bullygate affair exceptional in the way that it gained mainstream attention and dominated political programming for a number of days. This was a scandal of personal character and conduct which would not remain confined to the periphery of public consciousness. Blogs provide an ongoing churn of stories based on political rumour and gossip, ones which rarely break through into a wider public sphere. Not always able to predict which elements of backstage gossip will get picked up as 'genuine' gaffes and scandals, the blogosphere provides political chatter, an onstage chorus who seldom get to sing the aria. Deeply interested in the machinations of the political world, for some bloggers the overlap of interests with the mainstream media (MSM) can be dismissively portrayed as incidental to their project, but they are conspicuously precise when referring to their own past postings and when sourcing others' contributions.

While the clear 'political gossip' components of Bullygate give it an obvious appeal to bloggers, our case study will also illustrate aspects of the wider yet distinctive types of political mediation that bloggers perform in the digital media environment. In the following discussion, we explore the generic attributes of political blog posts under three general categories: the mischievous blog (post), the investigative post, and the visual post. The three categories are not presented as a comprehensive taxonomy of blogging, but are intended to provide useful distinctions under which to examine the attributes and attitudes of contemporary political blogging.

Mischievous blogging

In this example from 18 February, three days before Rawnsley's book serialization, Paul Waugh provides his own take on a recent post by Iain Dale, while recalling an earlier posting of his own[2]:

Don't forget the PM has form on the c-word
18 February 2010, 19:53:56
Number 10 have today <u>denied</u> claims by <u>IainDale</u> that Gordon Brown called a key aide a 'c*nt' during a rant in Washington.

But for those who doubt that the son of the manse would be even capable of such a thing, here's a wee reminder of a blogpost I filed last year. Strangely, it didn't get picked up at the time, but it was July...

'Apparently, just over a year ago, ahead of the knife-edge vote on the 42-days terror plans, Brown called [Norwich North MP Ian] Gibson in for a chat.

'Lefty Gibson was implacably opposed but Brown tried (and failed) in the one-on-one meeting to get him to change his mind.

'Eventually, Brown accepted that Gibson had a principled stance and would vote against the Government. But he was unsure about which way neighbouring MP Charles Clarke would vote.

'What about the c*nt next door?' he asked Gibson'....

UPDATE: Someone close to GB tells me that he has never heard him use the c-word. They say that Gordon preferred to use the word 'bastard' instead, pronounced with a hard 'ass' in the middle, Northern/Scots style.

The multilayered structuring of the text on the page, with the reverse chronological display of posts and (potential) comment threads, hyperlinks and the 'updates' at the end of the post, hint at the ways in which blogs blur the lines between orality and textuality; and so provide a form of political communication not available in either traditional print or broadcast media. In writing about blogs, it is therefore difficult to avoid allusions to both written ('text', 'comment thread') and oral forms of communication ('conversation', 'overheard'), with the expressive nature of the blog sitting somewhere between the two.

The dialogic/interactive properties of blogs are usually referred to the presence and use of a comment thread by readers, and these were certainly a feature of the blogs we looked at in 2010, but as this example suggests, often the more significant conversation is with a network of other bloggers and websites. Hyperlinks and blogrolls are generic devices that stitch the blog and its blogger into that network. The hyperlinks in this post are underlined in the version quoted here. The first one, on the word 'denied', links to a short article within the *Evening Standard* news site, by the Political Editor, Joe Murphy; 'No 10 denies naked Gordon Brown called aide C-word' (18 February 2010). The second link, on the proper noun IainDale, is to the relevant story in *Iain Dale's Diary*, and the third is to Waugh's own blogpost from July 2009, citing another occasion when Brown was alleged to have called a colleague a 'cunt'. Waugh also quotes at length from the earlier blog, and this doubling up is also a frequent feature in political blogging, the digital medium facilitating a 'cut and paste' approach to textual creation.

These hyperlinks may give a visual impression of offering evidentiary support for the anecdote, but the trails lead to equally uncertain prior texts: Murphy's article gives no source for the story, but writes that the claim is 'believed' to be in Rawnsley's book. Iain Dale writes in his blog that the incident 'may or may not appear' in Rawnsley's book.

The gossipy engagement that blogs sustain with politics is carried here in part by the adoption of a conversational linguistic style – also supporting boyd's argument that blogs blur the lines between literacy and orality (boyd, 2006). This blogpost shifts from the journalistically styled opening statement, 'Number 10 have today denied claims by IainDale that Gordon Brown called a key aide a "c*nt" during a rant in Washington', to a more colloquial tone ('here's a wee reminder'), with use of nicknames, of an ironic ('son of the manse') and adolescent ('Lefty Gibson') tenor. Waugh's citation of his earlier blogpost, while signalling his prior knowledge about how Brown treats his colleagues, also holds interest stylistically for the way the cited section reads like a shared joke, with the punchline 'delivered' in bold type for added emphasis.

In a discourse about bad language as bad behaviour, the choices that Dale and Waugh make in respect of their own linguistic practices are interesting. Neither spells out the swearword in full. Dale uses asterisks for all four characters in the title of his post and 'c***' in the body of the post (leading to one teasing comment from reader 'Jimmy': 'However bad the mistake, calling a member of his staff a conservative is simply inexcusable'). Waugh prefers 'the c-word' in his title and 'c*nt' within the post. Despite the usual tolerance of profanities in the blogosphere, the actual word is deemed off-limits in this context. The right-leaning bloggers appear to follow the style guidance of like-minded publications (*Telegraph*, *Mail*) in their reticence. These stylistic choices reinforce the very point at issue – the unacceptability of this word in speech or writing, except where shock or offence is intended. Yet another offensive word, 'bastard' can be spelled out in full, while Waugh even provides details on Brown's preferred pronunciation, almost prompting readers to try out the pronunciation for themselves. As befits an avowedly informal, even casual, contribution to political discussion, there is no attempt to draw out the implication of the fact that one supposed use of the word cunt is as a face-to-face term of address (Brown calls his addressee a cunt) and the other is as a term of reference (someone else, not present, is a cunt). Other things being equal, the former usage is very much more face-threatening to the immediate interlocutor – and more consistent therefore with the bullying charges.

The face-to-face social networks that foster gossip in its usual sense are premised on equalities and reciprocities so that gossipers and 'gossipees' can and do change places from one conversation to another. Because it is a public form of communication, because relations among contributors are unequal and because there are significant divisions of labour, political bloggery – even when it seeks to be mischievous – cannot not fully replicate such reciprocity. Care must be taken in revealing where information originated, for fear of poisoning the well. The 'update' section with which the account ends, about Brown's preferences in the matter of swear words, is protectively attributed to 'someone close to GB', since Waugh, as a journalist as well as a blogger, has a stake in the preservation of good relations with his sources and does not want to jeopardize this one by naming names. But the content of the update adds a note of authenticity to the account, signalling to Waugh's wider readership that his posts are read by persons within Brown's political inner circle, that those persons are in touch with Waugh, and sufficiently interested to offer him this titbit. Its new information challenges the very title of Waugh's post, yet is nevertheless included to indicate that he is part of an ongoing conversation; one which, for the most part, takes place between political insiders, but to which readers are invited along as eavesdropping participants. The blogpost allows space for this respected political journalist to appear to be reporting on political issues, while simultaneously indulging in a light-hearted foray into the overheard claims and anecdotes of the Westminster village. As a postscript at the end of the blog, Waugh's 'update' is not simply an afterthought, but an indication that this blogger is alert to developments in a fast-moving story, responsive to counter-arguments, and at the heart of the conversation.

The mix of journalistic phraseology with profanities and colloquialisms, in a story concerning the prime minister, and constructed entirely from hearsay, is indicative of the political blogs' in-between status or liminality; blurring and actively contesting the lines between private and public space, official and unofficial sources, constrained and unconstrained subjectivity, playful and serious, peripheral and central. Arguably such binaries are themselves contested from many quarters, but blogs have possibly served as precursors to the varied forms of digital media, which disturb and subvert traditional binary conceptions concerning political mediations: who are the legitimate commentators in publicly accessible space; what are the rules of engagement with public officials; what degrees of sincerity, gravity and impartiality are expected?

Investigative blogging

Our second right-leaning blog, *Dizzy Thinks*, also took up the Bullygate story with relish, producing a number of detailed blogposts, with seven posts (out of ten) relating directly to this story over a three-day period. While Paul Waugh's post above exemplified the mischievous side of blogging, the following examples from 'Brown admits his office has a bullying problem', a long post in the *Dizzy Thinks* blog (and some further posts intertextually related to this) are illustrative of another key feature in political blogging: the presentation of time-consuming research, often indicative of a deep interest and knowledge in the process of politics:

> So...Gordon Brown is accused of bullying, Mandelson says he's just passionate, then the head of the National Bullying Helpine contacts the BBC to say Mandelson is talking bollocks and that they've had people that work with Gordon Brown call them, and Downing Street refuses to comment.
>
> Obviously a much needed spin job will be at hand, and the ever servile Kevin Maguire is already noting that Ann Widdicombe is a patron of the charity and thinks they might have been duped – presumably he means that someone called, said they worked with the PM, but they were lying.
>
> [Kevin Maguire Tweet screenshot]
>
> Now let's get down to the nitty gritty as it were. The National Bullying Helpine [sic] told the BBC that 'over the last three or four years' the helpline had 'probably received three or four calls' from people working directly with Gordon Brown.
>
> This is quite funny, because for the last three or four years, I've been reading Hansard every day, and guess what, departmental bullying in Brown's offices has come up a few times.

Dizzy goes on to present his findings via a series of quotations from Hansard, spurred by the story's exposure to investigate whether Brown's bullying has been raised in Parliament. (Hansard is the official transcript of UK parliamentary debates, now available online.) This post summarizes the events of Sunday 21 February, with five verbal hyperlinks and one visual one in the text (the visual one is a Twitter screenshot). After setting the scene, Dizzy invites readers to 'get down to the nitty gritty' by perusing the evidence presented in his quotes. Unlike lobby correspondent Paul Waugh, Dizzy has a full-time job outside politics; for source material he relies not on insider whispers within parliament, but on publicly available data.

As with Waugh, Dizzy adopts a light-hearted, conversational tone ('this is quite funny', 'and guess what') as he echoes the phrasing of the 'last three or four years', for which he claims to have been reading Hansard every day. Given the number of transcripts and their generally routine nature, this is possibly written in jest, but with a serious point to make.

In May 2007, *before* he became Prime Minister and was still at the Treasury, the following was <u>revealed</u>,

David Simpson: To ask the Chancellor of the Exchequer (1) how many complaints of bullying have been investigated in his Department in the last 12 months; and how many complaints have been upheld;

(2) how many grievance procedures have been initiated in his Department in the last 12 months;

(3) how many complaints of sexual harassment have been investigated in his Department in the last 12 months; and how many complaints have been upheld.

John Healey: In the last 12 months fewer than five grievances have been raised and investigated. No complaints of bullying or of sexual harassment have been upheld. As the number of complaints of bullying and of sexual harassment was fewer than five, the exact number cannot be disclosed on grounds of confidentiality.

Dizzy cites two further instances, in February 2008 and March 2009, where similar questions relating to the prime minister's office (once Brown moved there) received similar answers, only confirming that 'fewer than five cases' were dealt with. Dizzy presents these formal, elaborate and non-revelatory exchanges to build his case against Brown, but also to demonstrate his powers of research (whether truly remembered from the time or collated during that day). He signs off:

I knew reading Hansard would pay off eventually! And for those in the national press .... yes, I love doing your research for you .... for free!

In Dizzy's personal blogging style the use of italics indicates emphasis and humour, often employed when asking a provocative question. In this case, the exclamation marks and spaces convey a boastful and teasing mode, with a direct address toward the national press, 'yes, I love doing your research for you'. Despite a convergence with the mainstream media in some respects, a number of bloggers continue to see themselves as upstarts and challengers to those in the journalistic professions. In longer posts, the shift to italicization can be read like a spoken aside or 'stage whisper', to use a theatrical reference, enabling the blogger to present a change of register, or even multilayered subjectivity, within the post (a posting by Dizzy on 7 February 2010, 'N for Vendetta?' provides a useful example of this feature). The dramatic pauses indicated in the extract above by the points of ellipsis ('dot-dot-dot') further signal aspects of implied performance in the blogpost, signalling pauses for effect. Not quite the script of a performer, nor the transcript of a potential broadcast, nor the online equivalent of print media (though bearing some similarities with colour writing in the press, as discussed in Chapter 2), the particular affordances of the blogpost enable its author to cultivate a personalized position of engagement with, and critique of, mainstream politics and media, often conducted with the dual force of being both mischievously provocative and well informed. Dizzy's Hansard research is recognized by fellow blogger and journalist, Paul Waugh:

> Amid the sound and fury about 'bullygate', Brownie points should go to Dizzy, who spotted last night that there is real evidence that bullying has indeed been a problem at both the Treasury under GB and at Downing St/Cabinet Office.
>
> (From 'Brown and Bullygate' post, 22 February)

'Brownie points' indicate kudos or credit for Dizzy; although in this case, there is possible additional punning on Gordon Brown's name. According to Waugh, Dizzy's digging provides 'real evidence' of a problem of bullying in Downing Street, but there is no direct confirmation that Brown is the culprit. As the story progresses, Christine Pratt of the National Bullying Helpline continues to give media interviews, and to come under scrutiny regarding her own conduct and ethics (possible breaches of confidentiality, inconsistency of allegations, links to the Conservative Party, past bullying claims against her, suspect business practices). Pratt temporarily replaces Brown as the prime target for the investigative effort of bloggers and others, with the professional integrity of the helpline service itself eventually called into question. *Liberal Burblings* provides one such example, complete with 15 separate links or credits in a 1,200-word post ('Hold on a minute: Was Brown actually PM when the bullying complaints were made?' 22 February). The helpline immediately lost all of its patrons in protest at Pratt's media intervention, and, according to its website it no longer has charitable status or, indeed, a helpline (http://nationalbullyinghelpline.co.uk/about.htm).

Pratt disappeared from the media spotlight just as quickly as she entered it, and it is likely that she is happy to remain out of sight and mind. While the story initially concerned Brown's character, who as prime minister was one of the most elite political actors in the country, Pratt's incursion into this elite political-media world, as an outsider and 'civilian', served to highlight the intense scrutiny that any person's character can be subjected to, instigated by those in the blogosphere and beyond (Thompson, 2005). This scrutiny was hardly undertaken in defence of Gordon Brown, although it did briefly shift attention away from Rawnsley's allegations, but instead was prompted by an overriding sense of disdain for an ill-conceived intervention.

While the political bloggers and 'Twitterati' were not alone in debunking Pratt's intrusion, described by Paul Waugh in one tweet as a 'slo-mo PR car crash', their particular mode of engagement can be characterized as superior, inquisitive, mocking and indignant. However, one of our core bloggers, Labour activist Luke Akehurst, notably posted only one response to the scandal. Titled 'People in glass houses...', the rest of the post finishes the phrase '...shouldn't throw stones', and then simply links to a *Guardian* article from December 2008: 'Ex-editor Andy Coulson bullied News of the World reporter, rules tribunal'. Luke's quiet position on this issue, realized both via a near-absence of posting and in his enigmatic, cautionary citing of the proverb, simultaneously presents an 'above the fray' moral superiority while also revealing his own political partisanship. Luke feigns a position of being both disinterested and uninterested while making his political point: two characteristics that are particularly unconvincing as articulations in the world of blogging. Even in these more restrained moments, blogs are often imbued with a sense of egotism (even narcissism – Cohen (2006)) precisely because the blog embodies strong personal–political stance-taking in a public space, where emotionally charged responses often come to the fore. Political blogging is not for wimps. Bloggers delight in finding inaccuracies, double standards, past misdemeanours and weaknesses, which they reflect upon by means of a variety of highly subjective and experientially informed positions (exasperation, irony, disdain) with the intention of encouraging others to join the fray. However, the caustic and superior attitude adopted toward 'the political' in blogs is not necessarily at odds with civically minded engagement. In this sense, blogs offer an exemplary expressive form through which to explore affectivity and politics in the contemporary media environment.

Visual blogging

On the next key feature we discuss in detail, the creative use of images in blogs, *Dizzy Thinks* provides a number of images relating to the Bullygate story over the three-day period during which the story qualified as a 'scandal'. Visual images can provide an instantly decipherable form of expression, especially those pictures with provocative or humorously distortive elements, such as cartoons or caricatures. Different types of visual distortion and exaggeration are utilized for political and humorous purposes in our next two examples, both from *Dizzy Thinks*. In the blogpost 'Gordon Adolf Stalin Brown' (21 February), Gordon Brown's portrait undergoes two transformations; morphed into the visages of both Adolf Hitler and Joseph Stalin. The Hitler image shows portraits of both Hitler and Brown-as-Hitler side by side, with the respective captions 'Reign of Terror' and 'Reign of Error'. The Hitler likeness was originally forwarded to blogger Iain Dale by artist, Louis Sidolo, hoping to attract attention to his 'political artwork', and published by Dale in 'Political Artist goes for Brown', 21 February 2010. Dizzy provides the link, but also reproduces the image in his own blog, in the context of reflecting on the negative reactions that Iain Dale has provoked. Dizzy's ostensible point is that this should be no more controversial than an earlier mock-up of Brown as Stalin; versions of which were used by both Channel 4 and *The Times*, and created with reference to the comments of senior civil servant, Lord Turnbull, who commented on Brown's 'sheer Stalinist ruthlessness' back in 2007 ('Stalinist' Brown, by ex-Cabinet Secretary, *Financial Times*, 20 March 2007). Images of Brown-as-Hitler and Brown-as-Stalin are both reproduced in Dizzy's blogpost, offering two direct visual exaggerations of Brown's political character, but within a meta-coverage angle which simultaneously opens up space for Dizzy to ridicule the reactions of those claiming to be offended.

> After all, in the murderous bastard stakes Stalin has Hitler totally owned. Hitler has what? Six to seven million dead human beings on his record? Meanwhile Stalin has around 40 million.

> *Shouldn't mocking Gordon Brown up as Hitler be less worse than*
> *mocking him up as Stalin?*
> I do love a good bit of synthetic outrage to point at and mock.
> It really lightens up an otherwise mundane Sunday afternoon.

Dizzy offers support to his fellow right-leaning blogger, pointing to a comparable case of media mock-ups of Brown, while also apparently enjoying the opportunity to publish both images and provide a facetious interpretation of their relative murderous capabilities, complete with street-style vernacular: 'Stalin has Hitler totally owned'. Dizzy also refers to 'Godwin's law' in passing, assuming reader knowledge of a tendency that predates the internet but has gained online status as a humorous 'law', coined by internet lawyer Mike Godwin: 'As an online discussion grows longer, the probability of a comparison involving Nazis or Hitler approaches one (100%)' (Godwin, 1994). Similar to the flaming or 'cyberpolarization' tendencies mentioned earlier, Godwin's wry observation on the tenor of debate in forums and comment threads contains a serious point: in promoting this 'counter-meme' Godwin appeals to users to avoid such distortion when inappropriate. While the 'law' foresees a Nazi association being made during an extended exchange, in this case Iain Dale's post (and Dizzy's in its re-presentation), makes the comparison between Brown and Hitler in a stark visual juxtaposition, collapsing Godwin's law into an instant, provocative image. Displaying the mocked-up image alongside the artist's own statement, in his blog-post Dale rather disingenuously claims a position of the 'reporter' of the artwork, rather than an 'endorser' – a position that earns him rebukes from bloggers of various political persuasions (e.g. *Harry's Place*).

Dizzy's own contribution to the discussion is later acknowledged by Dale, hyperlinked in the third of his four 'updates' to the post, as he responds to the torrent of the comments; many expressing views that such a posting was 'beneath' Dale, scornful of both the images as artwork and of the counterproductive political message. The mutual recognition by the two bloggers here is typical of the interplay between the leading bloggers of a shared political hue. With the images functioning as *reposted* material in his post, Dizzy avoids similar levels of admonishment by his own readers in their comments, a detail which demonstrates the significance of context and framing of content when bloggers choose to embed potentially controversial images within posts. Dizzy's assumed role as amused commentator, and specifically his penultimate sentence, 'I do love a good bit of synthetic outrage to point at and mock', discourage responses imbued with the already-mocked 'synthetic outrage'; instead the discussion rather predictably turns to the tangential issue of Hitler and Stalin's respective kill scores. With the next image that we discuss, Dizzy gained his own scoop, at least in the UK context, providing a link to an unusual treatment of political events (he is subsequently 'hat-tipped' by Iain Dale and Guido Fawkes for this discovery, although the two more renown bloggers are later credited as a source in mainstream media (e.g. Toby Young in the *Telegraph*)). A post entitled 'CGI fighting Brown!' is published by Dizzy on 23 February 2010. In this post, Dizzy lets the visuals do the work, his only commentary performing a 'check this out!' role with a small amount of text: 'Bullygate goes global! Wait until you get 30 seconds in and see Andrew Rawnsley's book dramatized in CGI! Yay Taiwanese News!'. The CGI animation, created by Taiwanese news site, *Apple Daily*, depicts Brown aggressively throwing aside staff, brawling in corridors and punching car seats in an exaggerated version of the anecdotes from Rawnsley's book. The YouTube HTML link is embedded so that the video can be viewed directly on Dizzy's page, and would have vastly increased traffic to his blog as the video went viral and websites credited Dizzy with the startling find. The dramatic computer-game-style visuals also attracted mainstream media attention, for example publicized on *The Daily Politics* twice that week, as well as *This Week* – while the writer who inspired the portrayal, Andrew Rawnsley, refers to the unusual news treatment in his column on 28 February (*Observer*): 'It's a treat'.[3] Creating digital avatars to act out political rumour and behind-the-scenes behaviour presented a spectacular version of politics, in which verisimilitude was downplayed (Brown's avatar bears little physical resemblance to the man himself) in favour of entertainment and heightened drama. The animation provided a visually startling reconstruction of imagined events, in which allegations regarding Brown's character were incongruously rendered in comic form (in both senses of the word). The network of bloggers, keen to seek out unusual material and provide their own fresh perspectives on mediated politics, can occasionally surprise and even influence the subsequent treatment of issues by their more powerful mainstream media associates.

The ever-evolving space of blogging in politics

This final section reflects on the affordances of the blog as a communicative form, and how blogs are adapting to pressures and

opportunities in an ever-evolving internet and hybrid media environment. In summarising these considerations, the discussion is divided
into three sections: the autonomy of the blogger; blogs as medium or
genre; and blogging in the social-media era.

The autonomy of the blogger: Being relatively cheap and easy to produce
(with templates on offer meaning that computing-programming skills
are no longer required), blogs provide a platform to present yourself
and your views to a potential audience (Rettberg, 2008, p. 84). Unlike
older participation methods, such as letters to the editor or phone-in
shows, bloggers possess editorial control over their blogs. However, in
contrast to other forms of blogging where the primary function is personal self-presentation or narrative-based (as a diarist, or overcoming a
challenge, for example), for bloggers writing on *politics*, there are varying
constraints on autonomy. Working within the parameters sanctioned
by defamation laws, 'independent' bloggers may be bolder in profanities and outspoken opinions than blogging MPs, journalists and party
activists, with commenting readers bolder still. However, unlike open-
discussion forums, the blogger is the principal contributor, with readers'
comments subject to monitoring and rejection.

Moreover, a blogger operates as an incomplete fragment in a wider
interconnected and multi-temporal media environment. Blogs are best
thought of as 'natively digital' in their mediality and practices (Dean,
2010, p. 29), as parts of an ongoing conversation across the mediascape.
Although their typical presentation on the webpage emphasizes their
linearity or chronology, their distinctively non-analogue nature means
that they simultaneously operate in a space that enables oscillation,
selectivity and fragmentary readings. Blogs encourage both diachronic
and synchronic readings: in addition to sustaining a readily accessible archive, bloggers are known to refer to past blogposts (especially
when it supports their argument or demonstrates foresight) by inte-
grating a hyperlink or quoting directly; and also to provide immediate
updates or corrections to blogposts as a story develops. Responding to
posted comments, other blogs and media sources, the initial posting is
not entirely fixed in time and space, or necessarily offering a definitive
take on events. The self-assertive tendencies of the blog's presentation
and content are often juxtaposed with their transient form. Indeed, the
ephemeral nature of blogs was highlighted for us when one of our key
bloggers left his position as Political Editor at the hosting media institution, *Evening Standard*, to blog for the online magazine *PoliticsHome* –
Paul Waugh's blogging archive disappeared from public view, but not,
incidentally, the online versions of the articles he wrote for the same

newspaper. In addition to highlighting how even the most popular blog archives can become inaccessible, this movement raises questions about control and ownership, in cases when bloggers operate as part of a parent media institution.

Are political reporters who also blog or tweet attracting readers due to their personal style, or because they write under a respected media brand? Waugh is an established political journalist, as is Laura Kuenssberg, who moved from BBC to ITV in 2011, raising similar issues.[4] Both were writing for 'old' media in 'new' media forms, in a more personalized space than that afforded by their 'official' reports or articles. Different media institutions vary in the degree of control they have over the content that appears under their brand (e.g. whether to 'scoop' on Twitter rather than their own website), with some organizations appearing to trail behind the technology, with no consistent policy on social media beyond broad issues of legality and ethics.

Similarly, the annual *Guide to Political Blogging in the UK*, edited by Iain Dale for the last five years at the time of writing, often recounts instances of how a blog considered influential in its field can drop out of the next year's tally of top blogs (e.g. Dale, 2010, p. 17). A number of bloggers who've gained status as 'influentials' in recent years have used their blogs as 'stepping stones' to other writing projects or computer work. Even the prime blogger and blogwatcher, Iain Dale, has recently distanced himself from the personalized blog: in July 2011 *Iain Dale's Diary* was wound down (although the archive is still accessible) and Dale's attention turned to *Dale & Co*, a new 'mega blog' that aims to showcase 'more than 100 writers, each with editorial independence, providing some of the best political, media, social and sports commentary on the net' (http://www.iaindale.com/). Another blogger from our sample, *Dizzy Thinks*, is currently a contributor to *Dale & Co*, writing as Phil Hendren rather than Dizzy. The recent move to 'mega blogs', in favour of individualized blogs, appears to be a significant trend in the UK political blogosphere, with a number of the more popular blogs now collaborative in nature. This is a shift that demonstrates the fluid and sometimes turbulent patterns of renewal and transition in the digital media environment. A *Guardian* article by Dan Sabbagh in May 2011 asked 'Is this really the death of political blogging?', as Dale's plans to leave his blogging 'diary' and launch the new site gained publicity. As is often the case with 'death of...' proclamations or questions, blogging was not pronounced dead in the final analysis, merely transforming and 'growing up', with trailblazers Dale and Waugh both abandoning the blog format to lead magazine-style collaborations, while the left-leaning bloggers claimed that it was merely the right-wingers who had 'lost momentum'. Despite noting the problems that bloggers face in turning their work into a viable business, and the ongoing 'churn' of neglected blogs being replaced with new blogs, Sabbagh concludes that 'blogging remains in vigorous health': 'The emergence of the Daley [pre-launch name for Dale & Co] also indicates that this is an activity that is growing up; as newspapers look more like blog sites – blogs are trying to look more like newspapers' (Sabbagh, 2011). This final concluding sentence hints at a convergence of media forms already touched upon (e.g. Jenkins, 2008); and how positioning bloggers in respect to the mainstream becomes ever more complex.

As recalled above, Paul Waugh moved from an 'old' media site, as the *Evening Standard*'s Deputy Political Editor, to a 'new' media magazine website. It is not only the 'look' of sites but the character, personnel and interests that overlap and switch in the digital trans-media environment. The recent shift to 'mega blogs' and online magazine-style formats can be linked to various economic, political, social and technological factors, including but not exclusively: professionalization of 'influentials' and concern for revenue prospects; sociability and mutual dependency within maturing networks (further encouraged in the era of social media); the 2010 General Election and subsequent change of government (with related power shifts); progress in web and multimedia design; and the embracing of mobile phones and tablets as key distribution channels. The 'growing up' that Sabbagh writes of, starts to look more like 'growing together' with the mainstream media, as collaborative blogging projects adopt the strength-in-numbers approach, along with aggregator sites such as the *Huffington Post* (with a UK version launched in July 2011), embracing the converged-media world of editorial policies, 'evidence based' analysis, visually attractive interfaces and even international audience reach. As blogging moves into a new decade in 2011, those deemed 'influential' have moved a long way from the stereotyped amateur ranting of the political anorak.

Blogs as medium or genre: whether blogs are a genre or medium (boyd, 2006) provides an intriguing point of contention from which to think further about their form, function and structure within the architecture of the web. Even in the space of a year or two, the political blog as a communicative form has shifted in character, with leading bloggers collaborating in mega-blogs, and adopting a style closer to an online magazine. At the same time political journalists working in mainstream media regularly update their Twitter feeds and in-house blogs alongside their traditional articles and broadcast segments. The ability of blogs to continue morphing and reshaping into a wide variety of expressive forms (micro-blogging, data-driven, video blogs) further complicates the task of devising a taxonomy of their distinctive affordances; as medium or genre. Blogs certainly comprise diverse generic recipes and languages (including the visual). Although often characterized as propositional in tenor, putting across an argument, blogs also often take a performantive stance: they frequently 'show' rather than 'tell'. However, the 'showing' can be accompanied with an ironic mode of address or sideways attitude, a 'go figure' approach to others' inanity and idiocy.

Blog posts are about connectedness and signposting, and there is a strong sense of etiquette when it comes to 'hat tips' for content. This form of camaraderie in the shared public–private sphere can be contrasted with the reputation for indignation and rudeness. However, there is an admittedly hierarchical element to the back-slapping and sharing of wry observations and comic images. Political blogs occupy a space not only 'beyond the news' but 'behind the news'; 'behind' in the sense of 'backstage politics' revealed, but also, 'behind' in the sense that they are often *reacting* to events, providing analysis that is in close dialogue with mainstream commentators and columnists. The combination of political rumour, speculation and sharp analysis, delivered with an attitude, which oft combines arrogance and high levels of political knowledge, is one that resonates with a niche, politically interested audience. Blogs in their own right might only resonate with relatively small and interconnected audiences directly, but their influence arguably goes beyond their own readers; bloggers make appearances as alternatives to other experts or journalists on political programmes; content highlighted by bloggers may later appear in mainstream political and comedy programming (such as the *Apple Daily* footage); the audiovisual remix culture of the internet (and popularized by bloggers) feeds back into the mash-up style of parody seen on TV (for example, Charlie Brooker on *Newswipe* or *10 O'Clock Live*). Although not provable without a longitudinal study able to track such trends, it is feasible that influence from bloggers has altered the language of mainstream commentators; an apparent preference among current newspaper columnists for a more colloquial and personalized style may be connected to the rise of the blogosphere, or the integration of the internet more generally into practices of interpersonal as well as mediated communication.

Blogging in the social-media era: Active bloggers have been keen to be integrated into the paradigm of the social-media era, rather than allowing themselves to be displaced by novel forms of consumption and interaction. This has changed the appearance and content of blogs (with new feeds to Facebook and Twitter, video links, and possibly shorter, more frequently updated blogs). Whether the rise of social media substantially disrupts the 'power law' tendency of the top blogs versus 'the rest' of the long tail remains to be seen. For now, aggregator sites (such as the *Huffington Post*) which include influential blogs, or collaborative mega-blogs (such as *Dale & Co*), appear to be more authoritative than ever in indexing stakes. All media institutions now appear to be responsive to the new possibilities afforded by digital technologies, especially the increased accessing of media content through smart phones (see Ofcom Communications Market report, August 2011), and in the case of broadcast media, the video-on-demand function (VOD) by which radio and TV programmes and films are experienced via websites.

The drive for interactivity has impacted on various forms of political programming and reporting, with those pursuing *topicality* and *immediacy* eager to integrate Twitter streams and web-based content into shows and commentary. Along with blogs, a number of networks or discussion forums, such as Netmums and Mumsnet, have also achieved a certain degree of visibility and 'expertise' kudos in mainstream media on social and political issues. In early 2010, the impending general election was even dubbed the 'Mumsnet election', as leading politicians (and their spouses, especially wives) took part in webchats on Mumsnet, attracting considerable publicity. The founders of such sites have also become occasional guests on news and current affairs broadcasts; possibly sidelining their blogging cousins as the new 'voice' of informed yet personalized opinion.

New web tools or platforms such as 'Storify' or 'Storyful', which allow users to create narratives from social-media postings, offer a visually appealing way to bring together the links that bloggers embed in their text; this move to *web curation* of multiple sources mimics the interconnectivity feature of blogs, and appeals to budding journalism students learning to incorporate textual and visual sources from social-media sites into digital storytelling in a transparent and traceable manner (see Sharma, 2011). As possible sources for information multiply online, and are available as instant 'updates', locating oneself as an authoritative *curator* of material becomes an attractive and worthwhile position, whether for serious or satirical purposes. Taking these trends together – the rise and imbrication of social media across web practices and beyond; an apparent move to collective blogs; the accessing of media content through a variety of technologies and platforms; increased visibility for interest group networks as political commentators; a curator role for bloggers and others linking to multiply sourced material – it would appear that the individuated character of blogging is fading into the background while interactivity, sociability and connectivity come even further to the fore.

4
Media Audiences and Public Voices – Terms of Engagement

In this chapter we turn our attention to 'media audiences', and develop an account of how audiences both *make sense of* and *evaluate* sources of the political portrayed in non-news media genres, working within the terms of our enquiry into the intersections and overlaps of 'political', 'civic' and 'popular' culture.[1] When it comes to posing questions about their varying relationships with mediated politics, we can construe audiences as citizens, conscious of their political rights and responsibilities and with expectations of the media based on that consciousness; we can construe them as primarily consumers, seeking pleasure, knowledge and information in a media marketplace. In their interactions with mediated politics, audiences also choose (with varying degrees of self-consciousness and in response to a range of textual and contextual cues) the manner of their engagement. They do this by identifying with or contesting political ideas and values (as individual viewers or through shared experiences); by adjusting their levels of attentiveness or interest; by making cognitive and emotional connections via a range of dispositions (empathetic, ironic, rational); and by choosing whether or not to participate directly in related activities, which may be productive (e.g. commenting on a blog post) or merely cathartic in dialogic potential (e.g. shouting at the TV).

In her introductory chapter to the edited collection *Audiences and Publics*, Sonia Livingstone argues for a radical re-thinking of what she perceives to be a too neatly separated conceptualization of 'audiences' and 'publics' as what is meant by the two categories becomes more densely interwoven and 'the media become ever more deeply embedded in all aspects of society' (2005, p. 35). Our own study is sympathetic to this position even though we recognize continuing and important points of differentiation relating to the fact that 'audiences' are essentially contingent collectivities, constituted in relation to kinds of performance while 'public' is the term used to classify the citizenry as a whole and is a grounding category for democratic polity. This is so, whatever the overlap occurring between the two in particular instances, an overlap further intensified by recognition of the fact that audiences can be variously 'active' and that 'the public' is regularly positioned as the recipient, sometimes the explicit addressee, of media performances.[2] Livingstone also notes how studies which are centred on news, public knowledge and formal political participation are often in danger of overlooking the cultural dimension to politics and political affiliation, the broader sphere of meanings, values, desires and satisfactions within whose terms people locate the activity of politics 'for themselves' and relate to it. She observes how an exploration of ideas of belonging and of the experience of belonging through mediation tend to be better addressed in analyses of other forms than the news (such as drama, entertainment and sport) where modes of affective involvement are recognized to be central. Drawing on the work of Peter Dahlgren (2003), among others, Livingstone discusses examples of inquiries with a research agenda that more broadly captures the experience of locating oneself within a 'civic culture' and of possessing and exercising modes of 'citizenship'.[3] Relating back to the points made above, we can see these experiences as involving ways of attending to the media that connect, often in shifting ways, the position of being a member of an audience with that of being a member of the public. Such an agenda is able to include a more comprehensive address to the diverse points of reference across which political and civic subjectivity is formed, sustained and revised. It also allows for the probability of multifaceted, inconsistent and sometimes contradictory dispositions at work, both in the construction of different citizen behaviours and (mostly unacknowledged) in the various normative prescriptions for 'good citizenship'.

With these general observations in mind, we hope in this chapter to explore the inter-relationship between modes of self-conscious citizenship and modes of 'audiencehood', drawing on responses to a range of serious, satirical and light-hearted political treatments, taken primarily from broadcast and print media. The chapter discusses interpretations and understandings of mediated politics obtained during group discussions, in many cases drawing on reactions to media materials analysed in the preceding chapters. In shifting our focus of attention 'beyond the news', we explore the various factors our respondents identified in relation to politics and political actors as portrayed by the media, including the deficits they perceived and those aspects of theme and form which gave satisfaction or pleasure. In this exploration we are interested in the ways in which different responses were prompted by the particular qualities (and limitations) of certain genres and media forms.

Our discussion in this chapter is guided by the following questions:

- How do members of the public relate to the various media portrayals of politics and politicians? In what ways, if any, do variations in generic 'recipes' prompt or encourage certain modes of audience engagement with the 'political'?
- How do members of the public position and present themselves, individually and collectively, in relation to the various portrayals of political elites? What kinds of knowledge, evaluations and emotions are drawn upon in this constitutive process?
- What do members of the public identify as problematic in the mediation of politics? Do they tend to blame the media, the politicians, or their own lack of competence, political understanding and engagement?

These concerns can be loosely categorized under three headings: comments on the impact of media form and genre for engagement with politics; self-reflective thoughts on identity, belonging, distance and knowledge, often expressed through contrasts between themselves, or 'ordinary people', and political elites; and normative evaluations on where mediated politics is 'going wrong' in Britain. Before turning to our respondent group analysis, we provide further contextualization on contemporary understandings of audiences in the rapidly evolving UK mediascape, and a brief introduction to our respondent groups.

Converging audiences and publics

Within the 'dips' into the political mediascape of our audit periods, we encountered a number of programmes, articles or cartoons where the role of visible and active audiences are structured into the text's rationale and format. Indeed, in relation to broadcasting, their active participation is integral to the values and identities of programmes such as *Question Time* or 'phone-in' segments found on both TV and radio (e.g. *The Wright Stuff, Any Answers*). Britain's public-service broadcasting ethos (epitomized most clearly by the BBC) has shifted its emphasis in recent years, to embrace the 'public' in more interactive modes of engagement, although arguably the 'top-down' reception model is far from being replaced. The BBC website claims as one of its six values:

'Audiences are at the heart of everything we do', while one of its six 'Public Purposes' is entitled 'Sustaining citizenship and civil society' (BBC, 2011). The broadcasting corporation's website reflects the vision set out in the BBC's 2004 document, 'Building Public Value'; its manifesto prepared as part of a consultation for the Charter renewal in the digital age (BBC, 2004). The BBC's ambitions are indicative of a wider shift, broadly social but enabled by new communication technologies, in which the participatory role for *public voices* (whether conceived individually or collectively), appears to be incompatible with older notions of mass-media audiences, and as public voices become entangled with their mediated figurations (Corner, 1991; Livingstone, 2005). Publics and individuals can, of course, be constituted and observed as entities separate to mediated spaces, and political elites periodically attempt consultation exercises in which they appeal to citizens directly in the mode of 'listening' governments or parties (e.g. see Coleman and Blumler, 2011, for an assessment of the Conservative–Lib Dem Coalition's performance as a 'listening government'), but the abundance of opportunities to identify and interact *across* and *within* mediated spaces means that the media play a central role in state–citizen relationships. The recent adoption of the term 'social media' to describe the character of what were seen as the growing applications of 'new media' technology exemplifies this emphasis on interactivity and a more flexible allocation of multiple roles.

In this context, the notion of 'media audiences' becomes uncertain and slippery given the expanding potential spaces available for individual and collective voices to adopt a variability of roles (activist, performer, spectator, reader); via differing modes of commitment and engagement (attentive, disengaged, aroused, outraged and amused); expressed across diverse times, places and media spaces, no longer tied to national boundaries or a limited format such as the 'letters page' in a newspaper. Studio audience members are able to participate at the time and location of recording within the broadcasting space, but also as audiences and publics at home, via emails, texts, letters and phone-ins, or in public online space, with comment threads, forums and Twitter feeds encouraging responses and initiating new topics for discussion. Website forums such as Mumsnet invite politicians into their own 'space', to take part in *live* online question-and-answer sessions (known as 'webchats'), which can be followed as 'live' discussion threads or reviewed later in archived form.

Mumsnet is an interesting case to consider briefly, due to the recent recognition of its users as citizens worthy of particular attention from political leaders. The discussion forum, originally conceived as a digital space in which 'mums' could share advice, information and sociability, had its moment in the political spotlight in the run-up to the 2010 General Election, and continues to organize its members around single-issue campaigns. For the live webchat event, the politician invited to take part in the webchat usually joins the Mumsnet hosts, co-founders Justine Roberts and Carrie Longton, in their office, with photographic and video images of their physical presence published on the Mumsnet website or 'broadcast' via their YouTube channel (and subsequently picked up by other media outlets). This particular merging of the audience or user-led 'grilling' of a politician via online communication technologies offers a hybrid mediated style of public engagement with political leaders, whose participation contributes a significant but ultimately small part to the ongoing discussion of issues within the forum.

Notably, such appearances generate publicity beyond the forum, albeit often tinged with derision, directed at both the 'yummy mummies' and the participating political leader. In autumn 2009, Gordon Brown's failure to answer a question on his favourite biscuit overshadowed his responses on diverse issues such as education, asylum seekers and welfare benefits, while David Cameron's appearance a month later attracted disdain due to his failure to answer questions quickly enough, apparently due to technical difficulties.[4] Both appearances prompted wider commentary on the forum itself as a political force (e.g. 'How much power does Mumsnet have?', Neil Tweedie, *Telegraph*, 19 November 2009), and an early assertion of the approaching general election as the 'Mumsnet election' (Rachel Sylvester, 17 November, 'This election will be won at the school gate', *The Times*) – a claim much repeated in early 2010 ('Meet the two Mumsnet founders, the women who could decide the next General Election', Beth Neil, *Daily Mirror*, 26 January 2010). Turning attention to the affordances of the forum, the online archive allows retrospective tracking of all users' comments in the thread, not only the questions and contributions made during the live webchat, but also the continuation of comments, which reflect on the featured politician's *performance* and on the *format* itself – crucially, aspects of participatory expression not so easily accessible or visible following traditional media audience appearances. The two examples below are in response to David Cameron's webchat:

posieparker Thu 19-Nov-09 15:18:15
I was hoping that this would allow me to entertain the idea of voting Tory, but it hasn't at all ... he does seem like a nice bloke, but

he really has no idea about the things that keep most of us from sleeping at night.

ZephirineDrouhin Thu 19-Nov-09 15:11:33

I'm starting to wonder whether this webchat format is even remotely suited to the grilling of politicians. Would it work better to have a Mumsnet interviewer or panel presenting questions from the discussion thread? They would have the ability to press said politician with follow-up questions, so we might have a better chance of cutting through all the flannel.

Following Nick Clegg's webchat as deputy prime minister in September 2010, the next user's posting expressed similar concerns, with added insight into the limitations from the politician's perspective:

pollycazalet Thu 16-Sep-10 22:04:24

I am just not sure it's the best format. We are all challenging and expecting a dialogue. He has an hour, is surrounded by advisors and the pressure not to say anything which will make the Today programme tomorrow (see biscuits passim).

I see how it's great for MN [Mumsnet] but struggle to see what he has got out of this.

Would really be great if he read the thread and came back with some more considered answers

During the online Mumsnet discussions, the website acts as a mediator between users and the invited politician, rather than allowing 'direct' access, performing a filtering role in the selection of the questions and in the deletion of inappropriate comments. Participants expressed frustration with the perceived limitations of the format, grappling with how to maintain the desired spontaneity and openness while ensuring that key issues are covered. For example, ZephirineDrouhin, cited above, suggests that follow-up questions would better 'grill' the politician, but require an increased mediator role for the Mumsnet interviewer or panel, while pollycazalet expresses empathy with the featured politician but questions whether the constraints of the 'live' element of the webchat enables considered answers to the questions asked.

Not only can discussion on certain issues continue beyond the live webchat (notably in David Cameron's case, over his lack of knowledge about the state provision of nappies for disabled children), but reflections on the *quality* of the dialogue and possible changes to *format* can be explored in the forum. The 'virtual' discussion can extend into 'real life' political events, even on rare occasions prompting the politician to personally attempt to recover support after a poorly received performance. In the example cited above, the Conservative Party leader later visited his questioner, Riven Vincent, at her home in Bristol to discuss nappy provision for disabled children; an issue where, as a parent of a severely disabled child (his son, Ivan, who died in February 2009), Cameron's original unsatisfactory answer was deemed to require a personal home visit in an attempt not only to re-establish his respect for Vincent and the issue she had raised, but to gain publicity and wider public support ('David Cameron goes back for round two after his Mumsnet gaffe', Laura Donnelly, *Telegraph*, 4 April 2010).[5]

Recent research has started to look beyond the narrowly conceived, invited 'audience participation' toward the more fluid and dynamic interactions that occur outside the confines of the broadcast studio or phone-in scenario, in response to both serious and more playful treatments of politics. Serious political programming such as *Question Time* encourages viewers to 'get involved in the discussion' through use of the Twitter hashtag #bbcqt, often attracting thousands of followers during the broadcast. In their study of what they dub the 'Viewertariat' responses to a particular episode in October 2009, controversial due to British National Party leader Nick Griffin's appearance on the panel, Nick Anstead and Ben O'Loughlin tracked real-time reactions to the broadcast events, noting how viewers used Twitter to express collective identities and to offer views on, or even pre-empt, the arguments made by panellists (2011). The nature of audience engagements with mediations of the political field has attracted research covering a range of media genres: in the case of *political drama*, Liesbet van Zoonen (2007) poses the question of what people 'do' with the popular accounts of politics offered in films and series such as *The West Wing*, by examining postings on the IMDB website. Likewise, fan forums for *reality TV* are suggested as sites for 'political talk' (Graham and Hajru, 2011); online communicative spaces that manage to harness levels of emotional investment and 'affective intelligence' that political parties might only dream of attaining from voters (van Zoonen, 2004; see also Coleman, 2006). *Comedic treatments* of politics have attracted renewed scholarly attention, notably into the popular phenomenon of late-night US comedy shows such as *The Colbert Report* and *The Daily Show*, and their impact on young people's attentiveness to politics (Feldman, 2007; Feldman and Young, 2008; Cao, 2010; Landreville et al., 2010; Holbert et al., 2011). Also with an interest in young citizens' attitudes to politics, Sanna Inthorn and John Street's (2011) focus group study of young people's attitudes towards celebrity politics found that, along with feelings of alienation and suspicion toward formal political structures, only those celebrities who performed a mature, entrepreneurial masculinity (e.g. Simon Cowell) were deemed worthwhile alternatives for political leadership.

A thread running through this research agenda is the consideration of a much-voiced concern for citizen estrangement from traditional politics; and the ways in which entertainment or popular culture genres might be construed as sources for political learning, meaning and identity formation. It is not only the informative, affective or symbolic forms of politics communicated *to* audiences that hold analytical interest here, but the opportunities for audiences to identify (with) a sense-making role for themselves. In making connections across political themes, interpreting and sharing thoughts and feelings about political ideas and values, or significantly, choosing not to do either, members of media audiences filter what is politically meaningful or civically useful to themselves; whether by choosing to view or listen to the mediated content, by participating in interpersonal communication sparked by what they have read or heard, or contributing to online forums where discussion can be taken outside of the temporal and spatial constraints of traditional media and immediate life-worlds. Thinking, then, of the media forms that we discuss here as *resources of mediated politicality*, the 'users' of these resources (whether encountered via TV, press or the web) can still be thought of as 'media audiences', albeit with an acknowledgement that a vast array of engagements are constituted under this frame.

A note on the groups

Our analysis is based on seven semi-structured respondent groups, held across Merseyside, Knowsley, Cheshire and Shropshire, with a total of 41 individuals taking part either in summer 2010 or in the early months of 2011. The majority of the groups consisted of people who already knew each other, meeting together regularly due to a shared common interest. We were keen to encourage discussion within groups of people who were already acquainted and comfortable expressing their views in a familiar environment; for example, groups were formed via an Older People's Voice forum, a reading group, or from members of an indoor climbing centre. We recruited participants from a range of age groups, from 17 to over 80 years old. The majority of groups were mixed-gender groups, with 26 female and 15 male respondents in total, and with a spread of participants variously in education, in employment, out of work, and retired from various occupations and professions. The membership of the groups, while not 'representative' in a sociologically robust sense, is sufficiently varied across demographic variables of age, social class, geographical region and gender for our current purposes. When quoting from our transcripts of these sessions, we have, in the customary way, changed all the names so as to protect the identities of our respondents.

Each session lasted around 90 minutes. We prepared short clips from TV and radio programmes, as well as newspaper extracts and cartoons, to prompt discussion in response to a selection of treatments of politics across different media genres and forms. For example, we presented clips from the reality TV programme *Tower Block of Commons* (*TBOC*) and the radio comedy show *The News Quiz*, both of which prompted heated debates concerning both the *content* and *form* of the programmes. We also invited respondents to give their own views on the way that politics is portrayed across a number of different media formats, and to discuss this within their groups.

In conducting this qualitative empirical research, we are interested in the ways that respondents describe and interpret the provided media materials, negotiate possible meanings, and interact with their fellow respondents. In this sense, we are interested in the various ways that participants talked together about their own experiences of mediated politics, with a sensitivity to expressions of the *emotional* dimension of engagement (enjoyment, outrage, annoyance, affinity), in addition to, and in combination with, the more sharply cognitive elements (e.g. issues of media bias, political affiliation, political knowledge and interest).

Generic appeals and limitations in political mediations

Our central interest in the range of generic offerings of mediated politics continues in this chapter, with the respondent-led sections below organized initially around comments which bring questions of genre and form to the fore. It is often in moments of difficulty in understanding, or, in response to comic forms, of 'not getting the joke', that we are able to note discussion of generic conventions, including playfulness and moments of perceived transgression, often leading to reflexive comments about political understanding in more general terms. Our selection of media materials presented to respondent groups represented a variety of generic 'recipes' and media forms, but also ranged from popular appeals to more esoteric treatments of the political. This meant that we were often noting reactions to the *unfamiliar* – personal unfamiliarity expressed towards a traditional media genre (e.g. editorial cartoons and sketch-writing); unfamiliarity due to the hybrid or innovatory nature of the material (comedy docudrama *Miliband of Brothers* (*Miliband*)); or unfamiliarity in finding aspects of 'the political' presented in an otherwise commonly recognized genre (e.g. the reality-TV programme *TBOC*, or Gordon Brown's celebrity interview on *Piers Morgan's Life Stories*). Respondents' comments on format-related or aesthetic qualities of the media materials they found puzzling, or even unsettling, offer worthwhile contributions in themselves; they also at times led to strongly expressed opinions about the essence of 'real' politics, and discussions on the suitability of certain generic types for constituting and shaping the political mediascape.

Television and the displaced politician

In this section we select respondents' comments relating to three TV programmes, all of which offer embodied performances of the political, with a dramatized version of 'real life' politicians, and politicians performing as themselves: the Miliband brothers' leadership contest is depicted in *Miliband*; Gordon Brown is interviewed for *Piers Morgan's Life Stories*; and an MP appears in the reality-TV series, *TBOC*.

As noted in Chapter 1, the generically innovative *Miliband* caused initial confusion for a number of our respondents, uncertain about the extent of its 'spoof' elements, especially among those who professed to have a limited knowledge of politics. Our first quotation comes from Olivia, in a group of health and beauty practitioners in Cheshire:

Olivia: You see, I thought they were spoof interviews as well. [Did you?] I didn't think it was them necessarily being that serious about it. [why was that?] Because they set the scene as being very light-hearted. And I didn't know whether they, because I don't know a lot of politics, I didn't know they were real people who were actually supposed to be important or not [laughter] but I just thought they were sort of taking the mick. When that first guy came on, he was like, I just thought that was part of the ... joke.
[...]
Olivia: I thought they were all, like, actors. Because I wasn't sure whether the Miliband brothers were actually them or if they were actors [laughter] [they were actors] [laughter] Sorry, man, I'm lowering the tone of our group.

Olivia's self-claimed lack of political knowledge adds to her confusion about the level of 'spoof' within the programme, not distinguishing the 'real' contributors (e.g. one by former Labour leader Neil Kinnock) from the acted segments. Along with Olivia's admission of her lack of understanding, her characterization of the talking-heads as 'people who were actually supposed to be important' suggests her own perceived distance from the political and media elites portrayed. Her confusion over the nature of the talking-heads' contribution – by people she did not readily recognize – is augmented by the unusual format of the programme, with its arch stylising of the interview segments. As her own misunderstandings become the focus of discussion amid good-humoured laughter, Olivia apologizes for 'lowering the tone of our group'; a semi-serious reflection on what her admissions possibly reveal about her own competencies, and those of the collective group of worker–friends, in their roles as citizen–viewers. The combination of a lack of political knowledge, here most clearly expressed as a misrecognition of the featured political personalities, along with the programme's distortive, farcical portrayals, contributed to Olivia's stated difficulties in assessing where the line was drawn between political joke and political commentary.

In another session, a reading group consisting of women aged 40 and upwards, the unusual formal and aesthetic qualities of the comedy docudrama again provoked initial uncertainty, with discussion leading onto how successfully the comic treatment worked with the 'real life' political events:

> *Alice:* the way you introduced it I thought it was going to be serious [what started to get in the way of that view?] It seemed to be, well, I'm not too sure what was going on, it seemed to be too lighthearted to be serious but, as I say, I'm not sure what was going on actually
>
> *Fiona:* I thought it quite quickly seemed to become slapstick in a way
> [...]
>
> *Emma:* I think it was funny right at the beginning because they were sitting in very small chairs and very small places. It gave the impression of being political comedy, it didn't look, to me, it didn't look right, I was ready to laugh at it, I thought it was very good
> [...]
>
> *Mabel:* I do think it's a very clever character assassination of the pair of them so you wonder where the makers of the programme are coming from really

Alice: Who's doing the assassination?

Mabel: well, I think, it's highlighting the rivalry between two brothers. It's not edifying anyway, these two brothers are trying to
become head of a political party and head of a country. Then that
is even worse, you want reason, don't you, you don't want fighting
siblings, Tweedledum and Tweedledee sort of thing.

We can note here the discussants swiftly negotiating matters of form and
politics: moving from initial uncertainty of not being 'too sure what was
going on' to a more confident and positive response from Emma who
points out the *visual* incongruity of their '*sitting in very small chairs and
very small places*'. Mabel then takes up this notion of caricature, adding a
literary/cartoon reference in her assessment of the programme's agenda
of 'character assassination': '*you don't want fighting siblings, Tweedledum
and Tweedledee sort of thing*'. In portraying the brothers' rivalry with
comic distortion, the programme depicts high-level politics as 'fighting siblings', rather than the politics of 'reason' that Mabel suggests we
would want ('*you want reason, don't you*'). This note of disapproval (possibly for the Milibands' decision to compete for the leadership as well
as the subsequent media portrayal) is a reaction found in other groups,
with one respondent getting 'quite wound up' by supposedly serious
news portrayals of political people and events being fuelled by speculation about behind-the-scenes motivations and *feelings* instead of 'real
politics':

[Drama documentaries are often quite serious, so going for comic
makes it quite distinctive?][6]

Sally: yeah, I mean it's ... I don't know, I got quite wound up by even
the news coverage of all the Milibands, it did become so much about
the, well, 'this rivalry might be this, might be happening behind
closed doors' and 'said to be feeling this that and the other'. There
was too much of that and there was actually nothing about any real
politics and I think the danger of programmes like that is that it just
feeds off that and then you become, it's almost like reality television
instead of thinking about ...

Matt: It's not real

Sally: yeah. It's ... I don't know.

Sally's comment presupposes normative judgements about what constitutes 'real politics' and the related civic role of the media, seeing the
'danger' in politics becoming 'almost like reality television', a trend that

Miliband 'feeds off' in its playful focus on the personal dimension of political events. The responses to *Miliband* hinted at the negative or limited aspect of comic treatments of politics, with mockery and ridicule of political persons in particular discouraging further serious engagement with politics, and alienating those who cannot 'get the joke' due to prior gaps in political knowledge.

There were a number of similar reactions to Gordon Brown's appearance on *Piers Morgan's Life Stories*, itself an unusual foray into celebrity politics for an incumbent prime minister, especially one famous for his discomfort at smiling for the camera (see, e.g. Letts, 2009). Echoing Mabel and Sally's comments above on the acceptable boundaries for 'real politics', some members of our sixth-form group objected to politics in this format, evoking a 'third person' who might vote for Brown based on enjoying this entertainment-led performance.

> *Lara:* I think it's a bit stupid, well not stupid. I think politics should be politics. I think if you make programmes like that, some people will be, 'ah he's funny, I'll vote for him'. I think it just seems a bit odd to interview a prime minister in a show like entertainment
> [...]
> *Peter:* I remember it being on, I remember deliberately not watching it because I think, personally that sums up the main problem with politics at the moment, it's all about personality, and you know, 'oh I like him' or whatever. Or, 'I've always voted this so I'll vote it again'. But, you know, I don't agree with that – because, I mean, there's nothing there about any sort of policy or anything. Which, you know, I don't think you need to know what the children of the prime minister are doing but you do need to know what his policies are and what his ideals are; that's the important thing [you think there shouldn't be a personality element to politics?] I think it's impossible to get rid of the personality element, but I think it's massively over-emphasized at the moment.

Peter points out that he chose 'deliberately' not to watch the programme, based on his opinion that such shows represent the 'main problem with politics', an overemphasis on personality and personal lives. Peter's rejection of the programme is coupled with a disdain for personality-led or unthoughtful political decision-making, by an imagined third person. Following on from Peter's comment, Alex is more accepting of politicians' desire to make a connection with people, although he has doubts about this particular programme.

Alex: I think they use it on purpose, because they want to show what personality they have, that they're not just machines working away somewhere, they can connect with people. I think it's a good idea in some aspects but I suppose that interview [there's a 'but'] yeah, I think there's a bit of collusion going on.

Respondents in a number of different groups commented on the reported friendship between Morgan and Brown, and the level of collusion or fakery around the programme. The noted level of collusion in the programme's format and style, for Alex, prevents a meaningful or 'true' representation:

Alex: They've had a conversation beforehand about it, whereas, if that interview was done on some other show like *The Politics Show* or *Question Time* people would believe, you know, it's... you'd say, well, what he was saying, you'd believe to be true, more than on that. The questions that he'd be posing on the Piers Morgan show, they'd be more for what people want to hear, rather than actually getting down into the situation and working, you know, getting proper answers from him.

In comparing the current programme with more politics-centric genres, Alex, along with others in the group, is critical of the questions posed by Morgan, evaluating the show against a journalistic frame in which 'proper answers' are drawn from politicians by keen interrogation, rather than agreeing to the questions beforehand, and colluding in giving people what they 'want to hear'. The premise of the programme, delving into aspects of Brown's life by means of a psychological–emotional interrogation rather than political interrogation, invites viewers to consider Brown as both a mediated political personality and a family man. Its brazenly melodramatic and populist chatshow format attracted criticism due to its strained blend of celebrity 'life story', recounted through personal anecdotes and high-emotion events, with high political office, all presented within a studio setting brimful with the trappings of a compliant audience, dramatic lighting and video montages. While commenting on a 'media view' of Brown, respondents revealed their own preconceptions of the prime minister in their evaluations of his performance, weighing up this unfamiliar offering against other mediated versions of Brown's persona. In the Knowsley Older People's Voice group, even those sympathetic to Brown suspected his motivations for appearing on the programme.

Clive: I say he's uncomfortable because that's not him, that's not him himself, that's a media view of him. As far as I'm concerned he's uncomfortable in that situation. He had to grin and smile there a couple of times, that's not like him. You've seen trying to grin. No, that wasn't him; that was stage-managed, everything to do with it. [...]

Margaret: Did anybody else see the full interview? Because they *did* interview him about the child that they lost. And that really, really was, I don't know, it was very sad because you could see his feelings were very emotional.

June: Well, do you think that wasn't done to make us feel sorry for him?

Margaret: most probably. I think we all knew, as an audience, (June: tugs at the heart strings) that that was going to come anyway and that it would pull at our heart strings, yeah.

Clive: They used a child as a political punchbag.

Margaret, who had watched the whole programme, recalls another moment in the interview, a moment much trailed in the print media before the broadcast, where Brown had been asked about the death of his baby daughter. Margaret's empathetically toned response, that it was really 'very sad', is immediately challenged by her fellow respondents, after which she is apparently persuaded that this moment has been designed to elicit a response of 'feeling sorry' for Brown, and therefore requires a more sceptical reading. Even where Brown is believed to be conveying authentic emotions, respondents objected to what they saw as a cynical attempt to manipulate their feelings, bolstered in many cases by a pre-existing antagonism towards Brown, in addition to the nature of the programme. Group members often disagreed about whether this interview could be counted as a credible performance for Brown, but even sympathetic appraisals of Brown's abilities as an effective communicator were couched in surprise and only a grudging admiration. This was particularly the case among our older participants.

Clive: He tried once on the questions, he looked at the camera direct; they get told to do that because you're getting to the audience inside that camera, and he done it on one occasion when asked a question, and he looked straight at the camera then realised he shouldn't do that and looked away straight away.

Damon: Purely from that clip, I think I said at the outset, I was surprised by it because I had this preconception that Gordon Brown

doesn't perform well in a situation like that and I thought he came across really quite well, on that occasion.
Cathy: He came across as a human being, didn't he, rather than a figurehead, type of thing.

Clive states his objections to this programme on multiple levels, based not only on Brown's concealed motivations and his failure to give a fully credible performance, but also on the constructed nature of the televisual appeal ('getting to the audience inside that camera'). Clive signals his defiance against such tricks of stagecraft (or TV-craft) by referring repeatedly to the presence of the camera and Brown's momentary direct gaze, imagining the instructions that Brown has been given to connect with his audience. Clive's scepticism is countered by Damon and Cathy, who are both more accommodating towards the performance, despite preconceptions, and the idea that this generic context allows him to come across as a 'human being' rather than a 'figurehead'. Overall, Brown's attempt to 'connect' more directly with audiences of popular rather than political programming appears to hold limited value as a tactic of mediated politicality, certainly among our respondents; the stripping away of associations with Brown's political roles or ideals leaves Brown in an awkward, displaced media space, with the effect of apparently encouraging charges of manipulation, inauthenticity and cynicism.

Where politicians appeared 'as themselves' in our respondent-group media extracts, the conversation often turned to the artifice of the representations on offer. Our second extract in which politicians 'played themselves' was the four-part reality-TV series, *TBOC* (although Neil Kinnock and Oona King also feature briefly in the *Miliband* clip). However, in this reality-TV format, where the 'displaced' politician is to be found living among 'ordinary' people in socially deprived areas of England,[7] concerns about the staging of behaviours and actions are directed, not at the politician, but towards the production team and the council tower-block residents; in this case, Sloane, the woman hosting Liberal Democrat MP, Mark Oaten. Before we discuss the comments on staging, we present the details of the short televised clip and initial responses to the programme.

In the *TBOC* extract shown to respondents (further edited by the research team, but showing all material relevant to the sequence featuring Mark Oaten and Sloane), Oaten is first shown helping Sloane with her weekly supermarket shop for the family in Dagenham. As we briefly outlined in Chapter 1, Oaten is initially pleased to have bought all the grocery and baby-related items required, spending just over £100 of Sloane's £150 budget; but his satisfaction is soon disturbed by Sloane's decision to spend the remaining money on cigarettes. Following a scene in which Sloane is shown angrily investigating his expenses, she challenges Oaten for claiming for two irons from the taxpayer. Numerous respondents evidently enjoyed this clip, with many choosing it as the most interesting extract at the end of the session, citing its accessibility and entertaining format.

> [Health-and-beauty workers group]
> *Olivia:* I think it's quite accessible for people that aren't necessarily interested in the ins and outs of politics; it takes it to real-life situations. It's quite shocking when she did spend all that money on cigarettes, but then in the same way, when she looked at his expenses, they're both as bad as each other.
> [Climbing-wall group 1]
> *Susan:* It's quite interesting that she said, 'you're taking money off the taxpayers' when she obviously doesn't work, for him to take the money, I mean these expenses and stuff, they do take the mick a bit with what they classify as, 'I'm going to get the money back'.
> [Reading group]
> *Anne:* Well, you did get a shock when she spent £40 odd on cigarettes, but she got back at him, didn't she? And he's just as bad as her. There's no difference. Everyone's out for themselves.

The responses above are indicative of many initial reactions, engaging directly with the discursive configuration set up by the programme-makers, in which we are invited to reflect on whether they are 'both as bad as each other'. This proffered 'trap' set by the programme, in which an initial conflict over 'unacceptable' spending of benefits is countered by an investigation into 'shocking' expense claims, is in itself a form of 'staging' albeit at a structural level. A number of respondents questioned the comparison:

> [Climbing-wall group 1]
> *Will:* I'm starting to think it's a little bit biased towards, what was her name, Sloane? [yes] I just think, from the way it started off and they edited it, but it's from his point of view, and with looking at the benefits thing, I think it's a different system to the expenses. I don't agree with the way expenses works at all but it's a different system.

[Climbing-wall group 2]
Sally: I don't know. I'm not sure the two things are comparable at all. I think that's being very...it's been put together and people will look at it and go, 'oh yeah if you're doing that, why should we'...I don't actually think that they're at all comparable. She's got her £150 for the week and the way that she budgets, and she's saying I have no spare cash from these living expenses, whereas he's got a very different lifestyle, not sure that it's comparable to say, okay I think the way that they claim money back and things is not good but it's a different thing. It's not the same, it's not money management in the way that he's judging her, because it's, you know, he would have the money to spend £40 on cigarettes if he wanted to, and actually I'm not sure that we have any right how to tell somebody how to spend their money.

The format of the show, with its direct contrast of two kinds of 'claimants' from distinct spheres of society, provoked wide-ranging discussions, mostly on the benefits system and the MPs' expenses scandal, which had dominated political news for the preceding year, but also on wider issues of wealth distribution in society, and on concerns such as the risks of smoking and the challenge of eating healthily on a tight budget. In their discussions, respondents referred to personal experiences along with recollections of varied media representations to support their positions: referenced programmes included fictional accounts, such as *Shameless*, a drama featuring families living on benefits in a council estate in Manchester; and 'true-life' depictions, such as Jeremy Kyle's daytime talk show, or documentaries, for example, identifying precedents in which politicians were filmed attempting to live on benefits for a short period of time. However, often without prompting, discussion swiftly turned to forms of staging and artifice in the show. In a majority of groups, the first note of scepticism centred on Sloane's decision to investigate Mark Oaten's expenses:

[Health-and-beauty group]
Jack: It looks like it's been kind of staged slightly. I wouldn't have thought that she'd come up with, not criticising, but 'oh, I'll just go and do some research on Mark Oaten' and yeah, so... [so you're coming round to the view that it wasn't spontaneous?] no, not spontaneous. I think it's been staged, but obviously when you look at it, it could be something that she does off her own bat.
[Climbing-wall group 1]

Sally: I think it's designed to make the politician look foolish, I don't believe for a second that she thought, 'I'll Google his expenses', I imagine that was suggested to her. You know, it's all done on camera very nicely, and you just, somebody in production saying, 'I wonder what he spends on...' and they plug those ideas to her, and actually, I think it does come across that he's being very judgemental and it's the way they put, and even like the music that they played over when he was pushing the trolley was kind of bumbly along music, was trying to make...I don't know, I'm being critical.
[Climbing-wall group 2]

Will: I'd be interested to know if it was actually her idea to research his expenses or whether it was someone behind the camera that said, here you go, this is his name, this is what you can Google.

Discussion on editing choices also led to evaluative comments about how such portrayals conform to an entertainment-based logic, characterized as a marked tendency towards sensationalism or overstated negativity to pull in more viewers, rather than privileging a more edifying or informative perspective.

[Older Peoples' Voice]
Clive: I mean it could be edited any way you want, any way that they want to portray it, they will edit it, so that you as a viewer are told what to watch, are told how the situation is by simply editing, where they cut bits out, to please you, but not the truth.
[Sixth-form group]

Peter: Well, it's an interesting idea, but the only problem is that the media is interested in getting higher viewers so they're not going to introduce a reasonable MP and a reasonable person to go and send them to live with. [...] I think, I mean, a lot of the issues are really very important but I think it's perhaps slightly skewed in its portrayal of some things.

Alex: They'll get higher figures by showing, I suppose, the negative aspects of what goes on. So for instance, they were showing his expenses, £116 for an iron, people think, you know, it's not right, but people are more interested to watch that, I suppose. If it was all about the good things that MPs do, not as many people would watch it but they don't really want to show that.
[Climbing-wall group 1]

Adrian: Em, I don't know, I sometimes, I feel a bit uncomfortable about those sorts of programmes, that they, just feel like people are being a little bit exploited perhaps, so I wouldn't have watched it and I don't think [who's being exploited, the MPs or...?] Probably a little bit of both, yeah... [five minutes later]... And I wonder when you get things like that, whether the viewer's also being exploited a little bit by it. Sometimes you're watching things like that and then you think [sighs] it just makes you feel a little bit dirty, just a little bit because you think, oh, I know what they're trying to do and I know how they've made me feel, and they've done their job.

Despite their scepticism towards the programme and its intentions, it provoked the liveliest discussion in comparison with our other excerpts. Wide-ranging discussion encompassed social issues, TV formats, media ethics and political values. A number of respondents, cited above, saw the pressure to 'skew' coverage of politics and social issues actually coming from the audience, entertained by a mix of combative extremes and simplified narratives. Taking a more critical view, Adrian found the programme exploitative for *all* those concerned, including the viewer, partly due to his recognition that the programme could succeed in manipulating his feelings, despite his professed discomfort with the format. We return to these issues in relation to *TBOC* later, in the section on audience identification and affective orientations, but Peter's comment below possibly points to one reason why respondents engaged so energetically with the scenes from the programme:

> Peter: It's interesting as well because it sort of shows real people, it's not just figures and stuff, it's a real person who's claimed money on expenses and a real person who is on benefits so it shows the human effect of policies, etc, etc, which is interesting.

Cartoons and sketch-writing

In contrast to responses to the *TBOC* clip discussed above, our newspaper excerpts did not always stimulate an exchange of ideas, but instead required a more active role from the facilitating researcher, to draw out preferences and understandings of the political connections being made in the material. In the case of the editorial cartoons, respondents' lack of familiarity, both with the generic properties (e.g. symbolic, often opaque, relying on visual cues) and the depicted political persons and themes, presented obstacles for comprehension and enjoyment. Parliamentary sketch-writing, with its strongly satirical and disdainful mode of writing, appealed to some respondents, but the ensuing discussion tended to take the shape of a collective text-focused decoding exercise, rather than evolving into conversations on broader political themes or ideas.

Two sketches were read out and displayed on a large screen to respondents: *The Times'* Ann Treneman's piece on Nick Clegg wooing Cameron and Brown during coalition talks (see Chapter 2), and a sketch by Quentin Letts in the *Daily Mail*, which swapped the whimsical romance pastiche favoured by Treneman for a more cutting and partisan treatment of the same period, focusing on Brown's reluctance to leave office ('New politics? It stinks like a prop forward's jockstrap', 11 May 2010). Their contrasting styles provoked disagreements as to the more effective or amusing approach. Below are reactions from the Birkenhead reading group:

[On the Treneman sketch]
Fiona: It draws that situation together and almost makes it like a children's tale and it's just funny and witty.
Emma: I didn't like it. I didn't like it all. I thought it was boring and it just didn't appeal to me. Like, the News Quiz makes it look a bit more subtle. I found my mind wandering quite quickly.
Alice: No, I didn't find it boring at all.
[On the Letts sketch]
Alice: I just didn't think he wrote as well as the first one.
Emma: But that's got your attention straightaway, look at the language, the first two sentences, 'it's stinks like a prop forward's jock strap', 'what a tarts' bazaar', and then the end, 'what a bar of soap that man is', so he's actually, what's the word, they're like the two brackets either side of it which really hold your interest, that's probably what kept me…
Alice: I don't think it did, it really didn't hold my interest.

Emma, Fiona and Alice disagree entirely on which of the two sketch columns holds appeal, although they like at least one of them. Various respondents criticized the sketches for being 'boring', while others enjoyed the 'tongue-in-cheek' and exaggerated style. Letts' piece in particular came under criticism for being 'vitriolic', 'vindictive' and 'angry':

[Climbing-wall group 1]
Marie: And it's just boring [general agreement] there's nothing… why make politics boring when probably, you know, most people probably think it is boring, make it…

Susan: ... fun, easy to understand.
[Climbing-wall group 2]
Sally: The second one is angry. The first one's funny and the second one is angry.
[Health-and-beauty group]
Jack: I don't like it at all. It is more of a dig with an undertone of politics.
Olivia: I think it's somebody who thinks of ... I don't know, it's like the writing's a bit too many, I don't know, like they're bigging things up too much, in too many words for what he's actually saying. And not funny and not serious completely. It just doesn't really know where it's at. It's just like a bit of a rant by somebody with a plum in their mouth.

Olivia struggles over her words in an effort to describe and evaluate the writing style; she appears to object to Letts as a rather pompous and verbose narrator of events, with neither an informative nor humorous contribution to make. Letts' brand of condescending commentary might claim an outsider status, but nonetheless it places him within a media–politics elite for Olivia – with a 'plum' in his mouth. Letts' strongly expressed views and his gossipy tone deterred a number of respondents, for whom the style of writing became the focus for discussions and was deemed generally to be neither accessible nor amusing.

Similarly, discussions on editorial cartoons often centred closely on the qualities of the depictions on the page, with collective work undertaken on identifying political persons and themes, and attempting to unpick the intended meanings. Here, the Older People's Forum group in Knowsley grapple with Martin Rowson's cartoon depiction of Nick Clegg as Pinocchio (see figure 2.1, Chapter 2):

[Which do you think is the most difficult to understand?]
Margaret: I think the Pinocchio one [agreement] I didn't understand that at all.
Robert: Because who's he supposed to be shaking? There's no real image. [June: no likeness] That's supposed to be someone but it's not a recognisable someone. [Damon: It's supposed to be Clegg isn't it?] It is supposed to be Clegg.
Margaret: He's got yellow on him.
Clive: That's Vince Cable, innit that?
Robert: Vince Cable, yeah, and he's shaking Clegg to get him into [shape] shape, yeah.

Margaret: But if you look at him, he's got all the colours on hasn't he? The yellow and the blue and the red [it's a complicated image].

Robert: What's the other fella in the background? [peering through the window?]

Damon: That's Cameron. [Yes, it's Cameron peering through the window.]

Clive: Is the cat for Mandelson?

Robert: Oh, it's a fox, isn't it? [Yep.]

Damon: It's working the theme, isn't it, of Pinocchio? [It is.]

Clive: It doesn't make sense that.

Margaret: It doesn't make sense to me, I'm sorry.

This extended extract is indicative of the problems encountered by respondents, admittedly in response to a number of cartoons displayed out of their original news context and with a time lapse of a number of weeks or even months. Despite working collectively to decipher the visual clues to arrive at the political persons and themes alluded to, discussion did not necessarily result in constructive and meaningful engagements with the material for our respondents. Our sixth-form group progressed more swiftly, possibly due to the environmental factors of a school-classroom setting, and certainly due to a familiarity at that age of conducting textual-analysis exercises, even if not as regular readers of newspaper editorial pages. Responding to minimal visual cues, discussion moved from identifying political persons to drawing out a range of intended meanings and political values underpinning the cartoons.

Alex: My favourite was the Pinocchio one. [You like Pinocchio?]

[*Kevin:* Nick Clegg] Yeah. Because although it's obviously having a go at Nick Clegg, but overall it's having a go at politicians, calling them clowns, liars.

Kevin: That's the interpretation of Nick Clegg, isn't it, that's the way they portray him.

Alex: It's actually having a go at him but overall it's having a go at politicians in general, saying you've turned into a real politician, now your nose is going to grow with lying, it's going to get worse.

Kevin: But I think it's saying that because, before the television debates necessarily people didn't know what Nick Clegg, they didn't know who he was as a person because he wasn't a big face in politics, and then soon as the TV debates came on, his face was televised, everyone knew him, everyone knew what he stood for, everyone

knew how he spoke [and that made him into a real politician].
Exactly, then he got himself elected in the hung parliament, he's
a 'real' politician.
[...]
[So tell me about your favourite?]
Peter: Well, I just remember actually, because I remember very much
on the news, on the BBC, etc, etc, when you had Nick Clegg and
David Cameron walking in the Rose Garden, with the civil partnership, etc, etc, and I found that quite amusing, I have to say. And,
you know, I think it sums up the media attitude towards the development, look at all this honeymoon period, and then we've got the
bomb underneath the thing, which I think is quite interesting.[8]

Members of the sixth-form group, cited in the extract above, not only
talked about the cartoon representations on the page, but also the
implied commentary that the cartoons offered about the nature of
politics, media portrayals and the 'media attitude' conveyed; their evident political knowledge of the election coverage enables a nuanced
and intertextual appreciation of the cartoons as in dialogue with varied political material across the mediascape. The respondents connected
the visual cues to particular media narratives from the election period,
but also to perceptions of politicians and politics more generally. As we
see in the next section, where the 'generic recipe' works to facilitate
what are often strongly personal connections, through humour or identification, respondents also express an attentive engagement with the
'political', in what is frequently articulated as an important, 'civic',
relationship.

Identifying attachments, connections and distances

We have already touched on comments in which respondents have
expressed a range of emotions towards the material we showed them.
In this section we further explore emotional connections, selecting quotations where respondents refer to their own values or sensibilities, and
how they intersect with their preferences for certain genres of political mediation. Arguably, the modernist ideal of serious-minded citizens
making rational decisions about their future government does not capture what happens in everyday experiences of mediated politics: instead,
the media's portrayals provoke feelings of anger, boredom, disbelief,
excitement and more. Our respondents expressed a range of emotions,
both as part of generalized discussion on attitudes to mediated politics, and in more specific cases to the materials we presented. In their

expressions of curiosity or dismay, we found that the negotiations of funny, symbolic or manipulative elements in the material are crucial factors to consider alongside the informative and politically substantive content. For example, respondents tended to connect on a personal level with political themes where they identified intentional, and sometimes not so intentional, humour. Undoubtedly, our discussions demonstrated how personal investments in politics are construed in affective as well as deliberative terms.

On the whole, where comedic treatments of the political were appreciated and enjoyed, they were also thought to provide a *civic usefulness,* in the sense that they might engage those who would normally turn away from 'straight' political programming. Comedy also featured as a key genre when respondents reflected on their own personal appreciation of politics, and even as part of a shared British identity. In this section, we draw on responses to the radio show *The News Quiz*, noting that respondents were largely positive in their appraisals of this more traditional form of satirical performance. In three out of the four groups that heard this particular clip of *The News Quiz*, there was a general consensus that it was one of the most engaging media extracts in the session.

[Reading group]

Fiona: I just love that programme. Absolutely love it.

Alice: It sort of makes – you're all sort of there, got your own feelings about the cuts, one way or the other, and it sort of exaggerates them and your own inner feelings of them, and you know it's exaggerating whatever but it's quite good that they're thinking the same way as you are, perhaps.

Emma: I think humour's a very good way to get the message across [yes] and Jeremy Hardy does it very well, and it annoyed me when comparisons were being made about the coalition government in the war and now, and I think he got to it so well, and he had us all listening. If a politician had been going on like that, I'd have switched off in about ten seconds, but I listened to the whole of what he was saying because the humour was there but he was also making a strong political point.

The three respondents here express strong emotional associations with the programme, expressing their love for it, and explaining that it exaggerates enjoyably their own inner feelings. The clear affinity with the programme operates at *affective* and *political* levels: enjoyment is expressed in the strongest terms ('absolutely love it'), while efforts to describe its attractions draw out the *exaggeration* of 'inner feelings' and 'thinking the same way as you are'; this noted feeling of alignment with the performers facilitates engagement with the 'strong political point' about imposed economic austerity made by the participant Jeremy Hardy, as he undercuts the Coalition's own positive analogy with household budgets and wartime experience, and so effectively taps into a fellow feeling of annoyance at both coalition policy *and* the politicians' mode of delivery (see Chapter 1 for the transcript of this extract). The idea that comedy treatments of politics evoke the feeling that they are 'thinking the same way as you are' was a common response across the groups. For example, in another group, a male respondent commented, 'I mean, that broadcast there, are things what I would say'. Respondents felt they could align themselves with the comedian's expressions of politicality, as opposed to 'switching off' when a politician talks about the same issues. Also worthy of note is how such affinity encourages attentiveness to the political points being made by the comedian; as Emma comments: 'I listened to the whole of what he was saying because the humour was there but he was also making a strong political point'.

Self-professed fans are a very particular constituency; but respondents with minimal interest in politics, and who would not usually listen to such a programme, also found themselves reflecting on the political point being made:

[Health-and-beauty group]
Olivia: Em, I laughed a bit. But it wouldn't be something I'd ever choose to listen to, but the bit where he was on about his house, well I presume it's a house that he owns, that, for a couple of seconds made me think, well, it's true that everyone's in debt but you don't suddenly stop, you know, living, so, but it wouldn't probably. [That's quite an interesting reaction in a way, because rather than responding to it as comedy, you're responding to it as making a serious political point, almost.] Yeah, I mean, I think it did, it was a well made point made as a joke, which makes you think, it is a bit ridiculous, the cuts, when, you know, every person is in debt who's got a house. [So he's made for you a successful point because of the particular metaphor that he used at that point?] Yeah, I'd say so.

Olivia is cautious in her appraisal, but Hardy's ridiculing of the household-debt analogy has prompted her to think about the cuts, even for 'a couple of seconds', leading her to question the cuts policy and see it as 'a bit ridiculous'. Before returning to notions of the 'ridiculous' in politics, it is worth including the reactions of another respondent with initial reservations about the programme, who puts an alternative spin on the feelings of affinity prompted by listening:

[Climbing-wall group 2]

Ben: Yeah, I know I said it was very stereotypical but at the same time, listening to it sort of makes me feel a bit, sounds stupid, a bit more British with the whole 'keep calm and carry on', kind of thing, it's like, yeah the country's gone to pot, what can we do?, let's joke about it. You know, it sort of gives you that sense of, yeah, everything's gone wrong but at least we can have a laugh about it. Yes, we've actually got terrible politicians but at least we can have jokes about them. It sort of, it does make you feel a little bit better in a twisted way. [It might be a good thing?] It's not good for the likes of Cameron and Brown who are getting slated in it, but for us lot, it's like, yeah, you know, we've got terrible politicians but at least we can laugh about them.

Laughing at politicians offers a way of feeling 'better in a twisted way' about our collective inability to prevent or correct the deficits of political life, by providing a release for our frustrations at 'terrible politicians'. Ben identifies this resigned outlook as a British trait, with comedy performing a kind of civic good insofar as it facilitates amused acceptance (a finally benign judgment, which might clearly not be shared by those with other political viewpoints). That which is deemed a good thing for 'us lot' is not so good for 'the likes of Cameron and Brown': multiple senses of identity, belonging and status thread through Ben's statement. While Ben's quotation above characterizes politics and our political leaders as 'terrible' in generalized terms, for one of our respondents in the Shrewsbury group, the ridicule of politicians in this manner was indicative of a wider problem in current public and political discourse.

David: No, I, my attitude was not positive at all, I just don't like that sort of thing full stop.

Mary: Oh, really? [What is it you don't like?]

David: I just don't like people making snide remarks about people in public life. I don't find any pleasure or entertainment in that at all.

Derek: Ah, because it inspires disrespect?

David: Yes, and derision. I think we've got enough of it.

As an example of a wholly negative response, this was a more unusual reaction, one which surprised other members of the group. David finds the remarks of comedians 'snide', referring to politicians as 'people in public life' and so foregrounding their role in civic society in his choice of words. There are no hesitations or hedging here, in fact 'at all' is used twice, in addition to 'full stop'. By also commenting that 'we've got enough of it', David links his displeasure to something he feels is problematic in public life, or at least in mediated public life. Unlike the negativity that we found in responses to say, cartoons, this dislike is not connected to issues of understanding or of not 'getting the jokes' through lack of political knowledge, but a strong rejection of this mode of humour when directed at public figures. David's comments spark further discussion on the merits of mockery and critique:

> *Derek:* Excuse me, I think, if you don't mind, I think the amusement is directed at politicians, it's like the coffee shops in the Georgian times. The amusement was directed at politicians. If they'd been to…at other professions, it wouldn't have been so amusing, but it's purely because it's politicians that they're on about. [You mean politicians are fair game?] Yes, and also they're not trusted, you see. They're not trusted and so therefore, they're fair game. Any other profession wouldn't be treated so lightly.
> *Mary:* The other thing is, they actually are there to represent us. And yet we're prepared to stick them up and pull them down, laugh at them, and…But in a way that's quite healthy, isn't it? In some ways it can be quite healthy.

Derek counters that the key factor is that the amusement is directed at politicians, rather than other professions. Derek repeats that 'they're not trusted' and so therefore they are fair game. His comment implies a notion of causality in his use of 'therefore', with lack of 'trust' repeated as a reason for politicians being 'fair game' and a cause for such amusement. Derek's reasoning shifts the 'deficit' onto politicians' behaviour, here all grouped together as a profession that is not trusted, alluding to the 'coffee shops' reminiscent of a Habermasian public sphere of the past, and so shifting what David sees as disrespectful talk of politicians into the sphere of 'fair' critique, rather than flippant mockery.

While Derek points to issues of 'trust', Mary follows this by mentioning their role as representatives of the people: 'they are actually there to represent us'. Initially this leads her to question how we 'stick them up and pull them down', echoing David's concern with how roughly we treat those prepared to work in public life on our behalf; but then she stops herself mid-sentence and repeats that, in a way, that can be 'quite healthy'. This comment is interesting as it reveals conflicting opinions on the values of mockery and critique in a single utterance. Not only are normative judgements about the role of comedy negotiated among participants in their discussions, but here we see one respondent negotiating these positions in her single response. This extract demonstrates how asking respondents to make an 'either/or' judgement would not always be an adequate way to gauge their complex engagement with this kind of material. Similarly, a propensity to find material amusing or offensive can intersect closely with political and moral values.

David's comments above were very much the exception – most respondents answered that they did not feel sorry for politicians who were targets for humorous or even disdainful treatment, with some even expressing surprise that we would ask such a question (Susan: 'It strikes me as weird that you ask that question, do you feel sorry for them.'). Indeed, *The News Quiz* radio extract also prompted discussion of politics as routinely funny or ridiculous in its own right.

> [Climbing-wall group 1]
> *Marie:* Yeah, I mean there was a point there which was like, mocking backbenchers. Well, if you look at the Labour backbenchers, they're just as bad. Backbenchers are, they're rowdy, they just go for it, you can't – but obviously, it's just comedy, it wasn't – you just laugh at it. [So, biased and being on one side?] It was just his opinion, he wasn't talking like an actual general fact, you know, so. [And you laughed anyway?] Yeah, because it is funny [laughs]. [And do you think there's a political point to it, he's not only funny but he's also right?] Yeah. Well, politicians are mad. I think they are. You watch Prime Minister's Questions on Wednesday and you just, ah, it's just unreal how like children, almost, they're up and they're screaming at each other, and...
> *Susan:* I've seen that show.
> *Marie:* ...Ah, they're just so – it's quite funny.

Marie begins by addressing a perceived bias in the programme's mocking of Conservative and Lib Dem backbenchers, pointing out that Labour backbenchers are 'just as bad'. However, her own political support for the Conservatives does not prevent her finding the clip funny, simultaneously pointing out how the comedy operates at the level of opinion rather than fact, and the inherent ridiculousness of the politicians' behaviour during Prime Minister's Questions (PMQs) in the House of Commons (broadcast on BBC Parliament and BBC2). As discussion shifts from the comedic funniness of *The News Quiz* to the absurd funniness of PMQs, Susan interjects 'I've seen that *show*' as Marie describes it as 'just unreal', adding to the impression that this is experienced as 'showtime' politics. Marie wasn't the only respondent to spontaneously refer to PMQs as unintentionally comic. Karen, in our reading group, also 'couldn't stop laughing' at the politicians' performances:

> *Karen:* Do you watch Prime Minister's Questions? I watched it by accident, I just happened to have it on by accident, and I couldn't stop laughing because I thought, these are running our country and they're standing there on each side, like that, and they're all going 'boo', 'hiss', clapping like that [slaps table] going 'boo hiss', and I'm going, they're in charge! [laughter] It's like a . . .
>
> *Anne:* It's like an infants' school, isn't it?
>
> *Karen:* It is, and I couldn't get over it, I couldn't stop laughing, and then I thought, it's not a comedy show really but I thought it was [no] I thought it was hilarious.

For Marie and Karen, their separate realizations that the politicians in the parliamentary 'show' are 'in charge' and yet appear to be acting 'like children' causes hilarity, rather than a level of concern which threatens a move to antagonism or even hostility towards political life. In this sense, the dramaturgical elements of PMQs invoke a response of *civic irony*, to adapt a theatrical notion, by which the supreme civic space for representing the people's interests instead becomes a televised pantomime or 'comedy of errors', provoking hilarity, not at the politicians' comedic capacities to make funny jokes, but at the ridiculousness of the parliamentary performance in its entirety.

In these collated reactions, although the respondents offer ostensibly positive feelings and thoughts about the intersections of politics and comedy overall, they hint at a problematic paradox of critique through ridicule. The pleasures of political comedy are often negotiated with a sense of (ironic) distance in relation to the formal structures of civic space, manifested most clearly in responses to political persons and their perceived failings. Many comic forms construct a community of 'complicity' among those who enjoy them which can strengthen a sense (if only temporary and partial) of 'us' against 'them'. The imagined 'us' is usually constructed as one distanced from, yet grudgingly accepting of, the power-elite, a position expressed through multifarious and sometimes contradictory orientations towards mediated political culture.

Comedic treatments allowed for a range of strongly affective involvements, provoking responses that connected with a sense of shared enjoyment and even a satisfying awareness of the British satirical tradition. Likewise, the *TBOC* clip invited identifications and evaluations of the subjects depicted, at times rousing an angry reaction, which evoked the politician as part of 'them', separated by privilege and what some respondents saw as a sense of superiority masking their own failings.

[Reading group]
Emma: My sympathy was with her, it's not often you have people with understanding of how people worse off live, and my instinct is, how *dare* he say she shouldn't spend that money on cigarettes? I know she's struggling but as she said it's her luxury, and what luxuries do we have? Okay, they're maybe not criticised in the same way but I'm really pissed off with that man, I thought, leave her alone.
[Older People's Voice]
June: Well I'm annoyed first, I'm annoyed at the lady spending £40 'cos she's got young children and she should try and give up smoking, on that side [...] And when she looked up what his expenses were, I was annoyed with him. But I'm more annoyed with the system. Because why are we allowing them to do that? You know, a few hundred people in parliament are governing millions of people, shouldn't our opinion be more than theirs because there are more of us. So why should we allow them to do that, every week, every year, on and on and on? Well, we know what they're doing now, but they're still doing it.

Emma is defensive on behalf of Sloane, expressed in strong terms of being 'pissed off' with 'that man'. At the same time, she implies that the programme offers a rare understanding into how people 'worse off live'. Her response displays emotional affinities, but also discloses social and political underpinnings and a sense of injustice. Likewise in the second comment, June transfers her annoyance from those depicted in the televised sequence to a more systematic problem, exasperated at an unchanging situation where certain people continue to gain at the expense of 'us'.

Experiencing politics across diverse genres in imaginative, funny and provocative forms opens up space for those without specialized political knowledge to connect with aspects of the political in productive ways. Our respondents identified deficits in the media's own practices, such as staging and collusion, in addition to deficits in the values or performances of political elites. Respondents present themselves as variously aware or knowledgeable (as well as uncertain or ignorant) in different ways, alert to the aesthetic devices, limitations and promises of certain media genres, if not always knowledgeable of the political events or persons depicted. The variabilities of personal investment, knowledge and interest present problems in summarising findings from such a study, but in demonstrating how such material is appreciated and critiqued by a number of respondents, we hope to have shown something of the complexity of cross-generic mediations of the political at the level of the audience experience.

In sum, by presenting a range of responses to the kinds of media materials we have analysed in earlier chapters, we have drawn attention to how members of the national audience engage with forms of mediated politics, as citizens but also as entertained consumers, and with notable self-recognition of their own prior levels of interest or knowledge. Our respondents found affinities with mediated performances of the political, while also reacting, sometimes strongly, against what they perceived as unethical depicted conduct (the behaviours and actions as witnessed on screen) or unfair media treatment of this, or even in what the material allowed them to imagine was happening off screen and behind the scenes. We use the word 'affinities' here to acknowledge the role of affective response to the selected forms of mediated politics. Our audience research has helped to illuminate the complexities of how a range of contemporary political material is interpreted and judged. It also points to the civic values that can be prompted through shared audience experiences of pleasure, provocation and annoyance.

5
Mediation and Theme

In this chapter, we shift the emphasis from matters of form to matters of theme. So far in this book we have looked in detail at how mediations of politics outside of 'news' worked within very different generic models, articulating their material within a diversity of discursive, aesthetic and comic frameworks, often to distinctive audiences and readerships. What kind of thematic profile emerges from this heterogeneous activity? Across the kinds of generic space we have explored, what of politics and the political gets picked up and worked upon and what does not? Of course, some themes were articulated across many different generic formats, others were just identified by, for instance, a particular cartoonist, blogger or columnist. In nearly all cases, what we are terming 'theme' had a particular event or statement at its core, a piece of political specificity around which more general values and ideas were generated. As we have noted earlier, deciding what is and what is not 'political' can be an issue for research of the kind that we conducted given the interconnections between the political, economic, the legal and the broadly social that are always active. However, by focusing on accounts largely concerning Westminster and the major institutions of state, whatever else they also include, we hope to have reduced, if not eliminated, the vulnerability of our analyses to category confusion and category drift.

The discussion that follows is offered in two sections: an initial interpretative synopsis, followed by a more quantitatively grounded perspective drawing directly on our own coded database, which we have referred to previously (see Introduction). The rationale for this division is to allow us to develop the initial account in ways that go beyond the constraints of the data set, while also being able to indicate, separately, particular ways in which the corpus supports our observations. Our initial interpretative overview of prominent themes is divided into

134

two parts; first we consider the *politician* as primary substantive focus in political mediations, with subsections on the associated topics of leadership, suspicion and venality; second, we consider three broader *political framings* that each offer a particular lens through which to interpret political performances and events – affectivity, comedy and critique. We then draw on our database of media materials to present supporting quantitative data on political people, values and themes that we are able to track across a broad range of media formats and genres, revisiting affectivity, comedy and critique from this more formally 'grounded' standpoint. Inevitably this account is a selective one, but it is guided by our extensive and intensive scrutiny of primary materials, as well as by the literature of the broader research field.

Performing politics: politicians

We have seen how politicians, as bodies, faces and personalities, are the primary focus of generic attention to politics and the political in the media, including in those forms outside of core journalism, which are the subject of this book. This is not at all surprising since they are, literally, the embodiment of the political system and their own speech, behaviour and actions are regarded as a condensation of the various political values and positions available, and operative within the official political sphere. Although the weighting between media attention to politicians and direct attention to political systems and processes has justly been a focus of debate within media research and political studies (see, e.g. Franklin, 1994; Street, 2004), the notion that there might be a wholesale transfer of emphasis from, as it were, the physical to the abstract in political mediation, seems unrealistic within the contexts of history and of conceivable models of public representation. Politicians provide for generic work an extensive range of physical referents which, as we have noted, can either remain at the level of the 'personal' (politics as, essentially, politicians) or indicate through the mode of description and portrayal employed something more broadly about political structures, values and processes.

One important factor in the depiction of politicians, in whatever genre, is the degree of 'distance' at which they are depicted in relation to the 'ordinary' or explicitly in relation to 'us'. The idea of politicians as (too) distant is a recurring theme in political comedy as well as an element in serious political critique (including critique that uses the notion of 'the political class' (e.g. Beyme, 1996; Oborne, 2007). The view that politicians constitute an 'elite' comfortably removed from the real exigencies of everyday life has always been a judgment placed against existing democratic politics in many countries and in Britain it has been reinforced by a sensitive social-class agenda, compounding gender inequalities, in which active forms of family privilege through wealth and education have, in official political discourse, been downplayed in favour of appeals to versions of the 'meritocratic' principle.[1] In relation to this, it is important to note the difference between the perception that politicians constitute a self-formed elite, perhaps according to themselves unacceptable privileges, a view widely apparent in the work we looked at, and the perception that their ranks are largely drawn from a pre-existing social elite, a perspective that was also clearly active in some of our generic material. Identification of this second kind of elite formation produces a sense of structural skew at the very core of representational politics and it grew in prominence as a theme of mediation with the growing recognition, well before the period of our analysis, that the Conservative Party was likely to become a party of government again and that it contained within its senior ranks a number of highly privileged and wealthy individuals.[2]

The increasing visibility of politicians, through the intensive range of (often daily updated) audiovisual records of their public speech, demeanour and actions, projects them into public space as the familiar 'cast' of what is in effect the 'national politics show'. We have used theatrical analogies at several points throughout this book, with their implications concerning the importance of various types of performance and the nature of political commentary as, in part, a kind of theatrical criticism. Familiar though it is, the 'theatrical optic' is a central one for understanding the kind of mediations that we have set out to explore, ones in which not only an engagement with character but a construing (and sometimes an imaginative re-rendering) of story and plot are central (Goffman, 1959; Edelman, 1964, 1988; Meyer, 2002). The relatively uncontroversial observation that politics involves a good deal of performance relates to the more ambitious and debatable idea that politics is 'performative', a judgment that has been made by a number of commentators, including Arendt (1958), Butler (1997) Mouffe (2000, 2005, 2007) and Hampton (2009). What is meant by this is that an emphasis on the *constitutive* function of speech and action needs to be introduced and that traditional emphases on institutions and formal procedure need at least slightly to be adjusted with this in mind. In this view, politics is essentially constructed out of its performances rather than the performances largely being in a relationship of reflection to pre-given structures (Hampton, 2009). Certainly, the scale and intensity of contemporary political mediation, aided by digital technology, has brought regular and extensive political performance into the media, and the circulation of recordings of it (leading to counter-performances and re-performances) have more centrally entered into daily public space. During periods of perceived 'crisis' (at the individual or party level if not the national), the 'tour of the studios' both by those seeking advantage and those seeking damage control reaches unprecedented levels of relay and repeat performance.[3] The new terms of mediation have also increased, as our material shows, the range of informal as well as established modes of political discourse. With the arrival of David Cameron, there was a new 'colloquialization' of Conservative address, a strengthening of the 'relaxed' mode following on in many ways from the demotic re-styling that Tony Blair had introduced into the policy language of New Labour but which had not transferred itself smoothly or convincingly into the period of the Brown premiership (see Busby, 2009). It was Cameron, not Brown, who was regularly dubbed the 'heir to Blair', a title Cameron even awarded himself privately (Helm, 2010).

Of course, we are talking here primarily about 'visible' performance designed to advance policy initiatives, justify decisions and counter the sources of criticism rather than the range of 'invisible' performances that are generated as part of political office (some of which unintentionally enter public space through the now routine episodes of leaked emails, Freedom of Information requests and leaked conversational exchanges). In a recent review of the ways in which theatrical metaphors apply to politics, Martin Jay (2010) has noted how 'like the historical narratives that are so often mobilized as a rationale for political action, [political performances] can be understood as expressing a finite number of tropological emplotments that recur again and again, albeit with infinite variations' (p. 108). This sense of repetition or near repetition, both in political performances themselves, the tropes and narrative patterns they employ, and then in the generic rendering of them across the media according to different imaginative recipes, is something that is amply borne out by our analyses, as is the capacity of digital archiving to make performative 'inconsistency' immediately, embarrassingly and often comically visible. The remediations of Bigotgate, discussed later, brings to mind Marx's oft-cited quotation that history repeats itself, 'first as tragedy then as farce', with digital technologies condensing the experience to a single week in a politician's life. We look now at three dimensions of the theming of politicians across the genres.

Leadership

During the period of our audit, the portrayal of leadership achieved what was perhaps an unprecedented prominence due to the way in which the

Leaders' Debates dominated coverage of the general-election campaign. (For a varied discussion of these debates see, for example, Wring and Ward, 2010; Bailey, 2011; Boulton and Roberts, 2011; Coleman et al., 2011; Lawes and Hawkins, 2011; Pattie and Johnston, 2011.) Previous elections had, of course, always put the matter of the leadership qualities of party leaders (and therefore of potential prime ministers) into the spotlight, leading to strenuous 'leaderly' claims-making and display. However, by having three major TV events at which the three party leaders made their pitch alongside each other and according to an agreed protocol, the issue of leadership was projected with a new directness of comparative performance. The widely used analogy of the 'talent show' (*X Factor*) model, often employed disparagingly but not always, is testimony to this and we have discussed the ways in which parliamentary sketch-writers and cartoonists, as well as a variety of generic forms in broadcasting, made great imaginative play with the nature of the events, including their character as visual spectacle. What the *Leaders' Debates* brought out, albeit in a heightened form, were some of the tensions around 'democratic leadership', which we tracked at several stages throughout our analyses. Prominent here is the play-off between leadership as telling and leadership as listening, and between leadership as ideologically firm, or as flexible and pragmatic. The *Leaders' Debates* introduced a new and demanding dimension to the performance of leadership potential simply by requiring questioning and interchange between the three leaders, making it necessary not just to make an effective pitch to the studio and TV audience directly but to manage 'leaderly' relationships with fellow competitors in a way that accorded maximum comparative advantage. As some of our material noted and worked upon, 'reasonableness' and 'agreement' became important features of performance as well as 'strength of opinion' and disputation. Perhaps one of the most notable features of this was the 'I agree with Nick' phrasing used both by Brown and by Cameron in the first of the *Leaders' Debates*, in part a strategic device to construct some bridging between their own positions and that of a complicating (and formally equal) 'third party' within the adversarial frame, one with the initial advantage of novelty and little previous contamination by the exercising of direct political power at the national level. In Brown's case (his 'I agree' usage was by far the heaviest) this was reinforced by the need to shore up what was widely seen, on its own, as the diminished brief he had to put before the country for his re-election.

'Listening', a heightened responsiveness to public opinion and mood, was projected as a key part of governmental practice, a dimension of 'leading' rather than its reverse, in the last years of the Labour government, following a period in which there emerged a widespread, popular sense of policies being formed at too imperious a remove from realities and proper forms of consultation, including Parliament.[4] Interestingly, avowals of listening quickly became a central part of the coalition project (Coleman and Blumler, 2011). This partly followed from devolutionary, decentralising ambitions (within which the idea of 'the Big Society', with its implicit anti-statist sentiments, was a dominant Conservative theme). However, it was also, in its conveying of a withdrawal from bold assertion, strategically useful in the light of the compromises around policy made necessary by the coalition agreement. It continued to be so in 2011 when a number of policy initiatives, including those to do with the restructuring of the NHS, had to be slowed down and then substantially revised, attracting extensive cross-generic attention from the media.[5] In general, the media's portrayal of 'listening', as with the idea of 'the Big Society', was a sceptical one. The dominant interpretation taken, even by sections of the Conservative press made newly alert to signs of 'weakness' in political direction by the very nature of the coalition agreement, was that this was largely a PR exercise rather than a significant attempt to shift the character of politician–people relations and significantly revise the routes taken by decision-making.

It will be useful to comment here on how questions of 'party' figured in the material we examined, since 'party' remain a fundamental unit both of (antagonistic) political organization and of political commentary, however much strong individuals are seen to symbolize, essentialize and even displace it. Although we identify party allegiances, some explicit and some not, in the generic range, the period of our study saw long periods in which the public status of all three parties might be judged as moderate to low (according to a range of opinion polls indicating levels of satisfaction across all the policy areas), a factor which played into mainstream and alternative mediations. The Labour Party was clearly in difficulties during the period of its election defeat right through to the re-election of a new leader in autumn 2010. The victory of Ed Miliband over his brother, long predicted to be the next Labour leader, produced not only 'surprise' narratives but also 'concern', given the way in which union support had carried him through to a narrow win. As we illustrated in Chapter 2, a number of mediations positioned him firmly, if unfairly, as 'Red Ed', requiring him to make rapid and strenuous moves towards exchanging an ideological for a pragmatic identity to prevent the acquired label from becoming a serious constraint. This created challenges familiar from other attempts to rework leader identities and alignments with different constituencies, including that of 'over-correction'.[6] Even within party ranks, the revival of party fortunes is still, in 2012, widely seen as uncertain in direction and pace.[7]

The Conservative Party had entered the election with a good level of party confidence. This followed an extended period in which Cameron's attempt to 'decontaminate the brand' by distancing himself from Thatcherite policies, together with the taking up of a variety of Green initiatives and polices with a strongly social democratic character on social welfare and crime, had unnerved although not finally alienated a portion of the core membership holding more inflexibly to the traditional Conservative-policy agenda and values. With a widespread, earlier expectation that he would win the election decisively if not by a large majority, the 'hung Parliament' outcome was a disappointment to many in the Conservative Party and their media supporters, although it was an indication of an inability of the party to convince enough of the electorate, including many former supporters, that it should be put into government. Some of our analyses have shown how the spectre of a 'hung Parliament' and then the negotiated coalition with the Liberal Democrats, produced a sustained range of negative coverage, particularly within the Conservative media. Some of this negativity continues and in certain areas (e.g. aspects of social policy, taxation and attitudes to Europe) has worsened.

For the Liberal Democrats, the election campaign and then the coalition deal might appear to be an unqualified success, even allowing for the phase of 'excessive hope' following the first of the *Leaders' Debates*, when some indications suggested a massive swing towards the party on the strength of Nick Clegg's performance, a swing that was not sustained. However, the negotiated deal, although it brought a generally welcome and (given the final polling results) unexpected move into government, also produced anxieties within sections of the rank and file about unacceptable compromise and its implication for the independent future of the party. This concern continued, fuelled both by substantive worries about the abandonment of Lib Dem promises (of which that not to raise university tuition fees was the most dramatic instance) and a drop in popular support throughout the country. The position of the party within national civic culture is clearly more volatile than that of the other two parties, having a smaller base for retrenchment and having undergone a quite drastic (if avowedly temporary) change of political identity in relation to a number of core policies, among which are university tuition fees, regulation of the financial sector, deficit-reduction measures and welfare reform. In this context, it is not surprising that the position and performance of the Liberal Democrats, and particularly Clegg, was a recurring point of reference for generic work throughout our study. The involvement of the party in government created a new, uncertain and sometimes comic, dimension to what in many other respects were familiar elements of the 'national politics show', enriching the generic and tropological possibilities for portrayal.

Party alignments, then, were important factors in determining the character that mediations took, but they were less direct and predictable than in many earlier political periods, with high levels of internal dissent, public uncertainty and relative disenchantment being reflected in the kinds of descriptions and commentary offered both in the news and across the range of mediations we examined, including comedy. One continuing feature of the situation, reflected in some of the material from the latter part of our study, is the way in which the reporting of the government's actions routinely included speculation as to the involvement of both of the coalition partners, or of specific individuals from both 'sides'. This focus on internal tensions and differences within a two-party governmental frame has to some extent, and for the time being, displaced or decentred the model of the 'government (party) versus opposition (party)' axis which has provided the framework for political news, rumour, gossip, commentary and humour in the past, with the Labour Party reportedly making a 'serious complaint' to the BBC in January 2012 over the perceived imbalance in political coverage (Helm, 2012).

Suspicion

Principles concerning trust are clearly a core element of democratic political action, including claims-making and the kind of 'hearing' claims get. They involve, among other things, trust in the honouring of the representative function, a requirement that applies to all professional politicians as part of their basic role performance. In relation to political leaders, it becomes intensified and more strongly personalized as trust in the capacity and motives to make major judgments in the national interest. Trustworthiness is partly a matter of feeling able to 'take politicians at their word' and therefore matters of clarity, coherence, honesty and consistency in the words used run through a wide range of our material. It is also, of course, a matter of actions and therefore of the possible discrepancy between words and actions, another key feature of the generic work we have examined. Throughout the period studied, trust in British politicians to pursue the 'best' policies for the country was problematic. This was the result of a number of factors, including the continuing resonance of the decisions to invade Iraq and then to engage in major armed conflict in Afghanistan without, in either case, a clear equivalence of results to effort being widely perceived. The management of the financial crisis of 2008 and subsequent policy towards the banking sector and then towards public spending also led to doubts about the relationship between government pronouncements and effective action in the national interest. Perhaps, however, the most intensively mediated event concerning relations of political trust in Britain was the MPs' expenses scandal of 2009, which we have noted earlier and will touch on further below. This led to a major running story about the kinds of deception that MPs had used to gain optimum expenses within the Westminster system. The list of those involved was extensive across all political parties and at various levels of office. It was seen by some commentators to have caused an irreparable rift of trust between politicians and the people, a breach of the fundamental 'political contract'. However, despite the continuing presence of expenses as an active point of reference throughout our material, certainly in the period up to spring 2010, we were surprised by the extent to which the election campaign and then the formation of a new government were mediated within assumed terms of system and governance not greatly different from those that had preceded the scandal.[8] In that sense, the 'rift', the 'watershed moment', that some had seen in the 2009 events proved to be a misreading.

In much contemporary political analysis, assessing levels and kinds of suspicion might prove to be a more useful point of entry than levels and kinds of trust, given the extent of popular scepticism about official politics and democratic political efficacy, albeit a scepticism operating at different intensities and subject to periods of strengthening or reduction. Our material shows how the final months of the Brown government was widely portrayed as irredeemably undercut by distrust across a number of policy areas (a distrust that sometimes fed into directly personal gossip and leaks regarding the prime minister's own disposition and behaviour).[9] Following 'Bullygate', questions over Brown's character were to re-emerge in sensational form during the election campaign following a challenging on-the-street conversation about immigration with a lifelong Labour supporter, Gillian Duffy. In what he judged to be the privacy of his car shortly afterwards, Brown was heard on his clip-on radio microphone (which accidentally he had left on) referring to Duffy as a 'bigoted woman'. The incident became known as 'Bigotgate'. It was not so much the 'routine' hypocrisy of an overheard private judgment having to be retracted that was at issue in this case, but the sense of incompetence and of personal 'unravelling', which the incident served to portray.

The Coalition government's formation out of negotiated but continuingly uneasy bi-party agreement and the immediate framing of its policy within the terms of radical deficit reduction have clearly continued to provide ample space for suspicion as to the 'real intentions' behind ministerial moves and pronouncements, as well for continuing widespread public anxiety about national and household economies, and both the possibilities and the likely timescale for 'recovery'.

Among the established reasons for being suspicious of politicians is the possibility of deception (for recent commentaries, see Runciman, 2008; Corner, 2010; Jay, 2010). However, a level of mendacity in political claims-making (in relation, for instance, to motives, expected outcomes, what was known and when) has become an expected, edging towards 'accepted', part of political discourse. In this respect, a comparison can be made with advertising and other kinds of promotional work. Here whatever the sense of communicative misdemeanour which might follow from being led to believe something that later turned out to be untrue or unsubstantiated, perceptions of specific 'bad communication' occur in the context of the wider assumption that a measure of strategic deceit is an element of the entire field of practice and it would be a mistake (of naivety) on the part of the recipient not to relate to communications with this in mind. The extensive use of the term 'spin' in coverage of British political communications from the late 1990s through to approximately the mid 2000s bears witness to the ambivalent attitude to deception often taken (see Andrews, 2006, for a useful review). At one point in this period, 'spin' was the focus of sustained and critical media attention, as a new and potent threat to the democratic process. However, its steady, routine use to cover a very wide range of kinds of promotional strategy had the effect of at least partly naturalising it, of 'quietening down' the critical edge it once carried. Claims were made about a 'post-spin' politics by all parties, but these were widely seen as gestural rather than part of a committed attempt to revise the ethics and, more importantly, the structures of media–political relations. Only particular kinds and degrees of deception rise above the assumptions concerning the general pervasiveness of the 'strategic' in politics to become the object of specific complaint. As our material shows, certain modes of political deceit by exaggeration and omission (particularly in election campaigning) are widely treated by the media both as 'part of the game' yet also as 'fair target', and their trans-generic mediation reflects this ambivalence. We can contrast this with the kinds of 'un-licensed' deceit that appeared to be at work in the MPs' expenses scandal (a form of unacceptable 'fiddling') and the major strategic deceit suspected of being at work in the preparation of the case for invading Iraq in 2003. This latter was seen as a deceit too fundamental and grave to be adequately captured by the established semantics of 'spin' and it resulted in the widespread rendering of Tony Blair's name as 'Tony Bliar' together with a wide range of sharply critical treatments of Blair across the full generic spread at the time.

It is important to note that during the early months of our main study period, the political field was organized around an upcoming election and the campaign itself, thereby producing a strong politics of competitive 'selling', in which advertising and promotion models derived from commercial practice were dominant and widely perceived to be so. As with the Blair and Brown governments, it is the continuation of these models beyond the period of official party competition for office, and into 'normal' communicative relationship between government and public, that may continue to pose a problem for the Coalition, partly as a consequence of the way in which the 'permanent campaign' idea has become an established part of British politics. However, during most of our study period, questions of deceit did not become a major issue, perhaps only entering the frame significantly again in 2011 following questions about David Cameron's relationship with former and current News International staff in the wake of the phone-hacking scandal.[10]

Venality

Venality has a long history of being seen as a primary reason why people enter politics and/or stay in it. Clearly, the expenses scandal gave this position, most crudely expressed in the 'snouts in the trough' phrase, vigorous refreshment and many examples, particularly from the early period of our study, worked strongly with the idea. Along with the fallout from the MPs' expenses scandal, a Channel 4 *Dispatches* documentary broadcast in March 2010 and a *Sunday Times* investigation exposed four Labour ex-ministers (Geoff Hoon, Stephen Byers, Patricia Hewitt and Richard Caborn) for offering their services to lobbying firms for thousands of pounds per day in breach of Parliament rules. This 'cash for access' scandal became known as 'Lobbygate' (Wintour and Stratton, 2010). The 'corruptibility' of politicians in respect of monetary rewards shows diverse national histories, partly in relation to the nature of the inter-elite connections and opportunities available and seen to be at work. However, alongside the risks to political integrity posed by forms of bribery, fiddling and elite forms of 'moonlighting' (the legal taking on of paid roles in private companies and in the media while continuing to perform as a salaried politician), the broader relation of politicians and political parties to sectors of private industry, nationally and internationally, is frequently at issue. During the period of our study, the strengthening position of the Conservative Party, finally the dominant party of government, with its declared commitments towards the private sector and a known hostility towards areas of the public sector, was frequently a factor incorporated in the writing, speech and images we examined. The sense of a re-alignment in favour not only of the private sector but of 'fat cats' within it was inevitably compounded by the continuing suspicion about the firmness with which the finance industries would be regulated in the wake of the banking crisis of 2008.[11] Continuing indignation about the bonuses paid to chief executives whose institutions had drawn on taxpayer rescue packages, within a context now defined by governmental calls for austerity, was a strong element in the 'national political picture' as portrayed across a range of broadcast, print and web materials. Its generic formulation, even when extending to comedy, was often angry. More generally, claims to be 'all in this together' when it came to the need for economic restraint following excess, pushed the political rhetoric of national commonality regularly past the point of general acquiescence, creating a central point of tension and potentially of disorder, which is reflected in many texts from the latter part of our study, continuing through to the period in which we are writing.[12]

Political framings

Under this heading, we want to examine (in some cases, to re-examine) three broad ways in which the work we collected and analysed was framed in terms of what we can call its dominant tone and mood. First of all, we want to look at the question of the emotional and the affective within politics and within political mediation, since this came up on a number of occasions and is subject to radically varying judgments. We then want to explore further the ways in which comedy figured in generic approaches, since variations of the idea that politicians and political acts had a strongly comic, if not farcical, character was perhaps the most dominant tendency at work in the texts we collected. Finally, we look at the issue of critiques and alternatives, asking the question of how far and in what ways the mediations under scrutiny offered substantive criticism of political affairs and perhaps posed ideas about change and reform.

Affectivity

Politics has complex and shifting relationships with the realm of emotions, particularly during periods of relative systemic stability rather than periods of heightened conflict or transition, in which more 'passionate' forms become common both in the speech of politicians and in more general public expression. Although it is generally thought a good idea for politicians to 'feel strongly' about certain core political values, as one marker of their fitness for office, the appearance of the 'emotional' in political performance carries risks for the ways in which it will be mediated and perceived unless it is seen to be firmly contextualized by good levels of rationality and by 'self-control'. The strategic leaking out of personal emotion – of pity, regret or anger – into a phrase or gesture can work to 'humanize' political discourse, but within many political cultures, including the British, it can at a certain point begin to signal 'loss of control' and thereby undercut authority and status. Emotions are placed as the adjuncts to political values and positions, the dimension of 'feeling', which lies behind the thinking and the doing and which connects the politician as a person who professionally 'cares' for the well-being of those he or she represents and 'leads'. Their display in this respect and the open acknowledgment of them by politicians works usefully against ideas of 'coldness' and 'distance' within a media culture that has given increasing attention to emotional life across many different kinds of output and become steadily more suspicious of modes of emotional denial.[13] However, as indicated, the positioning, character and scale of the emotional can, by relatively minor shifts, move out of the current conventional frames for judging what is 'natural' and into a space where they generate concern and criticism. This is particularly true in a mediated political culture where, as we have indicated earlier, gossip and rumour play such a part in originating and sustaining stories, especially those about the 'true character' of political figures whose prominence places them within the contemporary celebrity circuit (among the many broad accounts of this phenomenon is Turner, 2004).

So far in this chapter we have referred back to the body of examples cited in previous chapters, rather than citing details of particular cases. However, in discussion of emotional display in political performance some specific illustration may be helpful given the relatively 'non-routine' nature of these instances. As we have noted earlier in Chapter 3, one running story during 2010, drawing on a number of sources of varying credibility and widely subject to generic, including comic, treatment, concerned the extent to which Gordon Brown could be considered a 'bully' (Rawnsley, 2010). The 'Bullygate' story was essentially one about Brown's personality and his 'affective management'. If his behaviour could be represented as a passionate commitment to getting results and an intolerance of delay and inefficiency (as Brown himself claimed in interviews) then it could be seen as 'justified emotion' in the pursuit of political solutions, an impatience and a tendency for occasional outbursts aligning positively with illustrious precedents, including Churchill, and having strong parallels both in the military and corporate spheres. However, if the stories suggested something 'wilder', as many did (involving allegations of verbal abuse and the throwing of objects), then a much more negative evaluation entered public space. In this framing, not only was Brown guilty of 'loss of control' in a way that questioned his fitness for office (and in an extreme reading, signalled a degree of 'personality disorder'), he was also guilty of seriously bad practice, bordering on the 'criminal', in his occupational behaviour towards juniors. Right to the end of his period of office, Brown was unable effectively to remove this dimension of 'emotional volatility', read as a *symptomatic weakness*, from his routine media portrayal.

Other politicians during our period of analysis were the subject of generic work around their emotional states, but most often these were tightly worked around isolated incidents (e.g. verbal outbursts of 'rudeness', especially in interview) rather than cohering into a pattern and a generalized interpretation of personality.

Within the world of political emotion, while the 'outburst' is nearly always newsworthy, crying constitutes a special and rare case, since, unlike the performative variations of anger or rudeness, involving different levels of self-awareness, tears usually indicate a temporary 'breakdown' of public persona, which will almost always be found highly noteworthy and carry attendant risks. Here again, Gordon Brown provides an illustration in his TV interview with Piers Morgan for the series *Life Stories* in February 2010. During this interview, the then prime minister started to become a little tearful when recalling the very early death of his first child, born prematurely. This 'revealing' moment had been extensively trailed in broadcasting and the press. In an edition of *The Andrew Marr Show*, Marr referred to the upcoming interview and cited the *Mail on Sunday*'s 'Exclusive' headline that 'Brown Weeps on Television' (7 February) in an interview with Alastair Campbell.[14] He pointed to Campbell's role in advising the prime minister on strategy and commented: 'This business that Brown weeps on television, I mean it's not what we really want in politics is it, that kind of heart on sleeve, he never wanted to do that?' In this judgement, not only is a 'we' readily established to disapprove of the action, but it is judged that Brown himself was somehow an unwitting or reluctant performer encouraged into the celebrity-style, intimate interview by Campbell and Piers Morgan. Another TV show going out before the interview itself, *The Daily Politics*, also posed the question directly and in a way that presumed a negative answer – 'Should politicians get emotional?' (8 February).

Across the period of our study, this incident, as with that of 'bullying' discussed above, clearly has distinctive features related to the prominence of Brown and the intensive scrutiny he was routinely receiving in the run-up to the general election. However, the character of the widespread media treatments given to the affair, some of them significantly working as 'trailers' in advance of the event itself,[15] brings out with illuminating directness the nature of the established public frames for assessing the role and fitness of emotional display by politicians and the criteria that might be used for judging 'acceptability'. It illustrates that not only may emotional display be viewed as 'weakness' but that, rather than being read as a strong sign of authenticity, it can be viewed as another deceptive ploy designed to win a positive response, one all the more cynical for its operation at the level of feelings rather than ideas (a reaction we noted in discussion of our respondent groups in Chapter 4).

It is not surprising, given the generally constrained, rather fugitive, role allowed for explicit emotions in political performance, that mediations of the political across a variety of genres regularly introduce, as a device of intensification and often of subversion, a strongly affective element in portrayals of politicians and political processes. Examples in all the preceding chapters show this at work in written, spoken and visual forms. Such elements can be seen, in some measure, as serving to 'put the emotion' back into politics, thereby 'correcting' the rationalist and rationalising tendencies of official political discourse, even allowing for the conventions of acceptable emotionality discussed above. The function of affective devices, as they occur for instance in descriptions, mimicry and fictional portrayal, is often to connect appearances back to realities, the controlled outer behaviour to the volatile inner state, the 'high' stated motive to 'low' primary drives. The sober and often ritualized discourse of official politics is thereby destabilized and undercut by, among other things, sheer affective energy, sometimes expressed in deliberate and vigorous vulgarity (as, for instance, in a sketch-show spoof). Indeed, the behind-the-scenes behaviours exposed in both the 'Bullygate' and 'Bigotgate' episodes appeared to replicate or imitate the plotting and coarse language of the popular comedy series about political public relations, *The Thick of It* (BBC2), compounding their dramaturgical resonances. Whatever may be the conventional protocols of civic orientation, such mediations cue an engagement with the political in which considerable emotional colour combines with the cognitive work of judging policy, performances and outcomes. This is clearly exemplified in the comments of our respondents, discussed in the previous chapter. Such 'colour' is, of course, a frequent ingredient in the various recipes for political comedy, a framing to which we now turn.

Comedy

At many points in our analysis, we have explored the comic dimension of mediations across a wide array of generic forms. Comedy has a long history as an approach to articulating political deficits, with forms of 'satire' accorded a key role as a mode of critique (see, for instance, Hodgart and Connery, 2009, for an overview and Day, 2011, for a recent commentary on satirical TV and politics). 'Satire' suggest a comedy of serious political intent but, as our examples in the earlier chapters suggests, within many modern societies there is a much broader and various comic realm in which raillery, mocking and spoofing of 'official' national life continues more as a routine accompaniment to governance than a critical threat to it. Viewed thus, it can be regarded as a cultural complement to the maintenance of established political structures, although it can also be seen, even by sections of the established order which might be thought to benefit from it, to risk trivialising matters that civic participation should take more seriously.

However articulated, comic mediations of politics are marked as strongly affective, working from, and upon, emotional patterns concerning politics and politicians. This differs radically from the appearance of emotionalism in political display (discussed above) since the emotion is generated in the *perceiver* (via mediation) of political performance, mostly a performance that has been projected as vigorously rational whatever the forms of distortion, addition and omission which have been introduced by the depictive work. As we indicated above, the humour to be found in contemplating (and enjoying) the 'obvious' deficits in political claims ostensibly grounded in 'public rationality' but where motives of self-interest and of narrow party interest appear to be primary is a staple of cartoons as well as other forms of generic practice.

Citizens may find many aspects of politics amusing in themselves but the 'culture of comedy' around politics is greatly encouraged and influenced by the range of comic treatments encountered in the routine mediations of broadcasting, the press and the web. Amusement and laughter, whatever their cognitive stimulation, can be seen to be positioned as moments of expressive 'release' within the broader context of individual civic consciousness. In part, the enjoyment of comic portrayals, as is evident in the accounts of our respondents in Chapter 4, are a way of 'getting back' symbolically at elite political managers (including their attempts at managing the terms of their mediation), temporarily re-balancing the experience if not the reality of power relations through phases of considered disrespect. Projected as aestheticized 'play' by their frequent recourse to forms of self-conscious exaggeration and the fancifully imaginative, comedic treatments can make connections with more serious, critical thinking about civic space, here combining with a range of other resources including the diverse inputs of 'news' as well as direct experience (forms of linkage which deserve further research attention). However, they can also work essentially as regular moments of 'fun' against the background of what is primarily a distant, resigned, acquiescent or even supportive perception of the dominant order. Here, as we suggested, they can operate in a way that is complementary to existing political arrangements even if this is not a planned outcome; an agreeable release of frustration, distrust and dislike that does not significantly re-orient civic sentiment or generate civic action. (In Corner et al. (2012), we explore the complexities of orientation involved here in more detail.)

Critique

The issue of critique clearly follows on directly from those we have considered above. Looking at the full range of the material we collected, what does it indicate about the way that the media, outside of their core news output, pose questions about the political scene and assess, more broadly, the prevailing character of 'the political'? Certainly, as we have shown, across the diverse generic work analysed, the political world is often placed at a distance, as a distinctive realm whose very disconnection with ordinary concerns and conventions provides ample scope for generic attention. In different ways, the broadcasters, writers, bloggers and cartoonists whose work we have looked at often make their main appeal to audiences and readerships by generating and sustaining (sometimes by exaggerating) this 'relationship of difference'. Insofar as this is a 'critical distance' it is primarily critical of political character and political behaviour rather than of political institutions and structures. A notable exception to this just outside the main period of our survey was the MPs' expenses scandal, to which we have frequently referred, a phase of political mediation in which deficits of personal character and behaviour were emphatically signalled but often in ways which connected outwards to perceived deficits in the expenses system and often more widely in aspects of the 'Westminster Culture'. However, we commented above how the 'structural' damage done to British politics by the expenses revelations does not seem to have been as widespread and fundamental as some commentators at the time predicted.

Alongside the highlighting of the inconsistencies, excesses and evasions of political claims-making, a direct and often obvious focus for attention, the most frequent and regular areas of critical comment are, not surprisingly, the spheres of policy. During the period of our study, the most important of these spheres was the economy, with the Labour and then Coalition strategy to reduce the national deficit a regular and dominant topic. Although there were sustained attempts by the Coalition to project the deficit as primarily the result of the Labour government's mismanagement and overspending, the narrative of the banking crisis of 2008/2009 still retained its prominence in mediated accounts across the genres and in a number of colourful ways. The issue of the extent and rate of cuts in public sector budgets, when placed in the context of the need to re-start economic growth and avoid the risk of a 'double dip' recession by measures of fiscal stimulus, was the focus for treatment within diverse generic approaches. Related to this was the policy on the City, or the financial sector, where mediations variously connected with a widespread public feeling that 'bankers' had got off too lightly in the kinds of regulatory measure introduced or proposed and that the continuation of large bonuses was an insult to any idea of a shared austerity. Whereas the area of macro-economic policy quickly became a matter of competing 'technical' abstractions and a transposition to shifting international (notably European) contexts, not easily represented in the kind of genres we looked at, the issue of the re-regulation of the City allowed a range of 'types', 'caricatures' and narratives of disgrace to emerge to provide accounts with a personalized and strongly ethical character, which would be worth a study of its own. The behaviour of the City became a realm of national moral drama equalling that of the MPs' expenses scandal a year earlier. A further development out of the economic policy area, continuing as we write, is what can be called the 'civil order' question, involving the extent and intensity of civil protest, including strikes, against cuts in public sector and welfare budgets, and the kinds of government response to these events, together with the broader public perception of them (the pattern of alignments and sympathies). What were essentially sub-areas of economic policy during the period, including most importantly the restructuring of the NHS and revisions to aspects of educational funding, also received attention (including in cartoons) at the points where they 'peaked' in relation to policy announcements and to reaction by public bodies.

Of the foreign-affairs issues that fed into mediation across the range we examined, 'war on terror'-related policies, including historical decisions, provided regular points of critical reference, with the hearings of the Chilcot Inquiry into the Iraq war and legal concerns over suspected MI5 involvement in the torture of Guantanamo detainees persisting as thorny topics. But it was the Afghanistan war that provided the most regular point of critical reference over the year. This continued the steady negative assessment of policy in the region, which had been a factor in all mediations, including importantly news output, from at least 2008. The sense of a conflict in which the losses (and the expense) increasingly outweighed any discernible gains either in regional stability or domestic security was a theme routinely present, including in 'angry' articulation. By contrast, British and European involvement in the Libyan conflict of 2011, after our audit had concluded, was perceived in rather different terms despite initial anxieties – as better managed strategically and politically, more successful in its outcomes, and of course entailing no loss of British military lives.

We have suggested that in none of these policy areas was criticism of such a kind to connect with a more fundamental questioning of the political and economic order. Only in respect of the banking crisis, the peak of which occurred before the period of our study, were there any suggestions within mainstream mediation that 'deep structural reform' was needed as part of the remedy, perhaps reform that reconsidered established forms of capitalist organization and the political commitment to growth.[16] However, for the most part even the very mention of 'capitalism' in public statements during the period of our study risked attracting a mainstream suspicion of moving towards an unacceptable radicalism of perspective. Vince Cable found this out, when as Industry Secretary speaking at his party's annual conference, he noted that 'capitalism takes no prisoners', before moving on to a more qualified and nuanced commentary almost entirely within the terms of market globalization. Deliberately provocative (although to what specific end remains a little in doubt) this was widely picked up in the Conservative press and led to a range of public criticisms from business leaders, some of whom questioned the fitness for office of anyone holding such views or perhaps even daring to name the dominant economic system.[17]

What about alternatives? Clearly it is not within the generic profile of most of the work we have looked at to outline alternatives with any explicitness or detail. Whereas critique lends itself to a variety of attractive polemical and comic stylings, alternatives require a degree of expositional sobriety and readerly engagement that restricts them to a quite narrow range of mainstream outputs, although as we have shown to some extent in Chapter 3, the web has significantly increased the options here. Alternatives to the specific speech, behaviour and policies critically portrayed are often implicit, sometimes trading on the 'obviousness' of the perceived deficits, as self-evident lapses against which more 'sensible' or more 'honest' options need little further specification. In some of the work we have examined, policy areas were judged deficient or even absurd according primarily to 'ethical' values (e.g. what is clearly 'fair'; what is 'just') although more deliberative, pragmatic grounds were also introduced (what will 'work'; what is 'realistic'; what represents an acceptable opportunity-cost).

We have suggested that across much of what we looked at, there was little sense that any major systemic reform to the present political order, as opposed to policy shifts or policy initiatives, was needed to produce, for instance, wider democratic participation or greater social and economic equality. Politics was seen as a flawed practice, an arena in which many flawed individuals operated, but this flawing was regarded as having a strongly endemic dimension and to be subject, in any case, to extensive qualification, thus limiting the imaginative sense of how the conduct of political business might be significantly different, let alone the offering of serious proposals for achieving this.

Under this heading, it is worth noting finally how the citizen was positioned in the material discussed. The citizen, as listener, viewer or reader, was situated at a distance from the political core, the authors of the material sometimes sharing this position but sometimes acting as a 'bridge', locating themselves, perhaps by tonal indicators of familiarity, closer to the political sphere than their audiences or readerships. A sense of public and civic identity, of 'us-ness', sometimes a baffled, indignant or angry 'us-ness', was at times explicit and at times merely a matter of tone and implication. That 'we' were affected by 'their' decisions was generally clear as a working assumption; professional politics 'mattered', it exerted its influence across national life in ways which provided the rationale for the kinds of mediation produced. However, a sense of distance was generally presented as something largely to be preserved rather than replaced by forms of active participation, particularly those forms extending beyond the established channels. Here, the non-news mediation of civil protest, including strike action, will perhaps provide an increasingly sensitive and significant dimension of generic work (including comic work) in the future.

Throughout the period we examined, all of the party leaders made claims and promises about a 'new politics', beginning with Brown. Some of these claims were reactive attempts at drawing a line under bad events, responding to circumstances like the MPs' expenses affair; some were clearly election oriented, or brought about by the novel circumstances of the Coalition. The phrase is a significant one for our study insofar as its sweeping generality, challenging any implementation even were that seriously intended, points towards the continuing *sentiment* of wholesale change which politicians have felt it necessary to articulate from time to time.[18] Here, they have taken their cue partly from their perception of a broader civic disenchantment and disconnection to which at least a degree of rhetorical attention regularly needs to be paid.

Re-framing our research along thematic lines in the present chapter has allowed us to synthesize observations on significant characterizations of politics, politicians and policy decisions across a range of media forms, foregrounding subject matter over the specifics of mediation and generic space. Our observations have reached not only across the year 2010 as a whole, but also back into the recent past, with reference to the 2003 war in Iraq, the 2008/2009 banking crisis and the 2009 MPs' expenses scandal; into the future with references to civil disorder in the summer of 2011; and outward to less directly political aspects of the cultural scene. These observations also map across from the synoptic to the specific, for example connecting general points about the role of emotion in political culture with the particular incidents of February 2010, which provoked media attention to just this phenomenon. In the latter part of this chapter, we retrace the above thematic discussion of politicians, political emotions, comedy, suspicion and critique, but here we return to the coded data set of texts that we assembled in 2010 as the core resource for our research, and thus provide quantitative support for our interpretative overview, and for the thematic interconnections that we are able to track across media forms. Below, we re-introduce the nature of the corpus and database before presenting findings on the prominence and treatment of key actors and themes.

Tracking political themes across our 2010 corpus

Our corpus was, as explained in the Introduction to the book, never intended as the sole basis for the analysis we proposed to undertake, but rather to contribute in two main ways to that analysis. We required the database to act as an archive for the instructively varied and characteristic texts in our corpus, which we could draw upon in the development of our enquiries into the generic forms of political mediation – the kind of work represented in Chapters 1–3. We also designed the database to provide a detailed profile of those generic resources, one which, through our own selections and codings, could then be interrogated quantitatively. So, in addition to storing digitized versions of our programmes, texts, cartoons and blogposts (i.e. the primary material in our corpus), the measures and variables recorded in the database enabled the quick and straightforward mark-up and retrieval of particular political performances or themes across a diverse range of media forms and genres. We anticipated that we would use quantitative information as a complement to predominantly qualitative analysis elsewhere in the research, and that this quantitative focus would be of more value on the thematic than the formal side of the research.

We coded the media content in our corpus as discrete 'message units' or records: for TV and radio, each unit was a single programme; for print the units were at article or cartoon level; for blogs, the units were the discrete blogposts.[19] We recognize a high level of commensurability is impossible to achieve across our diverse range of media forms, therefore, in the following discussion where we present percentages it is usually for a selected medium, rather than across the full data set. In addition to providing quantitative findings for a specific medium, we can note where and how key themes travelled across media forms and genres.

Due to the relative stability of our auditing sample across the three periods of data collection, we can track trends or differences not only cross-media but also across-time, by reference to numbers of 'mentions' of people or of themes. In the database we noted instances where certain types of actors appeared, both as 'participants' and as 'subjects' of discussion or dramatization. All actors were classed under six headings (Political People, Media, Interest Groups, Citizens, Celebrities and 'Other').[20] By removing duplicate codes within the categories for each record, we can determine which types of actors received attention, directly or indirectly, across our corpus. Likewise, for Political Issues, we can track which kinds of issues achieved a certain prominence across media forms and genres. It is these appearances that we have referred to as 'mentions' in the discussion below.

To offer some quantified thematic observations, we therefore now turn more specifically to the corpus, revisiting in the process some of the topics mentioned above, so as to give a firmer sense of the basis on which our earlier account rests, and to elaborate a little where it is possible to do so, with supporting data and examples.

Politicians

Given the selection of our media materials, it is perhaps not surprising that 'politicians' as a group garnered the most mentions as actor types. As an average across all three audit periods (February, Election, Autumn), TV was the medium most likely to feature political figures as participants or subjects, with 95 per cent of its programmes coded for the mention of one or more political actor. The Web was the medium least dominated by discussion of politicians, with 79.5 per cent of the blogs mentioning politicians (Radio had 93.8 per cent and Print 85.1 per cent). Only 'media actors' and 'citizens' come close to achieving the prominence of politicians in our broadcasting sample (with 76.6 and 71.1 per cent respectively on TV, and with 62.5 and 67.2 per cent on Radio), but this visibility is not replicated in Print media or in blog posts: as subjects, media actors achieve significant mentions in only 5.5 per cent of Print articles or cartoons, while citizens are mentioned in 15.4 per cent. In blogs, the figures are reversed slightly with 18.1 per cent for 'media actors' and 7.9 per cent for 'citizens'. So where politicians maintain between 80 and 95 per cent prominence across all media forms, other types of actor only manage substantial visibility in broadcast media – they feature much more sporadically in the mediated politics of cartoons, commentary, sketch-writing and blogs. In the kinds of media items we collected, politicians do appear to embody 'the political', as participants and subjects, with those people classed as 'citizens' gaining attention in TV genres (especially during the Election period), but not in the unregulated space of blogging.

Our auditing 'dips' into the mediated political year provided us with rich examples from which to explore aspects of political leadership: 'Bullygate' in February; the general election in April–May (including the *Leaders' Debates*, 'Bigotgate' and the coalition negotiations, the traditional focus on leader image during the election campaign and, finally, the Labour-leadership contest, with the added spice of a sibling rivalry played out at the highest public level. References to Brown, Cameron and Clegg were counted in the first two periods, while references to

Harriet Harman (as Deputy Labour Leader during the summer leadership contest) and Ed Miliband were included for the Autumn period (replacing Brown).

Interrogating the database for more discrete kinds of indicator, we can trace where political leaders featured as both subjects and participants. The findings support our earlier points on the dominance of political leaders in mediated political culture. This is especially marked in the Election period. Normally, third-party Liberal Democrat leaders rarely garner media attention outside of election time, and struggle for comparable coverage to the two main party leaders during the general-election campaign period, but in 2010 Nick Clegg's meteoric rise, from relative obscurity to 'Cleggmania', is a phenomenon supported by our figures. In our February audit, we recorded 'mentions' for Gordon Brown in 57.7 per cent of all TV programmes in our sample, with David Cameron also receiving sizeable coverage (at 42.4 per cent). In February, Nick Clegg is mentioned in only 15.2 per cent of the same programmes; and is further marginalized in other media forms, appearing in only 2.0 per cent of the blogposts, for example.

In the Election audit, the figures rise to 81.7 per cent for Brown, 84.1 per cent for Cameron and 85.4 per cent for Clegg, including their own appearances. The next named politician with the most coverage after the party leaders is Ed Balls, with 25.6 per cent of programmes. While these figures support the dominance of political leaders during election time, it is now the Liberal Democrat leader who achieves greatest visibility across TV genres. This pattern is repeated across our media selection: although Cameron garners more coverage than Clegg in Print media, the margin is surprisingly small, given Cameron's appointment as prime minister in this period (58.3 per cent of articles and cartoons, compared with 55.6 per cent for Clegg).

As we have noted in Chapter 2, editorial cartoons can offer a visceral treatment of 'the political' through depicting politicians in exaggerated and distorted forms; the resemblance to a real-life persona not always immediately obvious, but often heavy with symbolic and critical undercurrents. Out of the 118 cartoons coded in the Election period, 93 cartoons featured one or more of the three main party leaders (78.8 per cent). We should note here that inclusion could arise from being directly named in the caption, or the politician could be implied 'off-frame' but have some presence as the 'subject', perhaps on the other end of a pictured phone call. More obviously as an example of this kind of implied reference, on 2 May 2010, a Brown-shaped hole appears in the snow, rather than Brown himself (Adams, *Telegraph*). The televised *Leaders' Debates* likely played a part in this high number of cartoons depicting leaders – as Seymour-Ure has noted (2001, p. 348), cartoonists often draw on the TV image of political leaders. This would also help to explain Clegg's prominence in this media format, referenced in 53.4 per cent of all cartoons, compared with 59.3 per cent for Cameron and 38.9 per cent for Brown. In many cases the leaders appeared together in various combinations, with 26.3 per cent of cartoons depicting all three leaders together; while Cameron and Clegg's coalition agreement meant that a further 17.8 per cent referenced the two leaders together. In the same period, the next most prominent politician was Conservative front-bencher George Osborne, appearing (in some form of visual reference) in 11.0 per cent of cartoons.

By Autumn, Clegg's share of the media spotlight had diminished (mentioned in 35.7 per cent of TV programmes), with Cameron's prime ministerial role and Ed Miliband's victory in the Labour-leadership contest securing the two leaders a higher degree of visibility during the conference season (51.4 and 41.4 per cent respectively). This is the only period during which another named politician challenges the party leaders' dominance, with George Osborne's role in the Comprehensive Spending Review securing him *equal* coverage to Cameron across our TV sample, appearing as a subject or participant in 51.4 per cent of programmes. The nearest challenger to the top-four named politicians is, not surprisingly perhaps, Ed Miliband's brother, David (at 31.4 per cent).

As we have suggested, mediated politics is heavily focused on politicians as the primary focus of attention, and politicians do 'put themselves about' to get the right kind of attention for themselves, their parties and their policies. So far as party leaders are concerned, their visible and audible presence is managed much more via the news than in the kind of material we chose to audit. In February 2010, only Gordon Brown appeared as a 'participant' rather than as a 'subject' in a Radio or TV programme, and only once; interestingly, this is not in any traditional political genre, but on the celebrity chat show, *Piers Morgan's Life Stories* – an appearance we have already discussed. In the Election period, the leaders' presence as participants on TV and Radio was greater, due of course to their performances in the three *Leaders' Debates* as well as in the *Andrew Marr Show* (and in other interview programmes, e.g. with Jeremy Paxman, which we did not capture in the corpus). From the Autumn period we captured just one Radio appearance by Harriet Harman prior to Ed Miliband's election as leader, and one TV appearance each by Cameron, Clegg and Miliband, again on the *Andrew Marr Show*, part of the national ritual of the party-conference season. In the Autumn period, Cameron and Clegg also contribute their own columns in the Print media.

Political framings 1: emotion in mediated politics

Broadcasting is important here because it is the primary space where citizens encounter politics as public performance, and therefore where they might witness overt affectivity, as in the two notable cases of public 'crying' discussed in the preceding pages. The extent of media interest in these moments of public breakdown is itself testimony to the *rarity* of 'flooding out' or distress as a matter of performance, sincere or otherwise. Of course there is a distinction to be made between performers' emotions in respect of their own misfortunes, and their expressions of regret, sympathy, sadness, etc., for the misfortunes of others, where flooding out would be even more remarkable. We can take as an example an incident mentioned earlier in this chapter, Alastair Campbell's 'lapse' in an edition of the *Andrew Marr Show* on 7 February 2010 (see footnote 14), when he glanced down and started to become emotionally overcome after intensive questioning about Tony Blair's honesty in relation to the status and quality of the intelligence prior to the invasion of Iraq. This originates as no more than a few seconds of broadcast time, but recycling of it begins almost immediately via news broadcasts and online. Moreover, discussion of it spreads through the rest of the mediascape quickly and thoroughly. In our own materials we picked it up firstly in the blogosphere via '*Liberal Burblings*' on the same day as the programme itself ('Spare us the crocodile tears, Alastair'), then as part of the Monday daily media cycle (*Daily Politics, Daily Mail, Telegraph, The Wright Stuff*) followed later in the week by genres operating on a seven-day cycle (*Any Questions, Any Answers, Week in Westminster*).

If crying demonstrates vulnerability to the 'good' emotion of grief, then other things show vulnerability to 'bad' emotions in the general area of 'anger'. Gordon Brown was not so provoked as to publicly demonstrate the latter and was unwilling even to have it attributed to him, although his reputation for an off-camera bad temper was widespread. The 'Bullygate' episode therefore became a strong marker of his personal character, and not a positive one. 'Bullygate' was one of the political issues that we indexed, and in February 2010 when the story was current (see Chapter 3), it produced a full 83 mentions across all media platforms out of a total of 868 records or 'message units'

(9.6 per cent). Restricting the tally to the one week in which the story circulated, 21–28 February, its salience across our sample is striking – covered in 32.3 per cent of the 257 records. Ignoring all of the politics-as-process issues, only the economy, health, and MPs' expenses attracted a higher proportion of attention in the entire February period.

Political framings 2: comedy

Our attempts to classify the material in our corpus by 'media format' included two categories with a specific remit for humour: 'cartoons' and 'comedy/satire'. On occasion the parliamentary sketch-writer opted for a more critical or 'straight' tone, notably Andrew Gimson or Michael White, in which case it was coded as a 'Column/editorial/headline', otherwise parliamentary sketches were also coded as 'comedy/satire'.[21] The cartoons and comedy categories together amounted to 433 items across the corpus, accounting for 12 per cent of all items in February, 16 per cent in the Election period and 17 per cent in the Autumn. Since our auditing strategy remained consistent throughout these three periods, these figures suggest an increasing turn to the comic over the year.

Britain has a pervasive culture of topical comedy, with politics as its key but not exclusive focus. Our audit captured instances of several regularly produced comic formats on TV and Radio where the amount of specifically *political* comedy varied considerably (*Charlie Brooker's Newswipe* produced a 'political' episode on one occasion; *Bremner, Bird and Fortune* was dominated by politics, as was *The Heckler* during the election campaign; *Have I Got News For You*, *The News Quiz*, *Mock the Week* tended to lead with politics but then move into other areas). From the realm of broadcasting we captured overall 31 episodes of such comedy; 8 each in February and Autumn, and 15 programmes during the Election period. This sample can be investigated further in terms of the particular aspects of politics covered in such programmes. The February audit produces no single dominant theme, with 'Bullygate' occurring at the end of the sample period and so only *The News Quiz* on 26 February appearing late enough to cover it. That the affair received plenty of comic appraisals outside of the traditional political comedy is something we have already noted in Chapter 3 and in figures above. Issues that do appear are undoubtedly 'news-led', with the Election audit heavily dominated by the election-campaigning aspects, including 'horserace' elements and gaffes (referred to in 93.3 per cent of programmes), and of those, the *Leaders' Debates* in particular (66.7 per cent of programmes), rather than the policy issues. Of the substantive issues, it is the economy (including taxation, government spending plans, the credit crisis, etc.)

that is deemed most significant during the Election period (53.3 per cent). Immigration-related policies and MPs' expenses also attract sizeable comic treatment in broadcast material (26.7 per cent each). Not surprisingly, it is the economy that also dominates in the Autumn sample (87.5 per cent), while the party conferences and leadership contest provide substantial material (75.0 per cent).

Within our broadcast comedy sample we can also find support for our observation that British political culture is heavily focused on the *people* in politics, by cross-tabulating the comic items with mentions of British political figures. Cameron, Brown and Clegg dominate at election time, with their shifting political fortunes over the year meaning that Cameron is referred to in 87.1 per cent of programmes, compared with 71.0 per cent for Brown and 64.5 per cent for Clegg. Only George Osborne and Peter Mandelson came close as prominent figures of fun, with 45.2 and 41.9 per cent respectively. As Ed Miliband received no comic attention at all until the Autumn period, he appears in only 9.7 per cent of programmes overall. The data therefore support our sense that individual politicians had to be very prominent indeed to attract more than the tiniest fraction of comedic attention (and of course the comic attention then reinforces their prominence).

The classification indicated above is based on items in the corpus, identified by generic type as 'comedy'. It is also very clear that genres such as blogs, chat shows, reality programmes, newspaper editorials etc., would themselves from time to time take an opportunity for a moment of humour: this might be incidental and non-contrived in a TV programme like the BBC's flagship *Question Time*, with its live studio audience, but more deliberately planned in a late-night magazine show like *This Week*. One noted feature was the participation of comedians in programming not classed as comedy-based: seven politically themed programmes featured comedians in February, with 14 each during the Election and Autumn periods. Although *The Wright Stuff* accounted for a majority of these appearances overall, comedians also contributed to *This Week*, *Andrew Marr Show*, *Politics Show*, and *Daily Politics* on 12 separate occasions in our auditing periods. Established political comedians such as Mark Thomas appeared on the *Andrew Marr Show*, but also newer faces such as Shappi Korsandi, who contributed to *This Week* in February. During the Election period comedian Catherine Allen reported from Birmingham on the youth vote for the *Politics Show*; while impressionist Jon Culshaw joined the *Daily Politics* on 29 April, in a show dominated by Gordon Brown's 'über-gaffe' of 'Bigotgate'. Perhaps, then, it is no coincidence that comedian and *The Thick of It* writer Armando Iannucci was Andrew Marr's guest on the following Sunday (2 May 2010). We cite only a few examples here of where comedians are co-opted into the space of 'serious' political programming. Nor are they the only people offering wry takes on political happenings in these settings, with regular reporters such as Giles Dilnot for *Daily Politics* and Max Cotton for the *Politics Show* delivering reports heavy in visual, musical and verbal puns. In addition to creating their own mash-up style collages or musical sequences, televised politically themed programmes might also directly broadcast amusing clips from the web, just as the web borrows from TV for its humorous material.

An indicative way of using the corpus to explore the scope of *satire* in our material, rather than comedy in general, involved cross-tabulating the comedic items with another coding we developed to annotate 'political values' (greed, vanity, respect, sexism, etc.). Again, referring to our broadcast sample, we can note that some degree of coding for values appears in nearly all of our comic items, ranging from at least one 'value' annotated in 100 per cent of political comedy programmes in February, falling to around 50 per cent in Autumn. However, more detailed inspection reveals the nature of the comments made about political figures, and the degree to which they might be considered 'satirical' with politicized intent, rather than the broader 'mocking' of personality traits and appearance. In February, the MPs' expenses scandal was still current, and so issues of 'deceit', 'corruption' and 'greed' could be found alongside the personality-focused ridicule (which remained dominant). The inclusion of Charlie Brooker's *Newswipe* episode on 'Politics' significantly added to this critical emphasis. By Election time, issues of 'deceit' were still high on the agenda, with politicians' 'distance' from people becoming more of a concern than their 'greed'. The media's values also come under scrutiny at this time, with mentions recorded for media 'partisanship' and general 'conduct'. For example, in an episode of *Bremner, Bird and Fortune*, an item on the partisanship of newspapers during elections is followed later by a discussion filmed on location, as Rory Bremner travels in his own election 'battlebus' conducting interviews with various commentators. In the featured debate, writer Frederick Forsyth expresses his disappointment that the media, 'live inside their own little bubble and they share the bubble with the powers that be ... they are supposed to hold the establishment to account not join them, not go to bed with them' (2 May 2010). By Autumn, the comic focus on values comes to revolve almost exclusively around the personality traits of politicians, with Nick Clegg, Ed Miliband and George Osborne in particular facing personalized attacks. Overall, we find that general humour at politicians' expense is more common than humour with satirical intent. This would also be consistent with the accommodation of political humour within topical comedy shows which have a more inclusive remit. It also leads into the final topic for discussion in this section, which relates to critical framings of politics across genres and modes.

Suspicion and critique

Broadening out our discussion of 'political values' beyond comic or satirical treatments, we can look for trends across our generic range. In addition to values applied to politicians, we distinguished explicit mentions to political party 'core' values, those applied to democracy itself (e.g. democratic deficit), and those applied to the media (e.g. media ethics). Everything else was classified under 'other' – for instance, values as applied to the banking sector or European Union forums would be included here. We recognize that his type of coding of evaluative comments is not an exact science, and involves more of a qualitative judgment about treatment and appraisals. For this reason we note observable trends and patterns rather than detailed percentages.

It was the judgments that were made of politicians that dominated this index, and accounted for around two-thirds of all the mentions in our material. When the focus for evaluation is specifically on politicians, then the criteria of judgment were varied and the emphasis predominantly negative. Corruption, greed, racism, sexism, homophobia, inconsistency, hypocrisy and vanity/hubris were all variously brought into play. However, the majority of assessments offered were either on idiosyncratic personality traits and 'character', or the closely related category of leadership qualities. Thus, for example, there is in our material no evidence of a lasting media obsession with the greed of politicians in the wake of the MPs' expenses scandal. While politicians' greed is a recurrent value in February, along with 'deceit', 'distance', 'corruption' and 'competence', it is less prominent in the Election period (with 'deceit' and 'competence' still high on the list, alongside 'cynicism' and 'trust'). But by Autumn, 'greed' has all but disappeared from our sample, while 'competence', 'trust' and 'deceit' remain as critical points of reference. In February, politicians' 'distance' from the electorate was of greater interest than their 'competence'; in the Election period, these concerns were equally prominent, while in the Autumn, 'competence' was more than twice as interesting as 'distance'. Throughout, as mentioned above, it is personality traits and leadership qualities that dominate as explicit key concerns.

The judgments applied to the parties varied in prominence throughout the year, with the spate of book publications in early 2010 signalling the end of New Labour's 13-year government and producing a good number of reflections on Labour's core values in February; although the pre-election campaign from the start of the year also focused attention on Cameron's marketing of the Conservatives in this period. While the Lib Dems' values as a political party were barely mentioned in February, by the Election period, it is the Lib Dems who received most attention; much of this was in the form of critical appraisals of their negotiating stance and strategy during the coalition talks that followed the inconclusive election result. As the political year progressed, interest in party values increased slightly at the expense of interest in the values of politicians – the party-conference season offered another mediated opportunity to define and promote party values, especially for the Labour-leadership candidates. During the Election period in the spring, interest in the values of democracy itself also increased. While concerns over a 'democratic deficit' cropped up throughout the year, the Election period saw British democracy characterized not only as 'farcical' but also as 'enhanced' – both of these contrasting appraisals in many cases referring to the novel addition of the *Leaders' Debates* to the media campaign.

One incident that introduced an element of farce into the election coverage was Gordon Brown's 'Bigotgate' gaffe, already outlined above. While the *Leaders' Debates* provided a controlled environment for party leaders to promote their values, this unexpected episode generated intense scrutiny for what it revealed about Brown's character. Our database enabled tracking across media genres, with the story breaking while *The Daily Politics* was on air on 28 February, and dominating an entire episode the following day, as invited participants speculated on how it would impact on the final *Leaders' Debate*, as well as the election result beyond. Critical commentators claimed that the event revealed the 'authentic' Brown, 'thin-skinned, paranoid and perpetually on the hunt for someone else to blame' (Trevor Kavanagh, *Sun*, 29 February); an elite politician with 'cynical contempt' for the electorate (*Daily Mail* editorial). Humility and sorrow became the surprising values emphasized during an election-campaign period: seen in Brown's many apologies, widespread pity for Gillian Duffy, and even notional sympathy for the exhausted Brown, who, Rory Bremner suggested, just needed 'a cuddle' (*Bremner, Bird and Fortune*, 2 May).

Of course the proportionalities cited above do not tell us much about those specific failures of competence which were laid to the charge of politicians, or about what particular articulations of politicians and distance were generated. Such enquiry needs a more fine-grained or qualitative approach to the data, along with sensitive contextualization. But we take it as a useful corroboration of our analytic emphases that these are the patterns that the data revealed.

Theme through form, form through theme

We end this chapter with a few reflections on its value within the wider context of the book as a whole. We started with the question, 'what of politics and the political gets picked up and what does not?' and then sought to offer an account which answered that question in respect of our (circumscribed) interpretation of 'politics', as well as the particular moment in British political culture with which the book has mainly been concerned. The salience of politicians, especially celebrity politicians, was to be expected; their mediation in terms of leadership, trust/suspicion and money is likely to be a resonant one for some time to come in the UK.

The three framings, affective, comic and critical, are matters of theme for us inasmuch as they can each be realized in any number of formally distinctive genres. The 'pathos' of the scenes involving Alistair Campbell with Andrew Marr and Gordon Brown with Piers Morgan, although embedded respectively in a topical magazine programme and a celebrity chat show, was assimilated into the cultural conversation about politics and emotion without reference to that distinction, and for the purposes of this chapter we have followed suit.

However, to the extent that these distinctions also signify something about the *stance* towards politics of a politician, a citizen or a commentator, matters of form (certainly in relation to social address) are likely to be implicated too, and thus to lead back to textual concerns. For example, the suspicion that we noted, coming from some quarters, concerning the possible 'strategic' character of Campbell and Brown's pathos, took support from the televisual performative context in which this behaviour was put on display – within those formal terms which the 'accountability interview' (Montgomery, 2007) and the chat-show discussion have in common. It is in the second part of this chapter, where profiling of a quantified kind is attempted, that the pull *away* from specific textual form is at its strongest. This is where we found that the methodological justification for a quantified overview, importantly one that included formal elements, was most compelling.

We hope to have shown in this chapter, as in the ones that have preceded it, how themes and forms are interconnected in political mediation, here giving emphasis to the profile of the former across our study period. Some of the points we have raised and the questions we have posed will be developed further in our conclusions to the book.

The Forms and Functions of Genre
in Mediated Politics

Here, standing back from the detailed empirical work offered in the preceding chapters, we attempt to summarize what we have found out, reflect on its implications and develop points of connection with the existing research literatures to which we referred in the book's Introduction.

In discussing our findings we return again to the central concept of *genre* in our work. The key findings of the research respect the formation and development of particular genres in particular media, indicate the consequences of putting our genres to the 'test' of audience interpretation and response, and explore, from across the generic range, the major themes of political representation.

The broader issues we are able to address based on these findings have been assembled under three distinct headings (noting however the considerable overlap between what they variously cover). Under the heading *Generic work and civic orientations* we comment on how the work of media texts manages the relations between leaders and citizens as a matter of discursive organization. In *Political performances, subjectivity and affectivity*, we comment on the refraction of civic relations through entertainment media by focusing on the figure of 'the politician' in the era of celebrity culture. Finally, in *Masses, niches and elites*, we reflect further on what our study contributes to discussion of elite/popular tensions, as these play out within the mediascape, with some genres accessible on a much wider social basis than others.

It is our belief that the work presented in this book very much deserves to be extended and developed, with cross-cultural approaches that also carry forward our cross-generic emphasis, as well as more intensive ones which focus on particular genres and mediums. By way of preparation for further research, we have also included in this conclusion not only a short section reflecting on what we might learn through comparisons of the British case with other countries, but also one which deals with political developments within Britain (or affecting Britain) that have taken place since our primary research concluded at the end of 2010.

Key findings

We have located our study within the broad field of political-communication research, but distinguished it from the mainstream tradition in that field, where the principal focus remains, despite recent changes, on forms of political news – news as printed, as broadcast, and increasingly as circulated online. In this paradigm the specific features of news as genre(s) tend to become invisible, in being largely taken for granted, and the focus is mostly on the content and its discursive framing.

By contrast, we wanted to explore further what is, in general terms, a widely recognized if under-investigated feature of media–political relations – that the orientations of citizens towards politics, their interest, their knowledge, judgments, good and bad, of particular politicians or politics in general, are fostered not only in their encounters with news, but across a much wider range of mediations. In reaching out to connect with this range, questions of genre become more central, because generic contexts shape the politically sayable in important ways. For instance, the communicative affordances of a cartoon in terms of content and stance (see Chapter 2) are very different from those of a TV reality show like *Tower Block of Commons* (*TBOC*) (see Chapter 1) and audiences respond accordingly (see Chapter 4). As we noted in the Introduction, 'Genre' is a term around which a great deal of intensive debate has gathered in the humanities, particularly in relation to the kinds of 'separateness' in formal communicative character that the use of generic categories suggest, and the firmness and the stability of the 'generic conventions' that might underpin differentiation at the levels of both production and reception (see also Born, 2010). However, our usage here, while open to some of the questions posed in the wider debate, has largely been indicative rather than more ambitiously typological. That the different 'kinds' of thing that the media offer are subject to continual revision in their formal ingredients and recipes, that 'rules' and 'boundaries' are often uncertain, that cross-generic influences are widespread and that classifying all work in generic terms is sometimes difficult if not impossible, all these points we acknowledge. However, the term still offers a useful way of seeing media production and media consumption as organized, in part, by differentiating conventions of aesthetic and discursive practice, relating what is produced to different purposes, outlets, markets, audiences and readerships.

In the interests of coherence and consistency, our examples were mainly drawn from an archive of materials collected in the UK during 2010. As the study shows, a very large amount of non-news mediated politics is news-driven, in the sense that it picks up where news leaves off, extensively responding to it and commenting on it, within routine temporal cycles of media production. As a result, one key property that unites diverse materials across genres is their intertextual density. This is firmly established above, not only through the textual analyses of the 2010 materials, but through our account of what audiences were able to make of these materials when they were asked to read, watch and listen to samples of them. We have noted how their engagements were affected by their varying familiarity with aspects of the quite dense body of political information in circulation. Of course, the passage of time (though no more than a year and generally much shorter) between the original appearance of the material we selected and the focus-group exercises we conducted, worked to attenuate the strength of the connection between the content of the items from our selection and the news/current-affairs agenda of the day. This inevitably influenced the character of audience uptake and comment, though some topics, for instance the MPs' expenses scandal, had established themselves in memories more firmly than others.

To do justice to the generic repertoire it was necessary to begin with some initial framework for the classification and ordering of materials so as to better understand their substantive and formal interrelations. Separation by medium between broadcast, print and online materials made sense as the basis of a protocol for organising the chapters of this book. Our working assumption was that particular genres belong to particular mediums, so that reality-TV programmes, sketch columns and blog posts, for instance, belong respectively to broadcasting, the press and the internet. Whether the remediation involved in cross-media borrowings and recycling offers a serious challenge to this assumption is a relevant question, and any answer to it will need to ask about the extent of the textual reconfiguration involved as part of medium transfer, as opposed to the use of the 'medium' as a distribution channel (c.f. the established recycling of feature films via TV). Considerations at this level are not specific to political mediation, of course, but have far more general implications.

The rest of this chapter will maintain correspondence with the book's organization by continuing the use of these standard divisions despite our acknowledgement of their vulnerability in the evolving media ecology. We recognize broadcasting as the medium (or rather, two mediums, radio and TV), which commands the largest audiences; print as the most established, and the internet as the newest, most adaptable and fluid, and currently the most fascinating in media, culture and communication research.

Broadcast genres continue to offer the greatest opportunity for audiences to witness the embodied and envoiced performances of their elected representatives and candidates – as well as recycled and comic appropriations of these performances. The earnest presentations of their political selves that politicians attempt to sustain when fully in role (the BBC TV programme *Question Time* is exemplary here) are meant to be able to cope with equally earnest challenges from adversaries, interrogators and citizens, under disciplined conditions of participation. Rational argument is privileged, but incursions of strong negative emotion are often appropriate too, especially around points that are (or can be represented as) morally charged. Earnestness is vulnerable to occasional humorous deflation even in the 'serious' programmes, while genres less subject to the demands of official high-mindedness offer greater scope for displays of agonistic or comic political voices, including those where humorous display is the raison d'être – though the politicians themselves are less likely to be on-stage in these contexts (Coleman et al., 2009). Second-order performances (dramatizations) are an important part of the mix, though full-scale dramas with fictional narratives and characters are relatively rare (van Zoonen and Wring, 2012).

The modes of representation afforded by print permit greater authorial development than those of broadcasting, these authors sometimes speaking as the voice of the newspaper itself rather than as named individuals. Whether these pieces are primarily verbal (parliamentary sketches and leader columns) or visual (editorial cartoons), their mode of reception gives readers time, if they need/want it, to come to terms with what is being claimed. We have observed how much of this results in the production of comic (though not necessarily 'satiric') discourse of different kinds. The 'difficulty' or complexity of any argumentation varies with the target audience of the publication along what are familiar, if changing, demographic lines, as does the articulation of 'partisanship' in a context where there is a considerable amount of non-partisan humour produced at the expense of politicians/politics in general rather than it having any more specific political aims.

The internet has fostered one particular native genre that has been of importance in political communication – the blog. Although the newest of all the genres examined, blogging already has a history, and political blogging is continuing to move away from its origins as a place for the voices of individuals without access to institutionally supported publishing opportunities. A small collection of political blogs was sufficient to demonstrate: their extensive interlinking with other online resources, including social media as well as other blogs; the persistence of the individual voice (despite the above-noted drift towards more institutionally grounded forms of blogging); considerable informality of linguistic styling; reliance on visual as well as verbal representations; and an orientation towards the insider interests of the 'Westminster village'.

Our chapter on audiences started by discussing the limitations of this term for addressing new forms of online 'audience participation' in political mediation. Yet, recognising the still limited numbers of ordinary people who actually take part in Mumsnet-type webchats, or any of a large range of opportunities to be part of public and/or interactive political discussion, we still found ourselves able to employ, for much of our work in this area, the more conventional view of audiences as (diverse, active) consumers of media texts. It is an established part of media audience research to note and explore the variations of response within audiences and the variable ways they draw upon their own knowledge, experiences and values in making sense of and evaluating media materials. For this research we anticipated that the degree of interest in politics as such would be an important conditioning factor. The fieldwork produced participants with a range of positions, from apathy and cynicism through to activist. Lack of interest certainly entailed some ignorance of political people and events that given texts assumed a knowledge of, although it was the texts that added formal complexity or innovation to substantive demands which proved especially challenging, including certain editorial cartoons and the comedy-drama-documentary *Miliband of Brothers*. Participants' emotional likes and dislikes were usually articulated in relation to their civic values, so for example, reactions to comedy were not just about what was funny and therefore enjoyable, but also about whether, and to what extent, humour at the expense of politicians was good for the country's democratic health.

When we turned our attention to the themes rather than the forms of political mediation, we wished to avoid the risk of focusing too narrowly on the major events of British political life in 2010: the general election, the contests for the Labour Party leadership, and the Coalition government's first austerity budget. Our real interest was not so much in these events as such, but in the more general thematic characteristics given public expression (overtly or covertly) in the materials examined, with these events and others acting as conduits. Perhaps the most significant finding here, though not a novel one, is the deeply entrenched and persistent discourse separating 'us', the citizenry, from 'them', the politicians. 'We' in this discourse are largely the recipients of actions instigated by 'them', or else the victims of 'their' neglect, their failure to control banks/bankers, restrict immigration, prevent crime, and so on. We have also noted, in a way deserving of further comment later in this chapter, that there was little evidence of an actively oppositional or resistive orientation towards the perceived deficits of politics as currently constituted. Clearly, this does not preclude the likelihood of different forms of popular resistive behaviour, of expression and of action, developing in the hard economic times that are now anticipated for the medium- and even long-term future.

Generic work and civic orientations

Our study has illustrated, and tried to investigate, the very wide range of ways in which the political is mediated into civic space, the ways that various aspects and properties of 'politicality' are defined and represented, constructing 'politics' simultaneously as a profession, a set of institutions and processes, a specific sphere of social and economic life and a dimension of the everyday. John Ellis (2000), drawing on psychoanalytic categories, has written suggestively of the manner in which media forms act as means of 'working through' (of reflecting upon and dealing with, by modes of assimilation, displacement and refocusing) the topics and themes that often first make their appearance in public space within the frame of the news. Such 'working through' involves coming at the issues (pre-installed by journalism as 'significant') from different angles and with different emphases, reiterating them with lighter or darker toning and with varying degrees of confirmatory or questioning force at work in the aesthetic and discursive recipes employed. There is a sense in which our previous chapters have shown instances of the 'working through' of British politics over a particular period. The generic forms we have examined might be seen to have frequently been applied to the 'replaying' of politics in various pleasurable or satisfying ways rather than the 'relaying' of it, although we have also shown how an element of 'relay', of primary connection and of knowledge throughput, also inevitably occurs in the kinds of portrayal at work.[1]

The material we have explored sets up different cognitive and affective relations with its presumed audiences, readerships and site users, taking variable aesthetic routes to describe, imitate and 'place' the political, both specifically and in more general terms. Certain events or actions are positioned as 'routine' but some are highlighted as 'remarkable' and as deserving of a response across a very wide range of post-news treatments, whether this response takes the form of a sharpened comprehension of political events or the groans and laughter of intensified recognition.[2] Such a process can be seen as broadly 'civic' in character, in ways which engage both a sense of the civic collective ('public') and of the civic individual ('citizen'), the emphases here weighted in different ways according to theme and form. Civic subjectivity, in its collective and individualized interpellations, clearly involves ideas of political membership, of the affiliated self, in ways which often combine relationships of emotion, of affective investment, with relationships of knowledge – of system, process, people and events. Some of our examples have shown the variety of combinations here, which mediation can draw upon and re-project.

At several points in the previous chapters we have noted how the generic work we examined produces, or assumes, different kinds of distance in relation to the political. At times, we are brought 'close up' to politics, particular issues receiving an attention that moves, even 'intrusively', towards the 'private within the political'. A number of forms of imitative portrayal, including those of comedy–drama, cartoons and certain blogs, as well as the 'intimacy' of talk shows, work within the terms of this optic. However, at other times 'distance' is the dominant relationship, politicians seen not only as 'other' (maybe weirdly so) when compared with the 'ordinary people' who make up the civic collective but also as disconnected from them in ways that are to do with basic terms of understanding as well as social space. If the perception of such distance becomes too pronounced (politics, in more than one way, as 'unpopular') it can be seen as contributing towards the widely discussed condition of 'political spectatorship', in which a variable level of attention to the 'show' of politics dominates over any active ideas of membership, involvement and participation. Here the idea of citizenship shades into its established minimal form, in Britain as well as elsewhere – a rather bemused and regularly irritated electorate. In our inquiry, we have noted how different generic forms variously move people around, through the listening, viewing and reading positions that they cue, in relation to this idea of the 'show' – the management of political distances, and mobility across them, being an important feature of

generic work. But we cannot align distance directly with political judgment, since there are examples where we are placed at a distance in
order the better to engage with the full complexity of specific political
affairs rather than to register their lamentable remoteness, and examples
where we are brought close up to appreciate the detail and experience
of political decision-making as well as those in which heightened cause
for comic pleasure and for scorn is provided by proximity. We have also
been able to document, albeit selectively, how audiences variously take
up or refuse the positions and perspectives being offered them, with the
situation, again, further complicated by their own individual shifts of
alignment in relation to the same item, drawing on the diverse levels of
positive or negative evaluation which are brought into play.

Underlying the civic cross-current at work both in generic production
and in reception by specific media-user groupings there is at work a level
of the 'political imaginary' (on this notion see, for instance, Buck-Morss,
2002). By this term, we point to that broader apprehension of the political realm, its pasts, presents and futures, that transcends any specific
knowledge of a system, institutions and elites even though it is fed by
this knowledge, however sketchily. This is a level that is engaged when
relating to political events internationally (about which almost nothing
specific may be known) as well as at home. Rather than any substantive body of knowledge and values, this is essentially a hazy template
of assumptions, drawing on hopes and fears at the level of personal,
family and community experience, about the flows of power in society and perhaps the likely directions of any change. Perceptions of 'real
politics' can be seen to play out against the background of the political
imaginary, however softly and fluidly defined it may be.

Political performances, subjectivity and affectivity

In this section we expand on a number of points around issues of subjectivity, affectivity and political performance. Political subjectivity is
not only a matter of alignment in terms of proximity and partisanship, but also involves understanding differences of emotional response
their character and their intensity. Politics involves feelings as well as
thoughts, and its diverse ways of being portrayed and discussed raise
questions of aesthetics as well as of information and reasoning. We have
explored this dimension of political subjectivity both in our textual
studies and through our work with respondent groups. Prompted by
their encounters with the texts we showed them, our respondents frequently volunteered accounts of their emotional engagements with
forms of mediated politics, as well as indicating their political interests

and partisanship. Our interest in emotionality cross-connects with a number of interrelated research areas: the 'personalization' of politics; celebrity subjectivities in elite politics; and the issue of how both mediated and unprompted public ridicule can contribute (positively or negatively) to political appreciation.

In our Introduction, we placed our work within the context of a 'cultural turn' in the study of media–political relations, a move towards greater recognition of the importance of the broader settings of values and meanings within which political activity is situated. Related to this, we can also recognize an 'affective turn', a more intensive engagement with emotionality, in humanities and social-science research. This has been understood as a methodological repositioning, with early influence (and later criticism) from feminist writers in particular (Clough and Halley, 2007; Tyler, 2008), while recent studies have turned attention to emotionality as a resource in journalistic storytelling (Wahl-Jorgenson, forthcoming) and the ways in which news and non-news mediations shape affective responses (Barnhurst, 2011; Grusin, 2010; Papacharissi and de Fatima Oliveira, 2012). Our interest in 'affectivity' is meant in the broadest sense of being attentive to the meaning of emotional display in (mediated) political encounters and to the types of emotional response which political performance may foster in audiences (cf. Pantti and van Zoonen, 2006). Our corpus of media materials included televised moments where strong emotions 'leaked' into political programming, either directly portrayed or in the retelling of earlier incidents, with former Prime Minister Gordon Brown providing notable examples. The intense discussion brought into play through this mediated 'turn to the emotional' was expressed in ethical terms with reference to sincerity, appropriateness, empathy, self-pity and discretion, and in the aesthetic terms of personal taste and distaste, articulated together with political principles or partisanship. Drawing on resources of emotional knowledge when making sense of politics does not militate against the capacity to draw on political knowledge, or to craft opinions based on factual information rather than rumour or misinformation. We did not find that respondents chose between 'emotional' and 'rational–political' engagements – those with the strongest personal investments in politics often showed the greatest appreciation for achieving a degree of balance between political and entertainment values.

This 'turn to the emotional' attests to a related sense in which affectivity is core to our research: in the recurrent motif of politics as 'embodied' in the politician as mediated political subject. For example, the *TBOC* series, exploiting the popularity of reality TV and its links to the current cultural obsession with intimacy and confessional TV, brought the individual politician (as embodying a political class recently 'disgraced' as a result of the parliamentary expenses scandal) into the recognisable tableau of elite persons socially re-located and therefore 'out-of-place', embarking, often with some reluctance, upon a personal journey to understand how the 'other half' live.

The predominance of TV as the medium through which politics is encountered has been intricately linked to the related concept of the 'personalization' of politics, certainly within studies on news coverage (Thompson, 1995; van Zoonen, 2005; Langer, 2007; Karvonen, 2010; Langer, 2011; van Aelst et al., 2012; Stanyer, 2012). Our material shows that this personalization now extends well beyond the news. Politicians, as the embodied expression of political ideas and values, are found in all the comic and serious expressive forms that mediate politics. They are present as extended fictionalized recreations in works of drama, as distortive caricatures in cartoons and sketches, and as subjects whose personality traits are deemed worthy of extended commentary in press columns and documentary programmes. With such an emphasis on identity and character, the narrow social representation at the heart of British government (public-school- and Oxbridge-educated, millionaire, 40-year-old, white male) serves to accentuate the widespread impression of the professional modern politician as a predictable type. David Cameron's epithet 'call me Dave', epitomizes his efforts to alleviate the distancing effect of privilege with well-crafted performances of informality and intimacy.

For those attempting to rework and control the symbolic meanings of such performances, creative uses of verbal and visual imagery are crucial tools – for commentator and satirist alike (Rowson, 2009; Simpson, 2003; Parry and Richardson, 2011), and attention to the theatrical and the symbolic ingredients of political discourse now forms a significant part of contemporary political-communications research. Such imaginative usages, whether in broadcast, print or web-based genres, include those to be found in the comic treatment of politics, with the purpose of inducing laughter via a variety of argumentative, imitative and descriptive modes of delivery (see Corner et al., 2012). From Henri Bergson's (1911) essay on laughter through to Michael Billig's book on 'Laughter and Ridicule' (2005), there has been a strong emphasis on the corrective or disciplinary function of laughter as well as, and sometimes rather than, its affective aspects. Political satire, even more than ridicule, clearly entails a moral opposition, with recognition of the crucial, unspoken *incongruity* dependent on shared knowledge of appropriate ideas and values. In our media materials, satire with serious political intent coexisted with other kinds of humour, with ridicule especially prominent, appearing variously hostile, affectionate or ironically detached. As Jeffrey Jones (2010) has argued, a negative sense of cynicism is not necessarily the outcome of shared laughter at national politics – this can also encourage more constructive critique, and even contribute to political action or reform (Barnhurst, 2011, p. 585).

The mocking of politicians, delivered with a sarcasm that can range from irritation to vehement anger, is familiar ground for researchers of political humour, but our research has also drawn attention to more surprising combinations of ridicule and affection, as in most of the sketch-writing columns and some cartoons (which overall can range from populist vitriol to qualified gentle amusement). Our audience research revealed that respondents differed greatly in judging where acceptable lines had been crossed. Spontaneous publicly driven ripostes, such as the #nickcleggsfault Twitter meme instigated in response to negative right-wing coverage of the Liberal Democrat leader, demonstrate how a playful and heavily ironic tone can be directed at the mainstream media in *defence* of a politician (even if this particular joke lost its irony following the formation of the Coalition government). This public sense of politics as endearingly ridiculous, along with humorous treatments that consciously merge ridicule with affection, is congruent with the blending of mediated politics into the broader contours of celebrity culture. Politicians who are willing to participate in knowingly self-mocking comic performances, such as appearing on *Have I Got News for You*, or Tony Blair's memorable *Comic Relief* comedy-sketch cameo in 2007, trade on recognisable personae shaped *beyond* the news-oriented political field (Corner, 2003).[3]

Masses, niches and elites

Our enquiry has also indicated something of the range of generic practice not only formally but in respect of its demographic character. In some genres, the idiom and references that the journalists, broadcasters and bloggers seem to share with politicians have the potential to create an external impression of a grouping that only such insiders can understand and appreciate – an interest-based niche, comparable with any other specialist area of public communication, available in principle but exclusive in practice. Even the public service tradition in British broadcasting, with a remit to facilitate comprehension for the citizenry in general, recognizes different degrees of interest in politics and designs different kinds of programme to reflect this. The BBC's flagship *Question*

Time on prime-time TV has a very different communicative ethos from Radio Four's *The Week in Westminster*. But 'niche' and mass considerations are also relevant in the commercially driven print-media sector. We noted that the interpretative difficulties associated with some of the cartoons in our sample corresponded with the paper's position in the media marketplace, while the more accessible cartoons were to be found in the mass-circulation titles. The market for the satirical/critical fortnightly *Private Eye* is a very small one, but is likely to include some of the country's most politically well-informed citizens. Space on the internet for political communication is extensive and varied: it now includes subscription-based services like *PoliticsHome*, targeting journalists, politicians, academics – people (and institutions) with a professional stake in political affairs, rather than a general public readership.[4]

Summarising this, we may say that different types of 'audience' (we acknowledge once more the question marks that should be placed alongside this as a general category) are positioned economically and socially in relation to a diversity of media markets and perceived 'consumer' interests. This cross-connects with civic positioning, in which different sectors of the public are addressed through what can be very different lines of media engagement, carrying different civic values – and with public service broadcasting especially implicated in the challenge of harmonising 'audience' and 'public' identities, at the level of policy as well as of practice. As a number of writers have suggested (most recently, Corner, 2011; Livingstone and Lunt, 2011), the 'citizen–consumer' duality is a central and problematic one for much contemporary politics, including at the level of how the political is experienced, with differentiated patterns of media exposure and use and modes of media address an important part of the interplay of tensions and alignments.

National and international frames

The contribution of our study to the international literature in political-culture research consists in its intensive focus on the generic range deployed in one country at a particular point in time, for reasons explained in this book's Introduction. To 'internationalize' this is to ask, first of all, what kind of country we have been talking about, in respect of both its politics and its media arrangements, and what this means in a cultural perspective. As a 'mature democracy', Britain has a citizenry which is able to take democratic conditions very much for granted most of the time, in a way that (for instance), those of the post-socialist Eastern European regimes may not do. Against this settled background, events like the expenses scandal are able to take on foreground significance: the 'background' can also be brought into focus when constitutional arrangements (Britain's place in the European Union, reform of the House of Lords) are on the national news agenda. Something similar may also be the case in public attitudes towards the country's current media settlement, with audiences making individual consumption/participation choices without much conscious reflection on the underlying conditions which structure those choices until provoked into such reflections by, for example, the recent 'phone hacking' events.[5] Britain has also gone a long way in spreading the digital revolution throughout the population – the Office for National Statistics were reporting in August 2011 that 77 per cent of all households had internet access, up from the previous year's 73 per cent.

If safe cultural assumptions are disrupted for citizens/audiences by perturbing events, then for academic research, it is comparative studies that perform a similar function. Hence the importance of research such as the kind mentioned in our Introduction regarding analyses of news parody formats in a wide range of different countries, with their varying experiences of politics and media. Nationally grounded comparative studies which include broadcasting are also able to show the existence of transnational programme flows (Baym and Jones, 2012) as evidence of directions of influence between national settings, while also noting significant gaps in programme trade. The success of *The Daily Show with Jon Stewart* in the USA led to the rebroadcasting of this programme in the UK (on More4), but relative lack of interest for its predominantly American content led to the curtailment of this in favour of a weekly, global edition of the programme instead. Jon Stewart and Stephen Colbert (performing as his parody-persona in the *Daily Show* spin-off *The Colbert Report*) critique both a form of politics and a form of political reporting very specific to US political culture. This might explain why there has been no cloned British version of *The Daily Show* despite its notable success at engaging young people in politics, although its stylistic influences can arguably be witnessed in a range of British shows (*Graham Norton Show*, BBC1; *Charlie Brooker's Screenwipe*, BBC4). A weekly satire series for Channel 4, *10 O'clock Live*, first broadcast in January 2011, can be regarded as its closest equivalent, but since this show does *not* offer news parody as part of the mix, any comparability is primarily in terms of stance, tone, and intended audience, rather than at the level of genre/format. Britain has had its own, separate history of news parody on radio and TV and it is likely that satiric influences have travelled in both directions across the Atlantic in the recent past. Indeed, in terms of satirical drama, the British creators of the political sitcom *The*

Thick of It have produced a US equivalent set in the office of a fictional US vice-president, *Veep*, for HBO, while a US remake of *House of Cards* is currently in production, starring Kevin Spacey in the key role of MP Francis Urquart (Stiastny, 2012). This kind of transnational remediation mostly continues to conceal the extra-national format origins so far as viewers are concerned. Less common, though not unknown, are home-grown productions, which draw attention to national differences by introducing their own cross-cultural perspectives. Rory Bremner's three-part Radio 4 documentary on *International Satirists*, first broadcast in 2010, explored how jokes might travel beyond their originating national contexts (of Ireland, the Netherlands and Switzerland), while the same radio channel recently took its long-running comedy panel show *Just a Minute* to India, with panellists from the UK and India providing comic monologues on the consequences of British colonialism, among other less political subjects.

Only in relation to the internet can we begin to talk about an actual global communicative space. Here, too, for our kind of research it is currently generally preferable to conceive of this as *trans-national* communicative space, with individuals inhabiting national identities as they speak to one another across the internal lines of division within this space – country speaking to country at the level of individual citizen. Furthermore, since online resources do not prohibit intra-national discourse, plenty of what we found online had precisely this character. The extra-national readership of political blogs is publicly invisible until it offers thread comments, and thereby declares itself as external. Such declarations might come from the diasporic British or else from those participating as 'eavesdroppers' on national conversations. In the absence of any such declaration or marking, we would regard such commentary as 'virtually national'.

Continuity and change in mediated political culture: twenty-first-century prospects

In addressing what might be different in British political culture since our 2010 study was conducted, our sense is that the changes under way are gradual and modest in scale. At the structural level, we have already commented on the relative stability of British political life – a stability that has continued beyond the period of the original study. The formation of a coalition government in 2010 was a remarkable departure from tradition, but one which the population has accommodated with little perturbation beyond the areas of normal political debate and discussion – and satirization. With David Cameron and Nick Clegg on either side of a referendum campaign to change to a new voting system (Alternative Vote) in May 2011, the honeymoon period of the early cartoons came to a visible end one year on from the Coalition formation. In the years since the election result, strict austerity measures and proposed reforms to the health service, welfare system and the parliamentary system (including constituency boundary changes and fixed-term parliaments) have been met with resistance both within and without government, but mostly to the extent of delay rather than abandonment. Activist reaction to the controversial raising of student tuition fees up to £9,000 per year was conducted, reported and responded to in fairly conventional terms, albeit with Nick Clegg's Liberal Democrats attracting particular resentment due to their pre-election pledge to abolish fees altogether. None of the reported disagreements between the Coalition partners has been enough to bring down the government so far, but reporting of such tensions has arguably reduced Labour's contributions to media debates.

With the political scandal of MPs' expenses in 2009 preceding our study period, in 2011 negative attention shifted onto media practices and the tabloid press in particular. The media-political environment changed quite sharply in July 2011, when the phone-hacking scandal brought about the closure of the *News of the World*, a major, popular Sunday newspaper specialising in celebrity news. However, despite the damage to Rupert Murdoch's News Corporation, economically and in respect of its international reputation, the larger consequences for media in general and news media in particular lie in the future. The *News of the World* may have been re-born as the *Sun on Sunday* in February 2012, but Lord Leveson's enquiry into the general issue of press culture and illegal practices is ongoing at the time of writing.

Meanwhile, in politics and in the media, there is considerable 'business as usual', with the internet responsible for the most obvious innovations. In the British context, we have written about blogging as an established yet ever-mutating form of mediated engagement with the political scene, yet it is the micro-blogging site Twitter which currently attracts scholarly attention, as researchers grapple with its very nature and promise as a space and tool for political communications, among other uses (Anstead and O'Loughlin, 2011; Lim, 2012). Notwithstanding its diverse applications, the fact that Twitter users generally follow a *person*, whose tweets are limited in immediate space (to 140 characters) but unlimited in the sense of the other websites they can link to, aligns its communicative affordances with 'interpersonal gestures of pointing, nudging, and affirming' (Papacharissi and de Fatima Oliveira, 2012, p. 13). Although it is too early to assess the degree to which Twitter and other social media redefine or disrupt official political culture, certainly in the UK context, the generic affordances and possibilities promote an interpersonal sense of interconnectivity and informality that may further reconfigure the 'personalization' of politics for the twenty-first century.

It is rare for British politicians to gain a significant reputation, or even recognition, in the global online public sphere (certainly not since Tony Blair's premiership), so despite the expanded opportunities for political performance and participation, interest in political information online is still largely a national affair. Websites and blogs, and especially Twitter, give politicians (as well as their detractors) scope to hone their skills as engagingly personalized and humorous commentators, and also to 'converse' with other public voices in an open forum. Traversing what has been referred to as a 'hybrid' digital media environment (Chadwick, 2011a, 2011b), some Members of Parliament, such as the Conservative MPs Louise Mensch or Nadine Dorries, now move between news interviews outside the House of Commons, to appearances on *Have I Got News For You*, to Twitter 'spats' with other celebrity figures. Politicians able to navigate successfully such diverse spaces of mediated politics remain relatively rare, but the erosion of clear boundaries of political life is part of a wider social and technological shift, where the TV-driven visibility rules for politicians, defined by John Thompson (1995, 2000, 2005) are morphing at an accelerated pace. TV becomes one form of digital media among a variety available via multiple platforms and devices (Gripsrud, 2010; Bennett and Strange, 2011). Furthermore, the 'distinctive kind of fragility' (Thompson, 1995, p. 141) associated with such visibility is currently being augmented by the instantaneity, mobility and interactivity afforded by new communication technologies, providing opportunities but also pressures to be 'always-on' as a political performer.[6] The new forms of sociability in mediated politics, discussed with regard to blogging in Chapter 3, present both opportunities and potential dangers for elites, commentators and citizens, as digital media platforms continue to offer spaces for novel forms of engagement and connection.

We have noted both substantial generic continuities and new developments in the kinds of media materials analysed. In serious political programming, established staples such as *Question Time* have introduced innovations that complement rather than alter its format, and take advantage of media convergence, with use of both the official 'bbcqt' and the spoof 'dimblebot' hashtags on Twitter re-energising the pro-gramme for a large number of (crucially young) watchers (Anstead and O'Loughlin, 2011; Mangan, 2012). However, generic novelty was not the sole preserve of internet-based or convergent media: spoofery, irony and visual creativity were also evident in programmes such as *Miliband of Brothers* and *TBOC*. Comedy in Britain, including non-political com-edy, continues to enjoy a revival in terms of its diffusion and visibility in mainstream media, and in a thriving stand-up circuit. Since our audit period, Channel 4 has continued to nurture a satirical streak in its pro-gramming, with the launch of the weekly satire show, *10 O'Clock Live*, along with comedy–dramas satirising the 'Hackgate' scandal (*Hacks*, 1 January 2012) and the dilemmas of a hypothetical prime minister liv-ing in the age of digital media (*The National Anthem*, part one of Charlie Brooker's 'Black Mirror' series, broadcast in December 2011).

Further research

In this final section we offer a few brief comments on how the further extension and development of the field might progress. These include an indication of the potential insights to be gained from further inter-national comparisons; from work addressing the intersections of news and non-news genres, and from the introduction of production studies alongside textual and audience research.

There are a number of areas that would benefit from international comparative work across both 'mature' democracies and more turbulent states – either those moving toward democratization or those tighten-ing controls on power. In political communications, the mediatization of politics and the 'personalization' concept, or 'lifestyle' politics, are attracting critical investigation in a number of European and North American countries (Mazzoleni and Schulz, 1999; van Zoonen, 2005; Parotto, 2007; Barisione, 2009; Mazzoleni and Sfardini, 2009). We would expect internationally oriented research on political drama to consider not only the ways in which fictions dealing with political machinations in local and national governments are reaching audiences beyond their domestic context (e.g. *Commander in Chief* (USA), *Borgen* (Denmark), *The Wire* (USA)), but also the treatment of 'international' themes such as the 'war on terror', which continues to provide portrayals of international diplomacy and injustices (e.g. *Homeland* (USA), *The Killing 2* (Denmark), *Borgen* (Denmark)), in addition to docudramas and documentaries.

The wealth of research on US political comedy is well known, but the role of satire in other countries, including both mature and emergent democracies, is starting to attract attention not only in national case studies, but also in relation to the trans-national public sphere of the internet (Coleman et al., 2009; Papacharissi, 2010, pp. 150–151). The internet offers those living in stricter political environments an alternative outlet and challenge to national media restrictions, with playful or ironic styles of presentation often belying the serious nature of the issues (Kovalev, 2011; Lim, 2012; Narco News TV, 2011).

As we have noted, the cross-currents between news and non-news genres are viewed with suspicion in some quarters, with concerns over the expansion of 'infotainment' values degrading the informative and analytical qualities of news output, while others see democratising potential in a more accessible, informal and even increasingly participatory form of political information. Tensions and concerns in this area are worthy of further empirical and theoretical work, which would benefit from the kind of attention to generic properties and techniques that we have developed here, alongside traditional emphases on thematic content and audiences responses. The images of political leaders now attract intense scrutiny, as already mentioned, but such 'imagery' deserves an analytical attention to the forms of visual representations employed (literal and metaphorical), in addition to the forms taken by verbal information (Grabe and Bucy, 2009; Parry and Richardson, 2011). Alongside the growing empirical interest in the theatrical and symbolic expressions of politics (Fielding, 2011) there has been philosophical re-consideration of the Machiavellian themes of political hypocrisy and lying (Runciman, 2008; Jay, 2010; Corner, 2010; Elkins and Norris, 2012), with Tony Blair's former Chief of Staff Jonathan Powell entitling his memoirs, 'The New Machiavelli: How to Wield Power in the Modern World' (2010). The reasons behind this resurgence of scholarly and biographical re-assessments of political expediency and deception are worthy of further consideration.

Our current research has focused largely on the varied treatments of 'official' politics, but we also recognize the burgeoning interest in new forms of activism and political struggles 'from below'. A theatrical emphasis is similarly noticeable in recent scholarly work in this area, with online and offline 'repertoires of contention' (Tilly, 2005) performed by activists who share philosophies and spectacle-led tactics via social-media networks, in what W. Lance Bennett and Alexandra Segerberg (2011) have termed the emergent 'logic of connective action', rather than 'collective action'. Following the financial crash in 2008, the more recognisable G20 protests have morphed into an international Occupy movement against the global financial model, while the

Arab uprisings of 2011 are energising debate over the power of innovative media practices to spread protest, and even revolution, across national borders. Despite varying levels of success in terms of power shifts and political reform, the riots, protests and uprisings across the world have accentuated the carnivalesque in activist political culture and media practices, whether in the USA, Chile, Russia, Egypt or Greece.

Conceiving of generic work as a form of communicative social *practice* and not just as a set of texts, reminds us of how important it is to pay attention to the contribution of cultural producers – the writers, artists, designers, directors, etc. – who are responsible for the creation of the kinds of texts we have been exploring. While it is appreciated as a general principle that workers in the cultural industries are operating within a matrix of industrial, political and cultural conditions, relatively little is known empirically about how they themselves understand those conditions and the influence they exert on the work produced (Born, 2005; Hesmondhalgh, 2007, Kennedy, 2012). The sensibilities of those participants whose contribution to political discourse (certain bloggers and tweeters, for example) comes from a position of 'individual citizen' rather than cultural worker are likely to be significantly different from those whose contributions are underpinned by institutional arrangements. Further ethnographic and interview-based studies of cultural production across the generic range would significantly enhance our understanding in this area.

Finally, we should briefly comment on whether as a result of our research we are in a position to take an optimistic or a pessimistic view of the media's contribution to democratic health. As our chapters indicate, it has neither been our aim to mount a general case that non-news genres of political communication are causing harm to national political life nor to claim the reverse. The intrinsic variety of the materials reviewed makes such an overall judgment unwise, even without the complications of assessment involved when audience variables are introduced into the picture. Current levels of variety are strong, and our hope would be that this can be sustained – though clearly it will depend on economic and political factors as much as, if not more than, cultural ones. Attention to the specific, both in forms and modes of engagement, brings out sharply the current profile. To take the example of comedy, our survey has suggested that the current mix in Britain gives a higher profile to political ridicule than to satire, and that satirical material is more restricted in its demographic range to groups that already have high levels of cultural capital in this area.

As indicated in our Introduction, it is not just that some media critics are pessimistic and some are optimistic – those who are pessimistic vary in what exactly they take to be the problem. Some commentators have focused on poor standards of political information quality and quantity (e.g. Thussu, 2007); others are concerned about opportunities for citizens to participate meaningfully in public political debate (e.g. Coleman and Blumler, 2009). Our research relates only tangentially to the first of these critiques. We would endorse points that have been made elsewhere: (a) that if current information regimes are indeed tainted by the drift towards 'infotainment', a less tainted one would be no more successful in informing its citizenry if it demanded unrealistic levels of political interest from them; and (b) that the information content in genres that audiences also find pleasurable should not be underrated, though it should never be regarded as a substitute for high-quality journalism. We note also the relevance of genre considerations to this debate. 'Information' has to be designed to fit with pre-configured schemata of understanding and evaluation. This applies both to information that confirms existing views and to information with the potential to disrupt those views. Research of the kind presented here is intended, in part, to open up another line of enquiry into the character of these pre-configured schemata, as a precondition for evaluation of them.

Does our survey also speak to the issue of participation and engagement on the part of citizens? The structural opportunities for citizens to express their views in public discourse have certainly been expanded thanks to the rise of the internet, and many have demonstrated wit and imagination in their use of online resources for this purpose. Mainstream media continue to develop ways of including contributions from the public appropriate for their own forms of distribution. But 'speaking' and 'being heard' are two different things, and the individual message in a discussion thread is unlikely to find much of an audience, while citizens with large audiences (such as those who put questions to panellists on *Question Time*) are still operating within quite tightly managed parameters.

Appendix 1: Timeline for 2010

Chronology of events in 2010 UK mediated political year (with particular detail for audit periods). This list is necessarily selective, but it indicates those events that garnered significant attention and commentary across newspapers, the web and political broadcasting.

4 January:	Pre-election campaigns begin, as the Conservative Party launches new posters, with the slogan 'We can't go on like this...', and the Labour Party publishes 'Conservative Tax and Spending Promises' dossier.
6 January:	Geoff Hoon and Patricia Hewitt attempt coup against Gordon Brown's leadership.
21 and 29 January:	Tony Blair gives evidence at the Chilcot Inquiry into the Iraq war.
27 January:	Peter Watt's book *Inside Out* highlights troubled relationships in New Labour leadership, especially Brown's failings.
4 February:	Legg Report published detailing the expenses that MPs have been asked to repay.
5 February:	Labour MPs David Chaytor, Jim Devine and Elliot Morley, and Conservative Lord Hanningford to face prosecution on charges of false accounting, related to expenses scandal.
7 February:	Alastair Campbell gets emotional when questioned about the Iraq war on the *Andrew Marr Show*.
14 February:	Gordon Brown appears on *Piers Morgan's Life Stories*, tearfully recounting the death of his daughter.
21 February:	Publication of Andrew Rawnsley's book *The End of the Party* (with extracts in the *Observer*) leads to claims of Brown's bullying behaviour towards colleagues; soon coined 'Bullygate' as story develops, with anti-bullying helpline's claims that it had received calls from Downing Street.
23 February:	Alistair Darling tells Jeff Randall on Sky News that the 'forces of hell were unleashed' on him by Gordon Brown's aides.

22 March:	Stephen Byers, Geoff Hoon and Patricia Hewitt implicated in 'cash for influence' scandal, offering their services to lobbyists for cash.
24 March:	Alistair Darling announces the Budget, with a commitment to halve the deficit over four years.
6 April:	Brown announces general-election date: 6 May.
15 April:	First prime-ministerial TV debate, ITV: Nick Clegg surprises media pundits with strong performance.
22 April:	Second TV debate, Sky News.
28 April:	Gordon Brown recorded calling Gillian Duffy a 'bigoted woman'.
29 April:	Third TV debate, BBC1.
6 May:	Polling Day and Election Night: no outright winner emerges, leading to negotiations among the party leaderships.
11 May:	Gordon Brown leaves Downing Street with his family; Cameron becomes prime minister and forms a new coalition government with Liberal Democrat leader, Nick Clegg, as deputy prime minister.
12 May:	Cameron and Clegg's Rose Garden press conference.
25 July:	Wikileaks releases classified documents on Afghanistan war.
16–19 September:	The Pope visits the UK.
18–22 September:	Lib Dem Party Conference in Liverpool.
25 September:	Ed Miliband wins Labour Party leadership contest, narrowly beating his brother, David.
26–30 September:	Labour Party Conference in Manchester.
3–6 October:	Conservative Party Conference in Birmingham (with outcry over cuts to child benefit for parents in high tax band).
12 October:	Lord Browne's Report on Higher Education published, paving the way for a rise in fees.
19 October:	Strategic Defence and Security Review announced.
20 October:	Osborne announces details of the Comprehensive Spending Review.
23 October:	Wikileaks releases Iraq war logs (around 400,000 classified documents), with records of civilian deaths.
10 November:	First student protests organized against the cuts. A number of protesters occupy Conservative campaign offices at 30 Millbank. More demonstrations follow in November and December.

28 November:	Wikileaks releases more than 250,000 dispatches, known as the 'US Embassy Cables', reported over next few weeks, especially in the *Guardian*.
21 December:	Vince Cable stripped of role in BSkyB decision after he is secretly recorded claiming that he's 'declared war on Rupert Murdoch'.

We had three main auditing periods throughout 2010. The first period covered the month of February (a four-week period of Monday 1 February to Sunday 28 February inclusive); the second (Election) period covered the general-election campaign and formation of government (a five-week period of Thursday 15 April to Wednesday 19 May); and the Autumn period, to cover the party conferences and the Autumn Spending Review (an initial three-week period of Saturday 18 September to Friday 8 October and an extra week (Sunday to Sunday) of 17–24 October). Altogether, this gives us 13 weeks of core data, supplemented with other material of particular interest.

Appendix 2: Notes on the Auditing Process

Process for collection, analysis and archiving

All media materials were stored and archived, either as audio-visual files or text and image documents. We designed a Microsoft Access database to record details for each programme, article, cartoon, blogpost, etc., so that key aspects of the material were easily indexed and retrieved, rather than with the aim of conducting a detailed quantitative analysis. Drop-down menus with fixed variables ensured quick recording of this information, allowing for efficient coding and querying of the data, as well as the straightforward export of tables to Excel or Word (i.e. 'queries' are run to isolate certain features, or cross-tabulate data). During the early period of the project we devised various approaches to categorising and coding the broad range of media materials. A pilot study was conducted in December 2009, collecting and coding a week's worth of material. Following this trial, we introduced our 'macro-level' primary coding, where we could record political themes in a tighter 'closed' system, rather than the extended variables for coding more specific 'mentions' of people, issues and institutions. Respondent group transcripts were transcribed and coded using Nvivo 9.

Coding schema for media materials

All items were coded using the following measures:

1. ID:
2. Date:
3. Medium: (Periodical Print/Television/Radio/Web/Other)
4. Media Format: (e.g. blog, radio phone-in, panel show)
5. Title or name: (e.g. Wright Stuff, Telegraph)
6. Headline/Identifier: (e.g. DailyPolitics010210)
7. Total length of time (seconds) (*or page number for newspapers)
8. Length of time for relevant segment
9. Writer/author/presenter/chair/originator
10. Primary Level Coding

    (a) Dominant theme(s) or subject(s) (24 variables: e.g. Education, Terrorism, Electioneering)
    (b) Communicative Mode (e.g. dialogue, interview, expositional)

11. Secondary Level Coding

    (a) Political People (143 variables, under 6 main headings)
    (b) Political Issues (63 variables; under 12 headings)

(c) Political Values (42 variables; under 4 headings)

(d) Political Institutions (114 variables; under 8 headings)

12. Visual elements of interest (cartoon, photo, moving image): (open text box)

13. Notes on Intertextuality (to note instances of interdiscursivity or references to other programmes, blogposts, etc.): (open text box)

14. Further Comments: (open text box)

We do not reproduce the full list of variables here but they can be made available if requested from the authors.

Further notes on the database

Due to the varied nature of the material we are interested in, with variations in medium, form and genre, we recognized that a unified database for coding the material presented a number of concerns. For instance, this presented difficulties for what we would count as a single 'item' or 'message unit' (Neuendorf, 2002, p. 14) in the database, and we were concerned about the issue of comparability across our various media selections. For example, one short editorial counts as one 'record' in the database, but so too does an entire hour-long political magazine programme such as *This Week*, which by its very nature creates the space for a variety of participation modes and political themes. The flexibility of database design, with space for extended text rather than purely numerical data, enables the collation and organization of multiple types of print and broadcast material; we are not attempting to conduct the style of quantitative analysis that imbues each 'record' in the database with an equal status. Rather, the database provides the initial flexible yet systematic frame or profile from which we can approach the selected material in a multi-modal manner (with 'format' or 'theme' or 'expression' as primary interests), moving towards more detailed and selective techniques of analysis.

So, we can provide a general profile of political themes and modes of articulation across varied media forms and formats in the mediated spaces 'beyond the news' – we are not implying each record is equivalent in some kind of quantifiable way, or even that it would be desirable to try and produce that kind of mapping. Instead, we are utilising a quantitative approach, in which each item is selected and coded according to pre-arranged criteria. This allows for a certain level of comparison and tracking of trends across the sample, for example, noting a theme or treatment in a specific programme and tracing where other media formats might engage with or rework it. Contrasts and associations can be located with the confident knowledge that a selective and yet broad sweep of the mediated spaces for British political culture have been captured.

The database collection provides a profile of mainstream mediated political culture in Britain with some degree of systematic integrity, rather than relying on subjective and generalized conjecture about the range of mediated political culture. There has to be some degree of selectivity due to the limited nature of any project but here the selection is explicit, clarified and defendable. This approach does not negate the value of more exploratory and open-ended analysis. Rather, the adopted approach allows for movement between levels of analysis. On balance, we are not testing a set of hypotheses, but we are dealing with a varied range of materials from different media, and as such, a large array of media forms can be brought helpfully into a manageable and searchable corpus within the initial database frame.

Appendix 3: Audit Details

Table A.1 Number of TV programmes included in each sample period (plus total number of minutes recorded)

Programme/No. of Items	February	Election	Autumn
Mock the Week/HIGNFY	3 (90)	4 (130)	4 (130)
Question Time	4 (240)	4 (240)	4 (240)
This Week	3 (150)	7 (315)	4 (240)
Daily Politics	15 (630)	23 (1,200)	20 (1,260)
Wright Stuff	20 (1,800)	25 (2,250)	20 (1,800)
Andrew Marr Show	4 (240)	5 (300)	5 (300)
The Politics Show	4 (240)	5 (340)	5 (305)
Panorama	4 (120)	3 (90)	4 (120)
Tower Block of Commons	4 (240)		
Leader Debates		3 (270)	
Bremner, Bird and Fortune		3 (180)	
Other TV	5 (270)		4 (240)
Total TV	66 (4,020)	82 (5,315)	70 (4,635)

Table A.2 Number of radio programmes included in each sample period (plus total number of minutes recorded)

Programme/No. of Items	February	Election	Autumn
Any Answers	4 (120)	5 (150)	3 (90)
Any Questions	4 (210)	5 (250)	4 (200)
News Quiz/Now Show	4 (120)	5 (150)	4 (120)
Media Show	4 (120)	5 (150)	4 (120)
Political review*	4 (120)	2 (60)	4 (120)
The Heckler		3 (90)	
Total radio	20 (690)	25 (850)	19 (650)

*Political review includes *Week in Westminster* and *Beyond Westminster*.

Table A.3 Number of newspaper print items included in each sample period

Newspaper*	February	Election	Autumn
Sun	82 (72 A/10 C)	120 (111A/9 C)	96 (90 A/6 C)
Mirror	71 (65 A/6 C)	134 (110 A/24 C)	85 (76 A/9 C)
Mail	132 (123 A/9 C)	162 (148 A/14 C)	147 (133 A/14 C)
Guardian	155 (128 A/27 C)	203 (167 A/36C)	166 (136 A/30 C)
Telegraph	138 (110 A/28 C)	185 (150 A/35 C)	154 (125 A/29 C)
Total print	578(498 A/80 C)	804 (686 A/118 C)	648 (560 A/88 C)

'A' = articles and 'C' = cartoons.
*Includes sister publications on a Sunday.

Table A.4 Number of blog posts included in each sample period

Blog Name	February	Election	Autumn
Dizzy Thinks	55	77	16
Luke Akehurst	25	22	18
Liberal Burblings	32	52	47
Paul Waugh	74	95	50
Craig Murray*	17		
Total web	203	246	131

*Murray's blog was dropped from later sample periods due to lack of relevant content.

Table A.5 Totals for the audit

Medium/Period	February	Election	Autumn	Total
Total TV	66	82	70	218
Total radio	20	25	19	64
Total print	578	804	648	2,030
Total web	203	246	131	580
Total no. of records	867	1,157	868	2,892

Appendix 4: Focus Group Design

This section presents a summarized version of our protocol for the discussion groups. Overall, the researcher aimed to minimize involvement and the following questions were used as a guideline rather followed inflexibly. Selection of broadcast clips and newspaper items below are indicative; there was some variation, depending on whether groups were conducted in summer 2010, or early 2011.

Warm-up phase

Welcome; introduce project; ask each speaker to introduce themselves; any questions; general media habits:

- Does any of your regular viewing, listening and reading of various media include programmes or articles with a political flavour? What kinds of programmes/articles would those be?
- (Do you have any particular programmes or items that you feel you *have to* watch, listen to or read?)
- When the election was on, how did that change your normal viewing and reading habits?

Broadcasting phase: TV

Introduce clip

1. *Tower Block of Commons*

    - Does anyone have any initial reactions or opinions on this clip that they'd like to share?
    - Does it seem to be mainly about *entertaining* its viewers or about *educating/informing* them/us? OR Is it thought-provoking, or is it a good laugh – or both?
    - Do you think it *takes sides*, politically? Do you feel that *you* are more sympathetic to one side than the other?

2. Miliband of Brothers

    - What are your initial reactions to this clip?
    - Did you see this programme?
    - In terms of style or content, do you think this is interesting TV?

Broadcasting phase: radio

Introduce clip

1. *The News Quiz*
   - What did you *like* about this extract? (if anything)
   - What did you *not* like about this extract? (if anything)
   - Do you think this kind of programme assumes too much political knowledge (for you/others)? OR 'Do you think you got all the jokes?' If not, why not?
   - Does this extract make you feel sorry for politicians, as the victims of this humour?

Print phase: cartoons

'Here are five political cartoons taken from different newspapers during the election period and more recently ... We'd like you to look through the cartoons and think about which ones you like and dislike ... '

If you find it helpful, you can rank them 1–5 in rough order of how funny you find them. (Ask for tops and bottoms and then discuss variations among the group here and reasons for the highest and lowest placing.)

- Do you think the funniest cartoon is also the most politically perceptive cartoon? Why/why not?
- Ask if any are 'hard to understand'. Which, and why?
- How useful do you think political cartoons are in contributing to the public sense of 'what is going on'? (perhaps follow-ups here).

Print phase: parliamentary sketch-writing

Introduce two examples of sketch-writing from newspapers

- What did you *like* about the extract(s)? (if anything)
- What did you *not* like about the extract(s)? (if anything)
- Do you think this kind of writing assumes too much political knowledge (for you/others)? OR Do you think you got all the jokes? If not, why not?
- (Does this extract make you feel sorry for politicians, as the victims of this humour?)

Closing phase

Having seen all this material, we have a few 'winding down' questions that we would like to ask:

- Which of our extracts was the hardest to understand?
- Which of our extracts was the most enjoyable?

- We've included examples today with humorous content, do you think that politics can be funny/mixes well with humour? (examples?)
- Do you think that there's too much in the media which is making fun of politics and politicians?
- Do you think that the political programmes and articles you watch/read are influencing your own political attitudes?
- Do you approve or disapprove of how the mass media cover politics?
- (follow-ups if necessary, e.g. Do you find the media mainly fair or unfair? Are some parts of the media more objectionable to you than others?)

Notes

Introduction

1. Examining the various 'pro' and 'con' elements of current and emerging patterns of political mediation has become a familiar theme in the literature. See Brants and Voltmer (2011) for a range of essays around this vexed evaluative issue.
2. The literature is extensive, with Castells (2009) one of the influential discussions at a general theoretical level and Axford and Huggins (2001) Bimber (2003), Dahlgren (2009) and Coleman and Blumler (2009) indicative of a growing range of publications connecting theoretical perspectives to researched instances.
3. For a recent account of the issues surrounding the idea of politics as a distinctive sphere, see Thornhill (2009).
4. It is of interest here that what is the most frequently cited early reference for the idea of 'political culture' in empirical political science – Almond (1956) – is followed up by influential use of the term in a groundbreaking comparative study of five nations entitled *The Civic Culture*, co-written by the same author (Almond and Verba, 1963).
5. The concept of 'affordance' can be traced back to the work of J. J. Gibson in the psychology of perception (Gibson, 1979) though Oliver (2005) suggests that it has so far been extended from its original use in a variety of research contexts as to have outlived its usefulness. In the 2000s this concept was drawn into the general field of multimodal social semiotics (Kress, 2003) where the focus has rather been on the potentialities of communicative modes (speech, writing) and of technologies (the computer, the mobile phone) than on those of genres. Its applicability to genre rests on the fact that genres offer relatively stable modal configurations that form the basis of textual production and interpretation.
6. According to Hamo et al. (2010), mock interviews are those which are 'built around a fictional character who conducts interviews with celebrities – politicians included – in a vulgar, insolent and uninhibited style' (p. 250). Eponymous hosts of talk shows (in this context) include 'Ali G', who is really Sacha Baron Cohen, and 'The Great Pini', who is really comedian Gil Kopatch.

1 Broadcasting Beyond the News: Performing Politics

1. See Introduction.
2. By general consent, the *Leaders' Debates* were the defining event of the 2010 General Election, and attracted considerable commentary at the time, as well as subsequent academic interest (Pattie and Johnston, 2011; Chadwick, 2011b; Wheeler, 2011; Bailey, 2011; Boulton and Roberts, 2011; Coleman

et al., 2011; Lawes and Hawkins, 2011). The present book is not an election study, so we will be paying relatively little attention to this series and the genre it represents, in order to paint a broader picture of the contours of broadcast politics.

3. Elfyn Llwyd, MP, was on the programme as the leader of the Plaid Cymru party, which stands on a Welsh nationalist platform, contesting seats in Welsh constituencies.

4. The party achieved 3.1 per cent of the national vote in the 2010 election, 919,471 votes in all, and took no seats.

5. The agreement between all relevant parties spelling out these rules can be found online at http://www.bbc.co.uk/blogs/theeditors/pm_debates_programme_format.pdf.

6. A podcast on this programme's 80+ year history is currently available on the BBC website at http://www.bbc.co.uk/programmes/b006qjfq. It has not always taken its current form: for its first 40 years it was a 15-minute live scripted monologue from a Member of Parliament. Elder statesmen like Peter Tatchell and Roy Hattersley have memories of giving these monologues.

7. For a discussion of the relationship between the different 'personae' that politicians may adopt within varying contexts, including media appearances, see Corner (2000, 2003). A perceptive examination of how families are 'used' in political-identity work is given in van Zoonen (1998).

8. The episode reportedly achieved an audience of 4.2 million (*Daily Mail*, 15 February 2010), which is low for the series.

9. Coleman et al. (2009) have interviewed politicians appearing in this show and its Dutch counterpart, exploring what they see as the value of this kind of exposure.

10. BBC 4 is a free-to-air digital channel, a fairly recent addition (2002) to the two BBC channels, which date from the analogue era.

11. The *Telegraph*'s own journalists, Robert Winnett and Gordon Rayner tell their own Bernstein-and-Woodward-type story of this scoop in *No Expenses Spared*, Bantam 12. See, for example, Lucy Mangan's review in the *Guardian*, 24 February 2010.

12. As we have seen elsewhere in this study, the forms that comic treatments took drew heavily on the changing 'culture of comedy' more broadly at work across the genres, a culture with demographic variables. This connection is perhaps most noticeable in TV, where comic stylings and formats (in particular, in relation to the 'outrageous') receive regular revision as a 'cutting edge' to the industry's popular appeal.

13. In Corner et al. (2012, forthcoming) and in Chapter 4 below, we offer a discussion of how audiences responded to a screening of this opening sequence, drawing on our own fieldwork.

2 The Political World in Print – Images and Imagination

1. For details of the press materials collected, see Introduction – the section *Notes on data collection*, and Appendix 3.

2. During the periods that we audited, there were five sketch-writers regularly at work in the national press. These were Simon Hoggart for the *Guardian*, Ann

Treneman for *The Times*, Quentin Letts for the *Daily Mail*, Andrew Gimson for the *Daily Telegraph* and Simon Carr for the *Independent*.

3. It is, however, Bernard Levin, writing a political column (as 'Taper') for *The Spectator* in the late 1950s and early 1960s, who brings to the development of sketch-writing the degree of sarcastic wit, which is now seen as an essential feature. It is also of significance to his tone and stance that his previous writing included TV criticism. Another important figure in stylistic development was Frank Johnson, writing for *The Times* in the 1970s (see Richardson and Corner (2011) for further discussion).

4. *The Times* was not included in our routine weekly sample and its contents are omitted from all quantitative indications which we produce from our research. An example is included here because of the generic interest, for our ideas concerning 'colour' writing, of the particular approach taken.

5. In addition to being a regular columnist for the *Telegraph*, Boris Johnson currently holds the office of London Mayor, and is rumoured as a possible future Conservative Party leadership contender.

6. Within our audit periods, the *Guardian*'s regular editorial cartoonists were Steve Bell, Martin Rowson and Phil Disley, with Chris Riddell for the *Observer*. The *Telegraph* cartoonists are Christian Adams, Nicholas Garland and Michael Daley. Peter Brookes and Morten Morland are political cartoonists for *The Times*. Mac (Stan McMurtry), Michael Heath and Robert Thompson provide cartoons for the *Mail*, while David Trumble, Andy Davey and Tom Johnston draw for the *Sun*. Kerber and Black provide daily cartoons within the editorial section of the *Daily Mirror*, although these are smaller single-column 'pocket' cartoons.

7. Not surprisingly, during the period of our audit of the election campaign, the vast majority of the cartoons with political themes that we collected depicted party leaders. Looking at indications of the number of appearances by a political leader in a cartoon, cartoons showing all three leaders topped the list. Again, not surprising given the concurrent political situation.

8. The distortion performed here, on a face that would become more well known only after the establishment of the Coalition government, meant that several of our respondents were unable to identify who it was, a problem compounding that of being unfamiliar with the details of the Pinocchio story (see Chapter 4).

9. At the time of writing, some 24 months after the campaign, Rowson is still making use of the Clegg-as-Pinocchio figure, which has appeared in a variety of contexts in his cartoons.

10. Perhaps the most well-known example of this is the *Private Eye* cover, which mostly features a photograph to which has either been added a comic caption and/or a speech bubble coming from one of the people depicted. The effect is always subversive. So, for instance, the issue (30 April–13 May) covering the election campaign but published before the result, shows a head-on view of the three party leaders at the *Leaders' Debates* podia, with Clegg saying 'Vote for one party ... ' and Cameron and Brown jointly saying ' ... and get one free'.

11. An indirect reference to *The Times* writer Simon Heffer.

3 Politicality and the Web – Tracking the Cross-currents

1. Rawnsley's *The End of the Party* (2010) was just one book among many published during 2010 which give an insider view of the last years of the New Labour government, with the personalities of Blair and Brown a particular source for the most scandalous claims. Those published before the election included, in addition to Rawnsley's book, Peter Watt's *Inside Out: My story of betrayal and cowardice at the heart of New Labour* (2010) and Lance Price's *Where Power Lies: Prime Ministers v the Media* (2010). Price took a historical view of the relationship between prime ministers and the media over the past century, but his insider role as Alastair Campbell's deputy during the New Labour years attracted particular attention.
2. Presenting the text does not do full justice to the multimodal look and feel of the blogs, although blogposts mentioned in the chapter are available to view in archives online (bar Paul Waugh's, although the authors do have an archive for reference). We have indicated embedded links by underlining text. All embedded images are indicated but not reproduced here.
3. Following this episode, and the apparent delight experienced in this new way of 'seeing' political leaders, BBC's *Newsnight* commissioned *Apple Daily* to provide similar animations during the general election (depicting the campaign launches, 'Bigotgate', and 'Cleggmania'), and also for the Labour-leadership contest (http://news.bbc.co.uk/1/hi/programmes/newsnight/9038477.stm). Deliberate commissioning of animated content by the BBC, complete with subtitles and accented voiceover, creates a sense of artifice, which was absent from the original clip, whose entertainment factor relied on its unabashedly exaggerated realization, incongruity and internet 'meme' status.
4. In a more recent example involving the micro-blogging site Twitter, the move of political correspondent Laura Kuenssberg from BBC to rival ITV (as its new Business Editor) in June 2011 has raised the issue of her whether she should be allowed to take her 65,000+ Twitter followers (and past tweets) with her as she changes from @BBCLauraK to @ITVLauraK. Following her move, the @BBCLauraK account displayed the wry tagline 'Definitely not the next Political Editor of the BBC...', listing only one tweet: 'I'll be back...', while the new @ITVLauraK listed all her old tweets and her many followers. In this case, the ownership of the past tweets moved with Laura, rather than staying with the BBC. As Jemima Kiss noted at the time, the blend of personal and professional communication on social-media sites such as Twitter blurs the lines on ownership, control and branding (Kiss, 2011).

4 Media Audiences and Public Voices – Terms of Engagement

1. At several points in this book, including in the Introduction, we have referred to these categories, noting their varying usage and a configuration of relationships, which is sometimes the subject of dispute, as is frequently the case with terms using the idea of 'culture'. For instance, 'popular culture', while it

clearly covers a different range of artefacts and practices than 'civic culture', is nevertheless related to it in various ways, sometimes ways which are the subject of dispute in assessments of the 'state of democracy' in contemporary societies (see, for instance, Street, 1997; Simons, 2003; van Zoonen, 2004 and Herkman, 2010). As we have indicated earlier, 'political culture' is also a term used inconsistently, sometimes applied narrowly to the culture surrounding the formal political system, sometimes extended such as to cover 'civic culture'.

2. 'Publics' is often preferred to 'public' to indicate something of the diversity and complexity of contemporary civic space; however, the singular form remains a strong and politically potent usage in its reference to all those having 'civic membership' within a nation-state.

3. Engaging with the broader cultural, including affective and aesthetic, factors that bear on being a citizen has been a strand in recent writing. Here, there has been some use of the idea of 'cultural citizenship', initially in the USA and then more widely, to register the multicultural character of many contemporary civic orders and the particular inequalities and tensions which often follow from this. For recent perspectives on some of the key conceptual issues, see Miller (2007) and Stevenson (2010).

4. Gordon Brown's webchat took place on 16 October 2009, resulting in 1,058 posts to the thread; David Cameron attracted 1,230 messages, with a certain degree of hostility. In January 2010, Nick Clegg's webchat had only 257 comments, but his performance was deemed impressive; but by September 2010, Clegg's revisit to the format as deputy prime minister in the Coalition government was initially greeted with shock that he would dare to make an appearance, amassing 696 messages, with many expressing disappointment.

5. Riven Vincent's name has more recently cropped up again campaigning on the same issue, in an unusual political interview format, this time in the *Guardian's Weekend* magazine. Rather than a traditional interview, Vincent was among a host of celebrities, politicians and campaigners (or 'public figures') invited to ask Cameron a single question in an 'audio interactive' interview, with the audio files of Cameron's replies also made available on the *Guardian* website (http://www.guardian.co.uk/politics/2011/nov/25/david-cameron-answers-questions). Mumsnet co-founder Justine Roberts was another contributor.

6. Elements in brackets are questions or remarks by the researchers conducting the sessions.

7. While the Channel 4 website states that they will live 'in some of Britain's most deprived neighbourhoods', all the estates are actually in England (Hull, Barking, Birmingham, East and West London).

8. The cartoon referred to here is Figure 2.3 in Chapter 2.

5 Mediation and Theme

1. The term 'meritocracy' is attributed to sociologist and columnist Michael Young, dating from his 1958 essay 'The Rise of the Meritocracy'. Young has since pointed out (Young, 2001) the considerable semantic drift that the term has undergone from what he intended. So far from being the unqualified

'good thing' that it seems to be in contemporary rhetoric (success rewarding merit rather than being a gift of birth), the original essay described the rise of a flawed system in which a talent pool was identified early from a structurally unbalanced section of the population, undergoing disciplined and focused training for roles in government. This specialist sector of the population occupied all positions of power to the exclusion of anyone whose life experiences had given them an alternative source of understanding of society's problems and how to address them.

2. The thesis that British senior politicians of all parties were drawn from a narrow and shrinking social range, favouring the privileged (reversing an education-driven trend that had started after the Second World War to open up politics in this respect), was given a high profile just after our audit period in a documentary written and fronted by broadcaster Andrew Neil, which attracted much comment (*Posh and Posher: Why Public School Boys Run Britain*, BBC 2, 26 January 2011). Two years prior to this, it had been reported that Labour under Gordon Brown had been planning to fight the election figuring the Conservatives under David Cameron as the 'toff' party (see, e.g., *Daily Mail*, 3 December 2009, 'Gordon Brown targets Tory "toffs" in class war election campaign'). It remains open for debate whether Eton- and Oxford-educated Cameron won the leadership of his party because or in spite of his social privileges. And popular judgment here is ambivalent too, since for a certain kind of typically Conservative voter, politicians with personal fortunes may be seen as less corruptible than those who rely on their MP's salary for their main source of income, while the privileged education to which their backgrounds gave them access provides another kind of validation for their claim on power.

3. Within these periods of intensive activity, the shape and direction of the 'story' can change several times within a day, as new inputs produce fresh reactions, denials, repetition with strategic shifts of emphasis and further journalistic probing through interview.

4. Commentators in the elite press often used the phrase 'sofa cabinet' or 'sofa government' to describe the situation of an informal grouping of decision-makers around Blair. This connoted a rather more socially relaxed gathering than 'kitchen cabinet', a more established, informal usage for the inner grouping around a prime minister.

5. The NHS decisions received intensive media attention as they went through a series of delays and revisions. The attempt to pass matters off as part of the caution and reflectiveness of good government, unafraid to have second thoughts, largely failed in favour of the media's view that successful opposition by those in the NHS had halted an insufficiently prepared policy initiative.

6. Over-correction follows from so strenuous an attempt to create a distance between established public perceptions and 'real identity' that a risky alliance with 'reverse political space' occurs. In this respect, Ed Miliband, within days of taking over leadership of the Labour Party after receiving strong trade union support in his election, so vigorously denied any pro-socialist, pro-union, anti-business bias as to raise questions in some quarters about his basic 'Labour' credentials. David Cameron, wanting in his first years as Conservative leader to make his party have appeal as a 'party of the

centre' rather than (or as well as) the 'right' (discussed below), risked placing it on the 'left' in some policy fields.

7. Miliband faced a difficult start to 2012, with traditional Labour supporters and even his advisers expressed concern over his leadership skills. Len McCluskey, general secretary of the Unite union, penned a comment piece in the *Guardian* claiming that Miliband's leadership had been undermined by his support for a public sector pay freeze (2012), while his own adviser, Lord (Maurice) Glasman's comments in the *New Statesman* that there 'seems to be no strategy, no narrative and little energy' from Miliband's leadership were widely picked up across the press, despite Glasman claiming he was supportive overall (5 January 2012).

8. Following the 2009 revelations Parliament as an institution has sought to put its house in order, first under the Labour government with the creation of the Independent Parliamentary Standards authority, and the instigation of an audit of past claims under Sir Thomas Legg; and then under the Coalition as a handful of parliamentarians faced criminal charges as a result of the scandal.

9. The move to an 'interior' front against Brown, raising questions about his psychological and emotional stability, was finally in fatal combination with the established, 'exterior' critique of his policies and decisions.

10. The relationship between political leaders and the press has a long and controversial history in Britain but the phone-hacking affair raised questions about consorting with 'criminals' rather than simply with other members of the power-elite.

11. 'Fat cats' is an effective, if overworked, label for the corporate super-rich, one with enduring popular resonance. During the period of our study, it was a category portrayed in cartoons with (especially by Martin Rowson and Steve Bell in the *Guardian*) with a strongly critical comic force.

12. It is clear that, for some years to come, generating a rhetoric of commonality in face of austerity will be one of the key tests of the British government in getting acquiescence, let alone agreement, for domestic economic policy.

13. The development of a journalistic interest in the 'inner life' of public figures, even to the extent of a drawing upon psychological explanations, merits a study of its own. The dynamics of personalization and celebrity are clearly a dimension of this development.

14. Campbell's performance in this interview also attracted attention due to a moment of 'breakdown' from his renowned confident, if not combative, interviewee status. Campbell's temporary faltering of speech and head-lowering, discussed further later in this chapter, occurred while being repeatedly asked about the grounds on which Tony Blair could claim he knew 'beyond doubt' that Iraq possessed weapons of mass destruction prior to the 2003 invasion.

15. As intensified media competition has increased the need to preview upcoming stories, especially those having an 'exclusive' character, the idea of talking about a mediated event in advance of its actually being 'published' becomes an established strategy, following wider commercial practice. It develops anticipation and serves to pre-install the event in the public realm, as well as projecting brand identity. Politics, too, has an interest

in 'trailing' about-to-happen political performances but in most cases its priorities are clearly not those of media.

16. The degree of 'reform' needed to the existing economic system and the extent to which this involves core principles and structures is clearly a matter in which British political perspectives are positioned within European and then global contexts. The issue is likely to remain an important and sensitive one for many years to come. As this chapter was drafted in January 2012, Cameron was drawing increasingly on ideas around 'crony capitalism' as a defect in which failures in the management of the economic system allow unacceptable disparities of wealth to emerge without any attendant risk-taking by those accruing it. Clearly, this is a different diagnosis from one in which the system as a whole is seen to have failed.

17. The potential controversiality of even using the word within government discourse is illustrated by a much earlier incident. When, in May 1973, the Conservative Prime Minister Edward Heath remarked of a corporate scandal that it showed 'the unacceptable face of capitalism', the phrase was reported as newsworthy well beyond the level it would have achieved had it been 'the unacceptable face of business'.

18. Sentimentality is, of course, an important part of political claims-making, providing a broad and positive emotional frame within which particular policies and decisions, some of them lacking any affective appeal on their own, can be articulated.

19. See Appendix 2 for more details.

20. We do not suggest there is an exact science to categorising subjects and participants in their mediated roles, although we follow the labelling cues offered by presenters and authors. However, politicians and media workers can usually be defined by their chosen profession (or status as an influential blogger). Some individuals present difficulties: Boris Johnson is a Conservative politician, currently serving as the London Mayor. He also writes a regular column in the *Daily Telegraph* and is something of a celebrity. The political leaders' wives are classed as 'other people' yet they perform a political role, and featured in various media during the election campaign, gaining more attention than female politicians (Campbell and Childs, 2010, p. 774).

21. The other media formats we set out to collect were blogs, radio phone-ins, columns and editorials, radio magazines, TV magazines, panel shows with audience participation, drama/fiction and 'other'. See Appendix 2 for further elaboration.

The Forms and Functions of Genre in Mediated Politics

1. The idea of 'play' and 'playing' are clearly suggestive ones for a lot of the material we have examined, indicating not only what are often its entertaining features but also the transformative, creative energies at work.

2. 'Recognition', that which is already known and therefore confirmed (as well as perhaps modified) in fresh portrayal, is clearly an important element in the way generic representation of politics works. See, for instance, Honneth (2007). Recognition is sometimes accompanied by a sense of the ironic, often

intended in the media portrayals themselves, as we have frequently noted. Later in this chapter we talk more about the significance of irony in mediated politics, in relation to the broader idea of affect.

3. The comedy sketch was notable for the participation of a serving prime minister, appearing as himself. Blair not only aped his own media persona in the cameo but stole the well-known catchphrase ('Am I bothered?') from the fast-talking, uppity teenager he appeared alongside, Lauren, played by Catherine Tate. Comic Relief is a charitable enterprise founded in 1985 in response to the famine in Ethiopia, raising money to help with poverty and disadvantage on a global scale. It is fronted by major British comedians, and its centrepiece is a biennial telethon, 'Red Nose Day'.

4. PoliticsHome (http://www.politicshome.com/) operates as a news hub with a focus on national politics ('all today's politics in one place' is its tagline). Some of its resources are open-access but paying subscribers get updated information from the House of Commons, RSS feeds of relevant blog and twitter activity, customisable email briefings and more.

5. Following extensive investigative journalism at the *Guardian*, the term 'phone hacking' became shorthand for the practice of accessing private mobile-phone communications. The extent of this practice on behalf of certain newspapers over many years led to a government enquiry, headed by Lord Justice Leveson, and many successful lawsuits by individuals whose privacy had been thus infringed, as well as to the closure of the *News of the World*, the Sunday paper at the heart of this scandal.

6. Such dimensions of mediated political culture can be contextualized within wider social, cultural and technological trends, and recast within new disciplinary areas of study, reflected, for example, in the launch of two new international journals in 2010: *Celebrity Studies* (Taylor & Francis) and *Comedy Studies* (Intellect).

References

Almond, G. (1956) 'Comparative Political Systems', *Journal of Politics*, 18 (3), 391–409.

Almond, G. and S. Verba (1963) *The Civic Culture* (Boston, MA: Little, Brown).

Andrews, L. (2006) 'Spin: From Tactic to Tabloid', *Journal of Public Affairs*, 6 (1), 31–45.

Anstead, N. and B. O'Loughlin (2011) 'Emerging Viewertariat and BBC Question Time: Television Debate and Real-Time Commenting Online', *International Journal of Press/Politics*, 16 (4), 440–462.

Arendt, H. (1958) *The Human Condition* (Chicago, IL: University of Chicago Press).

Axford, B. and R. Huggins (2001) *New Media And Politics* (London: Sage).

Bailey, R. (2011) 'What Took So Long? The Late Arrival of TV Debates in the UK General Election of 2010', in D. Wring, R. Mortimore and S. Atkinson (eds.) *Political Communication in Britain: The Leader Debates, the Campaign and the Media in the 2010 General Election* (London: Palgrave Macmillan), 7–21.

Barisione, M. (2009) 'Valence Image and the Standardisation of Democratic Political Leadership', *Leadership*, 5 (1), 41–60.

Barnhurst, K.G. (2011) 'The New "Media Affect" and the Crisis of Representation for Political Communication', *International Journal of Press/Politics*, 16 (4), 573–593.

Baym, G. and J. Jones (2012) 'News Parody in International Perspective: Politics, Power and Resistance', *Popular Communication*, 10 (1–2), 2–13.

BBC (2004) *Building Public Value: Renewing the BBC for a Digital World* [Online], http://downloads.bbc.co.uk/aboutthebbc/policies/pdf/bpv.pdf, date accessed 17 November 2011.

BBC (2011) *About the BBC: BBC Mission and Values*, http://www.bbc.co.uk/aboutthebbc/insidethebbc/whoweare/mission_and_values/, date accessed 21 May 2012.

Beckett, A. (2009) 'Guido Fawkes: The Blogger Who Knows the Power of Gossip', *The Guardian*, 4 November.

Bennett, W.L. (1998) 'The UnCivic Culture: Communication, Identity, and the Rise of Lifestyle Politics', *Political Science and Politics*, 31 (4), 740–761.

Bennett, W.L. and A. Segerberg (2011) 'The Logic of Connective Action: Digital Media and the Personalization of Contentious Politics', Paper presented at the 6th General Conference of the European Consortium for Political Research, Reykjavik, Iceland, 25–27 August.

Bennett, J. and N. Strange (eds.) (2011) *Television as Digital Media* (London: Duke University Press).

Berg-Schlosser, D. (2009) 'Political Culture at a Crossroads?', in K. Mitra, M. Pehl and C. Spiess (eds.) *Political Sociology: The State of the Art* (Leverkusen: Budrich), 31–50.

Bergson, H. (1911) *Laughter: An Essay on the Meaning of the Comic, Project Gutenberg,* http://www.gutenberg.org/files/4352/4352-h/4352-h.htm, posted 26 July 2009, date accessed 29 March 2012.

Beyme, K. von (1996) 'The Concept of Political Class: A New Dimension of Research on Elites?', *West European Politics,* 19 (1), 68–87.

Billig, M. (2005) *Laughter and Ridicule: Toward a Social Critique of Humour* (London: Sage).

Bimber, B. (2003) *Information and American Democracy: Technology in the Evolution of Political Power* (Cambridge: Cambridge University Press).

Blair, T. (2007) 'Full Text: Blair on the Media', *BBC,* 12 June 2007, http://news.bbc.co.uk/1/hi/uk_politics/6744581.stm, date accessed 19 March 2012.

Blumler, J.G. and S. Coleman (2010) 'Political Communication in Freefall: The British Case–and Others?', *International Journal of Press/Politics,* 15 (2), 139–154.

Blumler, J.G. and M. Gurevitch (2001) 'Americanization Reconsidered: UK–US Campaign Communication Comparisons across Time', in W. Lance Bennett and R.M. Entman (eds.) *Mediated Politics: Communication in the Future of Democracy* (New York: Cambridge University Press), 380–406.

Bolter, J.D. and R. Grusin (2000) *Remediation: Understanding New Media* (Boston, MA: MIT Press).

Boorstin, D.J. (1961) *The Image: A Guide to Pseudo-Events in America* (New York: Harper Colophon).

Born, G. (2005) *Uncertain Vision* (London: Vintage).

Born, G. (2010) 'The Social and the Aesthetic: for a Post-Bourdieuian Theory of Cultural Production', *Cultural Sociology,* 4 (2), 171–208.

Boulton, A. and T.C. Roberts (2011) 'The Election Debates: Sky News Perspective on their Genesis and Impact on Media Coverage', in D. Wring, R. Mortimore and S. Atkinson (eds.) *Political Communication in Britain: The Leader's Debates, the Campaign and the Media in the 2010 General Election* (London: Palgrave MacMillan), 22–36.

boyd, d. (2006) 'A Blogger's Blog: Exploring the Definition of a Medium', *Reconstruction: Studies in Contemporary Culture,* 6 (4), http://reconstruction.eserver.org/064/boyd.shtml

Brants, K. and K. Voltmer (2011) *Political Communication in Postmodern Democracy: Challenging the Primacy of Politics* (Basingstoke: Palgrave Macmillan).

Buckley, B. (2010) 'Forum: Art and Politics', *Postcolonial Studies,* 13 (2), 121–131.

Buck-Morss, S. (2002) *Dreamworld and Catastrophe* (Cambridge, MA: MIT Press).

Busby, R. (2009) *Marketing the Populist Politician: The Demotic Democrat* (London: Palgrave Macmillan).

Butler, J. (1997) *Excitable Speech: A Politics of the Performative* (London: Routledge).

Campbell, R. and S. Childs (2010) " 'Wags", "Wives" and "Mothers" . . . But What About Women Politicians?' *Parliamentary Affairs,* 63 (4), 760–777.

Campus, D. (2010) 'Mediatization and Personalization of Politics in Italy and France: The Cases of Berlusconi and Sarkozy', *International Journal of Press/Politics,* 15 (2), 219–235.

Cao, X. (2010) 'Hearing It From Jon Stewart: The Impact of the Daily Show on Public Attentiveness to Politics', *International Journal of Public Opinion Research,* 22 (1), 26–46.

Cappella, J.N. and K.H. Jamieson (1997) *Spiral of Cynicism: The Press and the Public Good* (2nd Edition) (Oxford: Oxford University Press).

Cardo, V. (2011) 'The Amazing Mrs Politician: Television Entertainment and Women in Politics', *Parliamentary Affairs*, 64 (2), 311–325.

Castells, M. (2009) *Communication Power* (Oxford: Oxford University Press).

Chadwick, A. (2011a) 'The Political Information Cycle in a Hybrid News System: the British Prime Minister and the "Bullygate" Affair', *International Journal of Press/Politics*, 16 (1), 3–29.

Chadwick, A. (2011b) 'Britain's First Live Televised Party Leaders' Debate: From the News Cycle to the Political Information Cycle', *Parliamentary Affairs*, 64 (1), 24–44.

Clayman, S. and J. Heritage (2002) *The News Interview: Journalists and Public Figures on Air* (Cambridge: Cambridge University Press).

Clough, P.T. and J. Halley (2007) *The Affective Turn: Theorizing the Social* (Durham, NC: Duke University Press).

Cohen, K.R. (2006) 'A Welcome for Blogs', *Continuum: Journal of Media and Cultural Studies*, 20 (2), 161–173.

Coleman, S. (2006) 'How the Other Half Votes: Big Brother Viewers and the 2005 British General Election Campaign', *International Journal of Cultural Studies*, 9 (4), 457–479.

Coleman, S. and J. Blumler (2009) *The Internet and Democratic Citizenship: Theory, Practice and Policy* (Cambridge: Cambridge University Press).

Coleman, S. and J. Blumler (2011) 'The Wisdom of Which Crowd? On the Pathology of a Listening Government', *Political Quarterly*, 82 (3), 355–364.

Coleman, S., A. Kuik and L. van Zoonen (2009) 'Laughter and Liability: The Politics of British and Dutch Television Satire', *British Journal of Politics and International Relations*, 11 (4), 652–665.

Coleman, S., F. Steibel and J. Blumler (2011) 'Media Coverage of the Prime Ministerial Debates', in D. Wring, R. Mortimore and S. Atkinson (eds) *Political Communication in Britain: The Leader Debates, the Campaign and the Media in the 2010 General Election* (London: Palgrave Macmillan), 37–55.

Conners, J.L. (2005) 'Visual Representations of the 2004 Presidential Campaign: Political Cartoons and Popular Culture References', *American Behavioral Scientist*, 43 (3), 479–487.

Corner, J. (1991) 'Meaning, Genre and Context: The Problematics of 'Public Knowledge' in the New Audience Studies', in J. Curran and M. Gurevitch (eds.) *Mass Media and Society* (London: Methuen), 267–284.

Corner, J. (2000) 'Mediated Persona and Political Culture: Dimensions of Structure and Process', *European Journal of Cultural Studies*, 3 (3), 386–402.

Corner, J. (2003) 'Mediated Persona and Political Culture', in J. Corner and D. Pels (eds.) *Media and the Restyling of Politics* (London: Sage), 67–84.

Corner, J. (2004) 'Television's 'Event Worlds' and the Immediacies of Seeing', *Communication Review*, 7 (4), 337–343.

Corner, J. (2010) 'Promotion as Institutionalized Deception: Some Co-ordinates of Political Publicity', in M. Aronczyk and D. Powers (eds.) *Blowing up the Brand* (New York: Peter Lang), 53–71.

Corner, J. (2011) *Theorising Media: Power, Form and Subjectivity* (Manchester: Manchester University Press).

Corner, J. and D. Pels (2003) *Media and the Restyling of Politics: Consumerism, Celebrity and Cynicism* (London: Sage).

Corner, J. and K. Richardson (2008) 'Political Culture and Television Fiction: "The Amazing Mrs Pritchard"', *European Journal of Cultural Studies*, 11 (4), 387–403.

Corner, J. and K. Richardson (2009) 'Political Values and Television Drama', Political Studies Association Annual Conference 2009 Manchester: Political Studies Association', http://www.psa.ac.uk/Proceedings/2009, date accessed 12 March 2012.

Corner, J., K. Richardson and K. Parry (2012, forthcoming) 'Comedy, the Civic Subject and Generic Mediation', *Television and New Media*.

Couldry, N., S. Livingstone and T. Markham (2007) *Media Consumption and Public Engagement: Beyond the Presumption of Attention* (Basingstoke: Palgrave Macmillan).

Crabb, A. (2010) 'Art of the Poisoned Pen', *Sydney Morning Herald*, 14 January, http://www.smh.com.au/opinion/politics/art-of-the-poisoned-pen-20100113-m71i.html, date accessed 19 March 2012.

Dahlgren, P. (1995) *Television and the Public Sphere: Citizenship, Democracy and the Media* (London: Sage).

Dahlgren, P. (2003) 'Reconfiguring Civic Culture in the News Media Milieu', in J. Corner and D. Pels (eds.) *Media and the Restyling of Politics* (London: Sage), 151–170.

Dahlgren, P. (2006) 'Doing Citizenship: The Cultural Origins of Civic Agency in the Public Sphere', *European Journal of Cultural Studies*, 9 (3), 267–286.

Dahlgren, P. (2009) *Media and Political Engagement: Citizens, Communication, and Democracy* (New York: Cambridge University Press).

Dale, I. (2009) *Guide to Political Blogging in the UK 2009/10* (London: Biteback/Total Politics).

Dale, I. (2010) *Guide to Political Blogging in the UK 2010/11* (London: Biteback/Total Politics).

Danjoux, I. (2007) 'Reconsidering the Decline of the Editorial Cartoon', *Political, Science and Politics*, 40 (2), 245–248.

Dawkins, R. (2006) *The God Delusion* (London: Bantam Press).

Day, A. (2011) *Satire and Dissent: Interventions in Contemporary Political Debate* (Bloomington, IN: Indiana University Press).

Dean, J. (2010) *Blog Theory: Feedback and Capture in the Circuits of Drive* (Cambridge: Polity).

Delli Carpini, M.X. and S. Keeter (1996) *What Americans Know About Politics and Why It Matters* (New Haven, CT: Yale University Press).

Dodds, K. (2007) 'Steve Bell's Eye: Cartoons, Geopolitics and the Visualization of the "War on Terror"', *Security Dialogue*, 38 (2), 157–177.

Doyle, W. (2012) 'No Strings Attached? Les Guignols de L'info and French Television', *Popular Communication*, 10 (1–2), 40–51.

Edelman, M. (1964) *The Symbolic Uses of Politics* (Urbana, IL: University of Illinois).

Edelman, M. (1988) *Constructing the Political Spectacle* (Chicago and London: University of Chicago).

Edwards, J.L. (2001) 'Running in the Shadows in Campaign 2000: Candidate Metaphors in Editorial Cartoons', *American Behavioral Scientist*, 44 (12), 2140–2151.

Elkins, J. and A. Norris (2012) *Truth and Democracy* (Philadelphia, PA: University of Pennsylvania Press).

Ellis, J. (2000) *Seeing Things: Television in the Age of Uncertainty* (London: IB Tauris).

Feldman, L. (2007) 'The News about Comedy: Young Audiences, *The Daily Show*, and Evolving Notions of Journalism', *Journalism*, 8 (4), 406–427.

Feldman, L. and D.G. Young (2008) 'Late-Night Comedy as a Gateway to Traditional News: An Analysis of Time Trends in News Attention Among Late-Night Comedy Viewers During the 2004 Presidential Primaries', *Political Communication*, 25 (4), 401–422.

Fielding, S. (2011) 'Fiction and British Politics: Towards an Imagined Political Capital', *Parliamentary Affairs*, 64 (2), 223–232.

Franklin, B. (1994) *Packaging Politics: Political Communications in Britain's Media Democracy* (London: Bloomsbury).

Freedman, D. (2008) *The Politics of Media Policy* (London: Polity).

Gibson, J. (1979) *The Ecological Approach to Visual Perception* (Boston, MA: Houghton Mifflin).

Godwin, M. (1994) 'Meme, Counter-Meme', *Wired*, http://www.wired.com/wired/archive/2.10/godwin.if_pr.html, date accessed 21 May 2012.

Goffman, E. (1959) *The Presentation of Self in Everyday Life* (New York: Anchor Books).

Grabe, M.E. and E. Bucy (2009) *Image Bite Politics: News and the Visual Framing of Elections* (Oxford: Oxford University Press).

Graham, T. and A. Hajru (2011) 'Reality TV as a Trigger of Everyday Political Talk in the Net-based Public Sphere', *European Journal of Communication*, 26 (1), 18–32.

Gripsrud, J. (ed.) (2010) *Relocating Television: Television in the Digital Context* (London and New York: Routledge).

Grusin, R. (2010) *Premediation: Affect and Mediality After 9/11* (London: Palgrave Macmillan).

Haines, H.H. (1979) 'Cognitive Claims-Making, Enclosure, and the Depoliticization of Social Problems', *The Sociological Quarterly*, 20 (1), 119–130.

Hall, S. (1981) 'Notes on Deconstructing the Popular', in R. Samuel (ed.) *People's History and Socialist Theory* (London: Routledge), 227–240.

Hamo, M., Z. Kampf and L. Shifman (2010) 'Surviving the "Mock Interview": Challenges to Political Communicative Competence in Contemporary Televised Discourse', *Media Culture and Society*, 32 (2), 247–266.

Hampton, S. (2009) 'Performance and Rhetoric: Assessing Political Speech', *Affect*, 1, 3–25.

Helm, T. (2010) 'David Cameron's Critics Erupt After "Heir to Blair" Fails to Deliver Majority', *The Observer*, 9 May, p. 4.

Helm, T. (2012) 'Labour Turns on BBC Over "Pro-Coalition Coverage"', *The Observer*, 1 January, p. 1.

Herkman, J. (2010) 'Re-evaluating the Relationship Between Politics and Popular Media', *Media Culture and Society*, 32 (4), 701–710.

Hesmondhalgh, D. (2007) *The Cultural Industries* (2nd Edition) (London: Sage).

Higgins, M. (2010) 'The "Public Inquisitor" as Media Celebrity', *Cultural Politics: An International Journal*, 6 (1), 93–110.

Hill, A. (2007) *Restyling Factual TV: Audiences and News, Documentary and Reality Genres* (London: Routledge).

Hilmes, M. (2011) *Network Nations: A Transnational History of British and American Broadcasting* (London: Routledge).

Hodgart, M. and B. Connery (2009) *Satire: Origins and Principles* (New Jersey: Transaction Books).

Hoggart, S. (2010) *A Long Lunch: My Stories and I'm Sticking to Them* (London: John Murray).

Holbert, R.L., J. Hmielowski, P. Jain, J. Lather and A. Morey (2011) 'Adding Nuance to the Study of Political Humor Effects: Experimental Research on Juvenalian Satire Versus Horatian Satire', *American Behavioral Scientist*, 55 (3), 187–211.

Honneth, A. (2007) *Disrespect: The Normative Foundations of Critical Theory* (Cambridge: Polity Press).

Horton, D. and R. Wohl (1956) 'Mass Communication and Para-Social Interaction: Observations on Intimacy at a Distance', *Psychiatry*, 19 (3), 215–229.

Inthorn, S. and J. Street (2011) 'Simon Cowell for Prime Minister? Young Citizens' Attitudes Towards Celebrity Politics', *Media, Culture and Society*, 33 (3), 474–489.

Jay, M. (2010) *The Virtues of Mendacity: on Lying in Politics* (Charlottesville and London: University of Virginia Press).

Jenkins, H. (2008) *Convergence Culture: Where Old and New Media Collide, Updated and with a New Afterword* (New York: New York University Press).

Jones, J.P. (2005) *Entertaining Politics: New Political Television and Civic Culture* (Lanham, MD: Rowman and Littlefield).

Jones, J.P. (2010) *Entertaining Politics: Satiric Television and Political Engagement* (2nd Edition 2005) (Lanham, MD: Rowman and Littlefield).

Karvonen, L. (2010) *The Personalisation of Politics: A Study of Parliamentary Democracies* (Colchester: ECPR Press).

Kennedy, H. (2012) *Net Work: Ethics and Values in Web Design* (London: Palgrave Macmillan).

Kiss, J. (2011) 'Who Controls Laura Kuenssberg's Twitter Account?', *The Guardian*: PDA The Digital Content Blog, http://www.guardian.co.uk/media/pda/2011/jun/22/laura-kuenssberg-twitter-account, date accessed 27 July 2011.

Kolbert, E. (2009) 'The Things People Say: Rumors in the Age of Unreason', *The New Yorker*, http://www.newyorker.com/arts/critics/books/2009/11/02/091102crbo_books_kolbert, date accessed 10 November 2011.

Kovalev, A. (2011) 'Russians Express Their Frustration with Explosion in Political Satire', *The Guardian*, 22 December, http://www.guardian.co.uk/world/2011/dec/22/russia-frustration-leadership-political-satire, date accessed 21 May 2012.

Kress, G. (2003) *Literacy in the New Media Age* (London: Routledge).

Kumar, S. (2012) 'Transgressing Boundaries as the Hybrid Global: Parody and Postcoloniality on Indian Television', *Popular Communication*, 10 (1–2), 80–93.

Landreville, K.D., R.L. Holbert et al. (2010) 'The Influence of Late-Night TV Comedy Viewing on Political Talk: A Moderated-Mediation Model', *International Journal of Press/Politics*, 15 (4), 482–498.

Langer, A.I. (2007) 'A Historical Exploration of the Personalisation of Politics in the Print Media: The British Prime Ministers (1945–1999)', *Parliamentary Affairs*, 60, 371–387.

Langer, A.I. (2011) *The Personalisation of Politics in the UK: Mediated Leadership from Attlee to Cameron* (Manchester: Manchester University Press).

Lawes, C. and A. Hawkins (2011) 'The Polls, the Media and Votes: The Leader Debates', in D. Wring, R. Mortimore and S. Atkinson (eds.) *Political*

Communication in Britain: The Leader's Debates, the Campaign and the Media in the 2010 General Election (London: Palgrave Macmillan), 56–76.

Letts, Q. (2009) 'How Gordon Brown's "Weird" Web Video Message to the Nation Will Leave You Chuckling', *Mail Online*, 22 April, http://www.dailymail.co.uk/debate/article-1172398/QUENTIN-LETTS-Gordon-Browns-appeal-nation-Number-10-TV.html, date accessed 18 May 2012.

Lewis, J., S. Inthorn and K. Wahl-Jorgensen (2005) *Citizens or Consumers: The Media and the Decline of Political Participation* (Milton Keynes: Open University Press).

Lim, M. (2012) 'Clicks, Cabs, and Coffee Houses: Social Media and Oppositional Movements in Egypt, 2004–2011', *Journal of Communication*. Early view: doi: 10.1111/j.1460-2466.2012.01628.x.

Linford, P. (2009) 'Political Bloggers and the Next Election', in I. Dale (ed.) *Guide to Political Blogging in the UK 2009/10* (London: Biteback/Total Politics), 70–73.

Littlejohn, R. (2010) 'The New Politics? More Like Brokeback Mountain'. *Mail Online*, http://www.dailymail.co.uk/debate/article-1278266/COALITION-GOVERNMENT-The-new-politics-More-like-Brokeback-Mountain.html

Livingstone, S. (ed.) (2005) *Audiences and Publics: When Cultural Engagement Matters for the Public Sphere* (Bristol: Intellect).

Livingstone, S. (2009) 'On the Mediation of Everything', *Journal of Communication*, 59 (1), 1–18.

Livingstone, S. and P. Lunt (2011) *Media Regulation: Government and the Interests of Citizens and Consumers* (London: Sage).

Lloyd, J. (2004) *What The Media Are Doing To Our Politics* (London: Constable).

Louw, E. (2005) *The Media and Political Process* (London: Sage).

Mancini, P. (2011) *Between Commodification and Lifestyle Politics: Does Silvio Berlusconi Provide a New Model of Politics for the Twenty-First Century?* (Oxford: Reuters Institute).

Mangan, L. (2012) 'How Twitter Saved Event TV', *The Guardian*, G2 section, 19 January, p. 10.

Marshall, P.D. (1997) *Celebrity and Power: Fame in Contemporary Culture* (Minnesota, MN: University of Minnesota Press).

Mason, P. (2011) *Why It's Kicking Off Everywhere: The New Global Revolutions* (London: Verso).

Mazzoleni, G. and W. Schulz (1999) ' "Mediatization" of Politics: A Challenge for Democracy?', *Political Communication*, 16 (3), 247–261.

Mazzoleni, G. and A. Sfardini (2009) *Politica Pop: Da "Porta a Porta" a l' "Isola dei famosi"* (Bologna: Il Mulino).

Meyer, T. (2002) *Media Democracy: How the Media Colonize Politics* (London: Polity).

Miller, T. (2007) *Cultural Citizenship: Cosmopolitanism, Consumerism, and Television in a Neoliberal Age* (Philadelphia, PA: Temple University Press).

Montgomery, M. (2007) *The Discourse of Broadcast News: A Linguistic Approach* (London: Routledge).

Mouffe, C. (2000) *The Democratic Paradox* (London: Verso).

Mouffe, C. (2005) *On the Political* (London: Routledge).

Mouffe, C. (2007) 'Artistic Activism and Agonistic Spaces', *Art and Research: a Journal of Ideas, Contexts and Methods*, 1 (2), 1–6.

Narco News TV (2011) *Egypt: How We Did It When the Media Would Not,* http://www.youtube.com/watch?v=WAyZ9OXIJgE, date accessed 21 May 2012.

Naughton, J. (2011) 'The Death of Web 2.0 is Nigh', *The Observer,* 7 August.

Neuendorf, K. A. (2002) *The Content Analysis Guidebook* (London: Sage).

Nikolaidis, A. (2011) 'The Unexpected Prime Minister: Politics, Class and Gender in Television Fiction', *Parliamentary Affairs,* 64 (2), 296–310.

Oborne, P. (2007) *The Triumph of the Political Class* (London: Simon and Schuster).

OED (2011) *Oxford English Dictionary,* http://www.oed.com/view/Entry/256743#eid11173991, date accessed 21 May 2012.

Ofcom (2011) *Communications Market Report 2011 (August).*

Oliver, M. (2005) 'The Problem with Affordance', *E-learning,* 2 (4), 402–413.

Pantti, M. and L. van Zoonen (2006) 'Do Crying Citizens Make Good Citizens?', *Social Semiotics,* 16 (2), 205–224.

Papacharissi, Z.A. (2010) *A Private Sphere: Democracy in a Digital Age* (Cambridge: Polity).

Papacharissi, Z.A. and M. de Fatima Oliveira (2012) Affective News and Networked Publics: The Rhythms of News Storytelling on #Egypt, *Journal of Communication.* Early view: doi: 10.1111/j.1460-2466.2012.01630.x.

Pariser, E. (2011) *The Filter Bubble: What the Internet Is Hiding from You* (New York: Viking).

Parotto, G. (2007) 'Corpo politico e corpo mediale. Profili biopolitici nell'era virtuale', Metabasis. Filosofia e comunicazione, anno II (3).

Parry, K. and K. Richardson (2011) 'Political Imagery in the British General Election of 2010: The Curious Case of "Nick Clegg"', *British Journal of Politics and International Relations,* 13 (4), 474–489.

Pattie, C. and R.J. Johnston (2011) 'A Tale of Sound and Fury, Signifying Something? The Impact of the Leaders' Debates in the 2010 UK General Election', *Journal of Elections, Public Opinion and Parties,* 21 (2), 147–177.

Perlmutter, D.D. (2008) *Blogwars: The New Political Battleground* (New York: Oxford University Press).

Plumb, S. (2004) 'Politicians as Superheroes: The Subversion of Political Authority Using a Pop Cultural Icon in the Cartoons of Steve Bell', *Media Culture and Society,* 26 (3), 432–439.

Powell, J. (2010) *The New Machiavelli: How to Wield Power in the Modern World* (London: Vintage).

Price, L. (2010) *Where Power Lies: Prime Ministers v the Media* (London: Simon and Schuster).

Rawnsley, A. (2010) *The End of the Party: The Rise and Fall of New Labour* (London: Viking).

Rettberg, J.W. (2008) *Blogging* (Cambridge: Polity).

Richardson, K. and J. Corner (2011) 'Sketchwriting, Political "Colour" and the Sociolinguistics of Stance', *Journal of Language and Politics,* 10 (2), 248–269.

Rowson, M. (2009) 'Dark Magic', *Index on Censorship,* 38 (1), 140–164.

Runciman, D. (2008) *Political Hypocrisy* (Princeton, NJ: Princeton University Press).

Sabbagh, D. (2011) 'Is This Really the Death of Political Blogging?', *The Guardian,* http://www.guardian.co.uk/media/2011/may/13/iain-dale-returns-the-daley, date accessed 10 November.

Seymour-Ure, C. (1972) 'The Politics of the Fool', *Political Quarterly*, 43 (3), 282–294.

Seymour-Ure, C. (2001) 'What Future for the British Political Cartoon?', *Journalism Studies*, 2 (3), 333–355.

Sharma, R. (2011) 'Web Curation Tools for Journalists', *BBC College of Journalism*, http://www.bbc.co.uk/journalism/blog/2011/08/web-curation-tools-for-journal.shtml, date accessed 10 August 2011.

Shirky, C. (2003) *Power Laws, Weblogs and Inequality*, http://www.shirky.com/writings/powerlaw_weblog.html, date accessed 10 November 2011.

Shirky, C. (2008) *Here Comes Everybody: How Change Happens When People Come Together* (London: Penguin).

Siapera, E. (2008) 'The Political Subject of Blogs', *Information Polity: The International Journal of Government and Democracy in the Information Age*, 13 (1–2), 51–63.

Simons, J. (2003) 'Popular Culture and Mediated Politics: Intellectuals, Elites and Democracy', in J. Corner and D. Pels (eds.) *Media and the Restyling of Politics: Consumerism, Celebrity, Cynicism* (London: Sage), 171–189.

Simpson, P. (2003) *On the Discourse of Satire: Towards a Stylistic Model of Satirical Humour* (Amsterdam: John Benjamins).

Singleton, D. (2010) 'Bloggers Set to be Allowed Privileged Access to Westminster Lobby System', *PR Week UK*, 17 February.

Somers, M. (1995) 'What's Political or Cultural about Political Culture and the Public Sphere?' Toward an Historical Sociology of Concept Formation, *Sociological Theory*, 13 (2), 113–144.

Stanyer, J. (2012) *Intimate Politics: The Rise of the Celebrity Politician and the Decline of Privacy* (Cambridge: Polity).

Stevenson, N. (2010) 'Cultural Citizenship, Education and Democracy: Redefining the Good Society', *Citizenship Studies*, 14 (3), 275–291.

Stiastny, T. (2012) 'Where Are the Westminster TV Dramas?', *BBC News Website*, 13 January, http://www.bbc.co.uk/news/uk-politics-16529685, date accessed 21 May 2012.

Straw, W. (2010) 'The Internet Election?', in I. Dale (ed.) *Guide to Political Blogging in the UK 2010/11* (London: Biteback/Total Politics), 7–11.

Street, J. (1997) *Politics and Popular Culture* (Philadelphia, PA: Temple University Press).

Street, J. (2004) 'Celebrity Politicians: Popular Culture and Political Representation', *British Journal of Politics and International Relations*, 6 (4), 435–452.

Strömbäck, J. (2008) 'Four Phases of Mediatization: An Analysis of the Mediatization of Politics', *International Journal of Press/Politics*, 13 (3), 228–246.

Sunstein, C. (2001) *Republic.com* (Princeton, NJ: Princeton University Press).

The Telegraph (2004) 'Bernard Levin', *The Telegraph*, 10 August.

Thompson, J.B. (1995) *The Media and Modernity: A Social Theory of the Media* (Cambridge: Polity).

Thompson, J.B. (2000) *Political Scandal: Power and Visibility in the Media Age* (Cambridge: Polity).

Thompson, J.B. (2005) 'The New Visibility', *Theory, Culture and Society*, 22 (6), 31–51.

Thornhill, C. (2009) 'The Autonomy of the Political: A Socio-theoretical Response', *Philosophy and Social Criticism*, 35 (6), 705–735.

Thussu, D.K. (2007) *News as Entertainment: The Rise of Global Infotainment* (London: Sage).

Tilly, C. (2005) *Regimes and Repertoires* (Chicago, IL: University of Chicago Press).

Turner, G. (2004) *Understanding Celebrity* (London: Sage).

Tyler, I. (2008) 'Commentary and Criticism: Methodological Fatigue and the Politics of the Affective Turn', *Feminist Media Studies*, 8 (1), 85–100.

Van Aelst, P., T. Sheafer and J. Stanyer (2012) 'The Personalization of Mediated Political Communication: A Review of Concepts, Operationalizations and Key Findings', *Journalism*, 13 (2), 203–220.

van Zoonen, L. (1998) 'A Day at the Zoo: Politicians, Pigs and Popular Culture', *Media, Culture and Society*, 20 (2), 183–200.

van Zoonen, L. (2003) 'After Dallas and Dynasty We Have...Democracy: Articulating Soaps, Politics and Gender', in J. Corner and D. Pels (eds.) *Media and the Restyling of Politics: Consumerism, Celebrity, Cynicism* (London: Sage), 99–116.

van Zoonen, L. (2004) 'Imagining the Fan Democracy', *European Journal of Communication*, 19 (1), 39–52.

van Zoonen, L. (2005) *Entertaining the Citizen: When Politics and Popular Culture Converge* (Lanham: Rowman and Littlefield).

van Zoonen, L. (2006) 'The Personal, the Political and the Popular: A Woman's Guide to Celebrity Politics', *European Journal of Cultural Studies*, 9 (3), 287–301.

van Zoonen, L. (2007) 'Audience Reactions to Hollywood Politics', *Media, Culture and Society*, 29 (4), 531–547.

van Zoonen, L. and D. Wring (2012) 'Trends in Political Television Fiction in the UK: Themes, Characters and Narratives', *Media, Culture and Society*, 34 (3), 263–279.

Wahl-Jorgenson, K. (forthcoming) 'The Strategic Ritual of Emotionality: A Case Study of Pulitzer Prize-winning Articles', *Journalism*.

Watt, P. (2010) *Inside Out: My Story of Betrayal and Cowardice at the Heart of New Labour* (London: Biteback).

Wheeler, M. (2011) 'Celebrity Politics and the United Kingdom's Televised 2010 Prime Ministerial General Election Debates', *Celebrity Studies*, 2 (1), 91–93.

Williams, R. (1976) *Keywords: A Vocabulary of Culture and Society* (London: Fontana).

Winnett, R. and G. Rayner (2009) *No Expenses Spared* (London: Bantam Press).

Wintour, P. and A. Stratton (2010) 'Stephen Byers and other ex ministers suspended from Labour Party over lobbying allegations'. *The Guardian*, 23 March.

Wring, D. and S. Ward (2010) 'The Media and the 2010 Campaign: The Television Election?' *Parliamentary Affairs*, 63 (4), 802–817.

Young, M. (1958) *The Rise of the Meritocracy, 1870–2033: An Essay on Education and Inequality* (London: Thames and Hudson).

Young, M. (2001) 'Down with Meritocracy', *The Guardian*, 9 June.

Zhong, Y. (2004) 'CCTV "Dialogue" = Speaking + Listening: A Case Analysis of a Prestigious CCTV Talk Show Series *Dialogue*', *Media, Culture and Society*, 26 (6), 821–840.

Index